Laura C. Martin's Southern Gardens

Laura C. Martin's

Southern Gardens

{ *A Gracious History and a Traveler's Guide* }

Photography by David Schilling

Abbeville Press Publishers
New York London Paris

Pages 2–3.
Monticello represents an exciting time in the gardening history of this country. Here Thomas Jefferson grew new and exotic plants from around the world and paid tribute to much native flora by including it in the formal garden.

Page 4. A bank of lilies brings a sense of cultivated beauty to dark swamp waters at Magnolia Plantation. Mysteries of the past lend a special appeal to this garden that boasts grand floral displays as well as native wildlife habitats.

Editor: Susan Costello
Designer: J.-C. Suarès
Copy Chief: Robin James
Production Supervisor: Matthew Pimm
Line Illustrations: Bobbi Angell
Color Illustrations: Nina Duran
Maps: Sophie Kittredge

For additional photo credits see page 252.

Library of Congress Cataloging-In-Publication Data

Martin, Laura C.

    Southern gardens: a gracious history and a traveler's guide/by Laura C. Martin: photography by David Schilling.
       p.   cm.
    Includes index.
    ISBN 1-55859-323-3
    1. Gardens—Southern States—History. 2. Gardens—Southern States—Guidebooks. I. Title.
SB466.U65S66 1993
712'.0975—dc20   92–27281
              CIP

Acknowledgments

Grateful thanks go to the people who made this book possible. A special note of appreciation to my friend Sally McMillan and to my editor at Abbeville Press, Susan Costello.

Thanks also go to many people who shared their time, enthusiasm, and expertise: Pat Marshburn, Orton Plantation; Kay Williams, Tryon Palace; Elizabeth Sims, Biltmore House; Barbara Meeh, Elizabethan Gardens; Flora Ann Bynum, Old Salem Gardens; Robin Salmon, Brookgreen; Mary Martha Blalock, Heyward-Washington House; Betsy Veronee, Magnolia Gardens; Barbara Doyle, Middleton Place; Pat Ryan, Bellingrath; Peter Hatch, Monticello; Dean Norton, Mount Vernon; Kent Brinkley and Libby Oliver, Colonial Williamsburg; Don Smith, Dumbarton Oaks; Jacqueline Broughton, Cheekwood; Carol Griffin, Dixon Gardens; Will Mangum, Rosedown; Mrs. Morrell Trimble, Afton Villa; Mrs. Glen Haltom, Mrs. Grace MacNeil, Natchez; Ron and Lani Riches, Monmouth; Betty Bagert, Longue Vue; Ann Parsons, Fairchild; Ann Merril, Morikami; Bunny Graham, Society of the Four Arts; Doris Littlefield, Vizcaya; Ryan Gainey, Laura Rains, Gardens for Peace; Laura Brash, Cypress Gardens.

Opposite.
Brookgreen Gardens near Murrel Inlet, South Carolina, is one of America's most beautiful sculpture gardens. Plant material has been carefully chosen to showcase over 400 works of American figurative sculpture.

Contents

Contents

A thriving, growing garden is, perhaps, the most beautiful legacy that one can leave. Each of the gardens selected for this book was created by individuals who desired to leave the world a bit more beautiful because of their work. While the American South is blessed with a multitude of lovely gardens, it was not possible to include all of these within a single volume.

The gardens chosen vary from small to large, simple to intricate. There were two main criteria for selecting the gardens. First, each illustrates a different period of the history of the South. From the opulent plantation gardens of antebellum days to the stark utilitarian gardens of Old Salem, each speaks eloquently of the people and the times in which they were created. The Biltmore Gardens were built for a different reason than the simple, elegant modern Gardens for Peace, and each reflects the stories and the dreams of the people who created them.

The second criteria was that each of these gardens is still closely associated with their founders. Most were family gardens that grew into places of such beauty, the owners desired that they be opened to the public. Through the generosity of families such as the Bellingraths, the Vanderbilts, the Callaways and the Blisses, we can now share in the grandeur of these gardens. We are fortunate that we are the recipients of such a wealth of beauty.

Opposite.
Columns of chrysanthemums welcome visitors to Bellingrath Gardens in autumn. Thousands of bedding plants carpet this Alabama garden throughout the year, making it an unforgettable horticultural experience.

NOVEMBER 13, 1991

I sit and look out over the remains of my flower garden. It appears brown and sad on this brisk November day, for an early fall frost has extinguished the bright hues and sweet fragrances of my garden. Spoiled by life in the American South, I pout because nature has robbed me of my garden as early as the middle of November. Then I chuckle, remembering that my northern friends have been buried under a blanket of snow for a month now.

It is easy to be spoiled in the South. Our growing season is long, we generally have ample rain, and the sun is hot and good for growing a multitude of wonderful plants. The wildflowers of the fields and forests are spectacular in their natural glory, and more formal gardens nearly burst with the vibrant hues of pampered and cherished cultivated flowers. The South must be the most beautiful country on earth.

The settlers who first came here certainly thought so. They sent glowing reports back to the homeland, writing of the incomparable beauty of the area. John Archdale wrote, in 1707, "The road out of Charles-Town for 3–4 miles, called Broad-Way is so delightful a Road and Walk of great breadth, so pleasantly green, that I believe no princes in Europe, by all their Art, can make so pleasant a sight for the whole year."

The most exciting gardens in the South today combine a touch of the past and a hint of the future. Gardens like those at Thomas Jefferson's Monticello and George Washington's Mount Vernon are steeped in tradition and offer us a living reminder of the importance of these men and their love of gardening.

Throughout our eventful history the men and women of the South have been closely tied to the earth. The rich soils of the region made millionaires of those who planted such crops as cotton and tobacco. These people of wealth and prominence created gardens reflecting the money that was earned from the land.

Plantation gardens such as Afton Villa and Rosedown give us glimpses of an opulent and exciting way of life in the antebellum South. Although they have suffered from the ravages of war and time, these beautiful gardens today are living examples of the persistence and rejuvenating power of southern gardeners.

Opposite.
Longue Vue Estate is the former home of philanthropists Edgar and Edith Stein. The South Lawn shows a strong Spanish influence and is composed of a series of fountains, geometrically clipped box-wood hedges, and intricately designed pebble walkways.

Although southern gardens combine many rare and exotic flowers and shrubs from all over the world, the gardens themselves remain undeniably southern. Live oak trees dripping with Spanish moss, and huge, spreading magnolias can only mean a southern garden.

By the turn of the century the South had a different kind of millionaire. The money, this time, did not come from the soil, but from industry and mechanization. Many wealthy and important people came from the North and settled in the South. George Vanderbilt found refuge in the mountains of North Carolina. James Deering found peace in his Italian estate on Biscayne Bay in Florida. Other millionaires, such as Cason Callaway and Walter Bellingrath, were born and bred southerners who created their estates close to their homeland. We in the South are fortunate to live near so many beautiful gardens and estates. Many of these are breathtaking in their grand displays of flowers and plants. Others are smaller but no less pleasing in their intricate detail of design.

Peace and tranquility mingle with a sense of history, an aura that pervades the southern garden today. From the tiny swept yards of Old Salem, North Carolina, to the grand gardens of magnificent coastal plantations, the southern garden is a unique and beautiful entity where the seeds of yesterday have grown into the towering trees of today. And yet, a new chapter in history is written everyday. In the fall of 1992, Hurricane Andrew tore through southern Florida, causing extensive damage to both Vizcaya and Fairchild Gardens. With indominitable spirit and unending optimism, individuals at these gardens immediately began to pick up the pieces and plant again. To explore the southern garden is to discover the essence of the South. The men and women who created these gardens, though separated by time, geography, and social and economic class, shared a common love for the goodness of the earth.

Gardening in the South means having the sweet scent of camellias linger forever in your memory. To be a southern gardener is to love the mighty magnolia as well as the tiny trailing arbutus, and to appreciate each for its unique contribution to the southern garden. With the legacy of love and understanding left to us by our ancestors, we must face the environmental problems challenging the global community today. Through love of the earth and understanding of the delicate balance of nature, we must become good stewards of our planet.

Opposite. Middleton Place near Charleston, South Carolina, reflects the history of antebellum days in the American South. A timeless sense of beauty pervades the garden, making it easy to imagine the opulent splendor of earlier years.

Pages 16–17. Prized for its sweet scent and delicate beauty, the rose has been loved by gardeners since the Golden Age of Greece. The rose garden at Biltmore Estate boasts over 2000 bushes representing 80 different varieties.

{1}
The First Colony, 1587

The beginnings of the colonial South are also the beginnings of this nation, for it was along the southern coast of North America that the first European settlements were established. The fifteenth-century discovery of the New World sparked the imagination and inflamed the wanderlust of Europeans. The Spanish found fortune and treasure in Mexico and Peru and established settlements in what is now Florida. Under Elizabeth I, England too began a period of colonial expansion. The English were anxious to establish a settlement in the New World and to share in the riches that this country promised. With Elizabeth's support, Sir Walter Raleigh organized an exploring party to find possible settlement sites in the New World. Raleigh sent his best men, who explored the coast of North America and finally decided to settle on Roanoke Island, a flat and sandy expanse about twelve miles long and three miles wide, well to the north of the Spanish settlements.

The exploration party returned to England with news of their find, and later sent a fleet of ships and many men back to Roanoke Island to build a fort and prepare for the small group of men, women, and children who sailed from England in three tiny boats during the summer of 1587. When the colonists finally arrived on Roanoke, they found the fort in ruins, and the skeleton of one of the twelve men who had stayed behind to begin the settlement.

Undaunted, however, the new arrivals settled in to make the most of their new home. On August 18, 1587, Virginia Dare was born; she was the first white baby born of English-speaking parents in America. Her grandfather, John White, was one of the leaders of the expedition and eventually became governor of the little settlement.

Although the colony was doing well, the settlers urged White to return to England to ask Sir Walter to send more colonists and more supplies. White's return was delayed by more than three years, and when he and his men dropped anchor near Roanoke in August 1590, they found the island deserted. The only sign of the colonists was the word "Croatoan" or "Croatan," scratched into a tree, and five traveling trunks found flung into a ditch. The fate of the lost colonists has never been determined.

The Elizabethan Gardens carry to perfection the idea of the gardens of sixteenth-century England. Formal statuary and pools, geometric beds, and neatly clipped trees and shrubs are careful interpretations of this style of design.

Page 18. Virginia Dare, sculpted as she may have looked as an adult, watches over the Elizabethan Gardens. These gardens were designed in the style of an Elizabethan pleasure garden, and are dedicated to the memory of the Lost Colony of Roanoke Island.

Page 19. Crape Myrtle (Lagerstroemia indica)

Opposite. Native trees and shrubs blend well with cultivated plants in the garden. Many varieties of native oaks are found here, as well as pines, cypress, dogwood, and spicebush.

THE ELIZABETHAN GARDENS

Although the first colony of the New World was "lost," it has never been forgotten, and the influence of these brave men and women has been great. The site of this original English colony was honored by the creation of the Elizabethan Gardens, next to the Fort Raleigh National Historic Site. The idea for these gardens originated in 1949 or 1950, when Mrs. Charles Cannon (wife of a well-known philanthropist from North Carolina), Mrs. Inglis Fletcher, and Sir Evelyn (founder of the English Speaking Union) and Lady Wrench were visiting the site of the Lost Colony.

The gardens were to be "an imaginative concept of an Elizabethan pleasure garden, Elizabethan in spirit and style but adapted to the present," according to the *History of the Elizabethan Gardens*. To make their dream come true, this small group of visionaries asked the Garden Club of North Carolina to sponsor a two-acre garden on a tract of land next to the National Park. In 1951 the Garden Club voted in favor of the project and agreed upon a modest plan for the creation of a two-acre garden at a cost of $10,000.

These plans were soon altered, however, when the Garden Club learned of the possibility of obtaining some valuable garden statuary owned by the Honorable John Hay Whitney, ambassador to England in the 1950s. Whitney had originally thought of giving the statuary to the Metropolitan Museum of Art in New York City, but when he learned of the efforts of the Garden Club of North Carolina, he gave the statuary to the Elizabethan Gardens project instead.

Whitney's gift included an ancient Italian fountain and pool with balustrade, wellhead, sundial, birdbaths, stone steps and benches, all of which date back to before the time of Elizabeth I. With the receipt of this priceless statuary, the plans for the garden were enlarged and elaborated. The Garden Club of North

Carolina enlisted the help of the New York landscape architectural firm of Innocenti and Webel to plan and install the gardens, which were expanded to include a full ten acres.

The land was dedicated and work was begun on June 2, 1953, the day of Elizabeth II's coronation. The gardens were formally opened to the public on August 18, 1960, the 373d anniversary of Virginia Dare's birth.

The Elizabethan Gardens have benefited from much generosity over the years, a fact that is evident to visitors as soon as they arrive. The front iron gates, which once hung at the French embassy in Washington, D.C., were a gift from the Honorable C. Douglas Dillon, undersecretary of state and later treasurer of the United States, and Mrs. Dillon.

The gatehouse, of bricks made in a late nineteenth-century kiln in Wilson, North Carolina, was built to look like a sixteenth-century orangery. The flagstone floor and handhewn beams help to sustain the image. Above the entrance is the coat of arms of Elizabeth I.

The gatehouse is furnished with many fine English antiques, such as a small, elaborately carved English chest with handmade hardware. Hanging on the walls are an oil portrait of Elizabeth I, thought to have been painted around 1592; a 1663 map of Devonshire (the original home of many of the first settlers); and a list of names of the lost colonists: the 91 men, 17 women, and 9 children who first arrived on Roanoke Island in 1587. Just outside the gatehouse is the herb garden that contains medicinal and culinary herbs, many of which are identified and further explained by small plaques. Here the visitor sees wormwood—once recommended as an antidote for the bite of a sea dragon; horehound, which was made into candy; and soapwort, used by the settlers as a cleanser. Many other herbs give the visitor a sense of how important these herbs must have been to the early settlers.

The gardens are laid out in a fashion popular in England during the latter part of the sixteenth century. The highest part of the garden, known as the mount,

Crape myrtles, originally from China, are often called the "lilac of the South." The common name comes from the petals, which resemble crepe paper. These small trees turn summer into a celebration of pink and white.

Opposite. The mount serves as a central point, and four different paths lead to other areas of the garden. To the west, paths lined with bright red salvia lead to the Sunken Garden.

Pages 24–25. The Sunken Garden holds priceless antique statuary given by John Hay Whitney, ambassador to England in the 1950s. Framed by a double hedge, this garden is a picture-perfect example of a formal sixteenth-century English landscape.

serves as a central point from which four paths lead to different parts of the garden.

The layout certainly would have looked familiar to the Roanoke settlers, for the homes and estates of their native country had gardens very much like this. Thanks to the designers' strict attention to detail and the emphasis on geometric design, the Elizabethan Gardens on Roanoke could easily be mistaken for a grand English garden of the sixteenth century.

To the north of the mount lies Roanoke Sound. The path leading to the water is lined with yucca and century plants and a rare form of sea holly that is indigenous to this area.

Also to the north is the overlook terrace, where in 1981 a sixteenth-century-style gazebo was con-

Huge clipped columns usher the visitor from one part of the garden to the next. South of the mount is the great lawn where a drama, The Lost Colony, is performed outdoors each summer.

structed, using period tools and techniques. Great pains were taken to construct the gazebo just as settlers might have done. The materials of the thatch roof were shipped from Norfolk, England. The hand-hewn oak posts and beams are connected by joinery, rather than nails. The exterior is covered with wattle and daub.

South of the mount lies the great lawn, where theater groups sometimes perform Elizabethan masques. Paul Green's 1937 drama *The Lost Colony* is performed each summer at Fort Raleigh National Historic Site, a park adjacent to the Elizabethan Gardens.

At the edge of the great lawn is a giant live oak that is thought to have been living in 1585 when the first colonists landed. A multitude of woody and herbaceous plants surround the lawn. During spring this area is filled with the beautiful blooms of camellias and azaleas. Summer finds the blooms of oak-leaf hydrangea and lace-cap hydrangea gracing the garden.

East of the mount, at the end of an azalea-lined alcove, is an idealized statue of Virginia Dare as she might have looked as an adult. The statue was carved in Rome in 1859 by an American sculptor, Maria Louisa Lander. The sculpture has a history all its own, for it spent two years at the bottom of the ocean, the result of a shipwreck. Once retrieved, it went to the State Hall of History in Raleigh. Later it belonged to Pulitzer Prize winner Paul Green, who gave it to the Elizabethan Gardens in the late 1950s. Local legend says that Virginia Dare grew up among the Indians and that her spirit still runs free in these woods in the form of a white doe.

West of the mount, steps lead to the sunken garden, perhaps the most beautiful part of the Elizabethan Gardens. Dwarfed by a double row of giant hedges, the sunken garden is achingly neat; pristine symmetry and order are the rule. Arched windows are cut into the hedges at regular intervals, letting the gardener peek out, the visitor peer in. The flower beds—oval, triangular, circular, and square— are filled to bursting with white, yellow, and blue

pansies in spring. Crape myrtles are heavy with the promise of a summer of bloom while at their feet annuals fill the beds with a rainbow of colors.

At the center of the sunken garden is a lovely antique Italian fountain and pool from the Whitney Collection. Statues of Apollo, Diana, Venus, and Jupiter, also from the Whitney Collection, adorn the corners.

The formal Queen's Rose Garden was added in 1976. It contains a rosebush from the royal rose garden at Windsor Castle, sent by Elizabeth II.

In the wildflower garden south of the mount the visitor will find plants indigenous and naturalized in this part of North Carolina. Some of the more outstanding plants included within this area are pink lady's slippers, foamflower, cardinal flower, white fringed orchid, and partridgeberry. The wildflower garden has a boggy area whose plants are of particular interest and importance, for several of them are considered uncommon.

The Elizabethan Gardens are a beautiful place to visit, providing both a taste of history and a horticultural delight. At each bend in the winding pathways, we find something to remind us of the purpose of the garden—to provide a glimpse of the beauty and the hardships that confronted early settlers in this nation.

{2}

Eighteenth-Century Town Gardens, 1700-1776

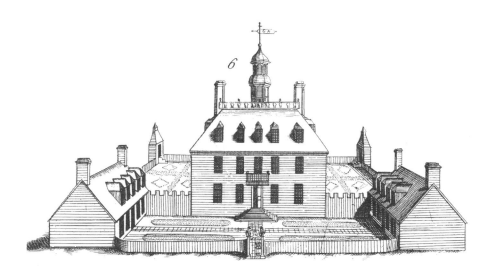

They had now no friends to welcome them nor Inns to entertain and refresh their weather beaten bodies. No houses, nor much less towns to repair to, to seek for succor. But they smelled the trees of the new land and rejoiced.

—FROM THE DIARY OF WILLIAM BRADFORD, ABOARD THE *Mayflower*, 1630

A hh, the trees. They stretched farther than the eye could see and must have seemed unending. It was said that a squirrel in eighteenth-century America could spend his whole life in the treetops and never come down once. What joy the scent of those trees must have brought not just to those aboard the Mayflower, but to other colonists as well. What fear this unexplored wilderness must have stirred in their hearts.

The first voyagers did not choose wisely when they determined places to begin their settlements. Jamestown, which was for a short time the seat of the Virginia colonial government, was founded on the banks of the James River in a marshy, unhealthful area. The population remained small because the mortality rate was so high. In 1699, after a disastrous fire in Jamestown, the government was moved to Middle Plantation, which later became known as Williamsburg.

Pages 28 and 29. Working at the edge of wilderness, gardeners at Williamsburg endeavored to bring a sense of order and formality to the landscape. The Governor's Palace Garden was planted with pristine precision. A copperplate called the Bodleian Plate shows the Governor's Palace as it looked in 1740.

To the south, the Carolina colony did not fare much better. The original settlement, Charles Town, was founded where the Ashley and Cooper rivers met and poured into the Atlantic Ocean. It was only a few years later, however, that the settlers left this marshy and unhealthful spot and moved across the Ashley River to the present site of Charleston. Here, at a place known as Oyster Point, the settlers laid out a walled town, using a plan they called the Grand Modell.

Because it was planned carefully and with foresight, the city grew gracefully and beautifully. The streets were wide and the house lots large, and spacious areas were set aside for churches and public buildings.

During the early eighteenth century, the settlers still feared attacks from native tribes and from the Spanish, who had settled in the area that had become known as Florida. For this reason, most new houses in Charleston were built within the city walls. Thus it was soon necessary to subdivide lots, and it became customary to build houses facing the street, with the gardens behind; many of these houses were attached. In 1740, the city was ravaged by fires; following these disasters, the houses were generally built with spaces in between to help keep fires from spreading. One added advantage was the greater availability of space for gardens.

The development of Charleston gardens was influenced by the presence of many different cultures. The early English and Irish settlers were soon joined by Dutch from New York and by a group of French Protestants. One of the most influential early groups was made up of English farmers who had originally settled in Barbados, departing for Charleston in 1680.

Both wealthy plantation owners and the well-to-do merchants of Charleston had a great love of gardening. By even as early as 1682, many European plants had been imported to supplement the lovely native plants that the settlers had found. In this year Thomas Ashe wrote: "The mulberry Tree everywhere amidst the Woods grows Wild. The planters, near their Plantations in Rows and Walks, plant them for Use, Ornament, and Pleasure…But now their Gardens begin to be supplied with such European Plants and Herbs as are necessary for the Kitchen, viz: Potatoes, lettice, coleworts, parsnip, Turnip, Carrot and Reddish; Their gardens also begin to be beautified and adorned with such Herbs and Flowers, which to the smell or Eye are pleasing and agreeable, viz: the Rose, Tulip, Carnation and Lily, etc." And by 1714 John Lawson had made this list of the herbs that he had in cultivation: "Angelica, balm, bugloss, borage, burnet, summer and winter savory, clary, marigold, pot marjoram, columbine, tansy, wormwood, mallow, lamb's quarter, thyme, hyssop, sweet bazil, rosemary, lavender, dill, caraway, cummin, anise, and coriander."

Constantly trying to encourage more settlers to come to Charleston, the colonists often sent fantastic descriptions of their new home back to Europe. In 1717 Robert Montgomery wrote a book entitled *A Discourse Concerning the Designed Establishment of a New Colony*. "English writers universally agree," he said, "that Carolina, especially in its Southern Bounds, is the most amiable country of the Universe….'Tis beautiful with odoriferous plants, green all the year. Pine, Cedar,

Cypress, Oak, Elm, Ash or Walnut, with innumerable other sorts, grow everywhere."

A general description of early eighteenth-century gardens appears in Loutrel W. Briggs's 1951 book, *Charleston Gardens.* "Usually a simple arrangement of walks and flower beds, arbors and bowers built for welcome shade and to support vines for fruit and beauty aka grapes and roses. As in England, arches and trellises placed throughout the garden, seats, summer houses and sundials were important ornaments."

High walls protected fruits and gave privacy. The lots were larger, and included small orchards and groves. Oranges were grown extensively, indicating a milder climate than Charleston has now.

By the year 1730 some Charleston residents were taking their gardening very seriously, as reported in J.E.W. Shecut's book *Medical and Philosophical Essays.* "Sometime in the year 1730 Mrs. Lamboll excited great interest in the science of horticulture and gardening by planting a large and handsome flower and kitchen garden upon the European plan. It was the first of the kind in Charleston and occupied the site, corner of King and Lamboll Streets. She was followed by Mrs. Logan and Mrs. Glopton, after which gardening was generally attended to by most families occupying suitable lands, both for pleasure and profit."

It is not always easy to determine what plants were used in eighteenth-century American gardens. Today's period gardeners are greatly aided in the search for authenticity by a series of letters written between Peter Collinson of London and John Custis of Williamsburg during the years 1734 and 1746. These letters indicate that the discovery of indigenous plants was only the beginning of the challenge of getting them to grow properly in the garden.

During the early years of the eighteenth century, the colonists desired to mimic the Old World in many ways. Certainly the gardens found in early American cities and towns resembled those of Europe. This basic pattern was followed in Charleston, in Williamsburg, in Tryon Palace, and in

a multitude of other places with close ties to England.

Many of these gardens reached their prime during the eighteenth century, but they declined in succeeding years. Restoration gardens have provided a clear illustration of what gardens were like when the American colonies were still happily tied to England. The English have richly influenced our ideas of landscape design, and it is a heritage that we are fortunate to have.

WILLIAMSBURG

The capital of the Virginia colony was moved from Jamestown to Middle Plantation—now known as Williamsburg—in 1699. This small town on the brink of the wilderness emulated England in many ways—not least in the style of its gardens.

The beginning of the eighteenth century in England was the beginning of what many consider the "golden age" of gardening. Stemming from the British love of the outdoors, gardening became a popular hobby and a form of artistic expression made even more exciting by the new plants brought to Europe by explorers from all parts of the world. Gardening became a passion, even an obsession, with many. Sophisticated clubs and the royal court echoed with conversations of new plants and new ways of putting these plants together.

In England, inspired gardening was practiced at the top of the social ladder. The aristocracy generally set the standards, supporting all forms of garden art—but their love of gardening united them with Britons from all walks of life.

Scholars believe that the climax of formal gardening in England occurred during the reign of William and Mary (1689–1702). There were several specific stylistic elements that found their way into most formal gardens.

One such element was the *parterre*, a geometric, often rectangular, bed with the hedges along two borders made up of small, close-growing plants. These hedges were usually created from thrift, thyme, or dwarf box. Another such element was the *knotte*, also composed of these miniature hedges, planted in such a way as to give the appearance of being overlapped, or tied in a knot. *Compartments* were borders of flowers set among grass.

Other features of formal late-seventeenth-century gardens included a bowling green, a mount (an artificial hill from which the entire garden could be viewed), statuary, urns, arbors, sundials, espaliered fruit trees, topiary, and dovecotes.

William and Mary themselves showed a great love of gardening. William took an interest in design, particularly French design, and he had a love of topiary. Mary's passion was for flowers and rare plants, which she kept in hothouses heated by flues and furnaces. Daniel Defoe, author of *Robinson Crusoe*, wrote that "all gentlemen of England began to fall in [with the King's taste in gardening]…and in a few years fine gardens and fine houses began to grow up in every corner."

By the time that Anne had assumed the throne in 1702, gardening in England was undergoing great changes, greatly influenced by the queen herself. In this century, between about 1720 and 1800, a more naturalistic look became popular. Gardens were to "blend in" with the landscape at large, rather than to be separated from it by tall hedges or fences. Straight lines and clipped, manicured shrubs no longer held favor with English gardeners.

But Virginians and other American colonists did not follow this new gardening trend. With a vast wilderness literally over the next hill, the colonists seemed to prefer more formal gardens and a clear delineation between civilization and wilderness. So while the majority of gardens in England in the seventeenth and early eighteenth centuries were transformed, leaving few formal elements surviving today, gardens in Williamsburg continued with the same earlier formal tradition. Eventually, the Williamsburg gardens became a window in time, offering a glimpse of a beautiful and exciting age.

Plant material for the Williamsburg gardens came from a variety of sources. Native plants dug from the surrounding fields and woods were used, and more exotic plants were imported from Europe. The nursery of Peter Bellett that existed from 1793 to 1808 was, at its prime, a large and bustling enterprise covering approximately fifteen acres. In 1805 its inventory included shrubs, flowers, vegetable seeds, and more than a hundred thousand trees of various types.

The modern restoration of the colonial capital of Williamsburg was made possible by the generosity of John D. Rockefeller, Jr. The first landscape architect hired by the Colonial Williamsburg Foundation was Arthur A. Shurcliff. Shurcliff graduated from Harvard University in 1896 and worked with Frederick Law Olmsted, Sr., who designed New York's Central Park and also developed the grounds at the Biltmore Estate in Asheville, North Carolina.

In Shurcliff's words, the recreated gardens were intended to "recall the period of the ancient dwellings and the old city itself." To do this he studied the layouts of thirty-eight different colonial and plantation sites and did thorough research and study of southern gardens and gardening traditions that might serve as examples and inspiration for his recreations.

The Governor's Palace

Perhaps nowhere in Williamsburg were the gardens more beautiful than at the Governor's Palace. Even today, the spacious grounds of the palace have a distinctly formal style reminiscent of seventeenth-century England.

The first royal governor to live in the Williamsburg palace was Alexander Spotswood, who moved into the mansion in 1716 (even though it was not completed until 1722). As the building neared completion, Spotswood showed more and more interest in the garden. He wanted to have the most elaborate grounds in the Virginia colony, including a formal water garden, which boasted terraces leading to a canal and a fish pond on the west side of the mansion. Enormous amounts of public money went to pay for this grand scheme, provoking ire among the members of the

The garden was a place to sit and dream but was also a showcase for exotic plants shipped to Williamsburg from around the world. Native plants were often given a spot of honor in the garden.

Alexander Spotswood, first governor at Williamsburg, wanted to create the most elaborate grounds in the Virginia Colony, including terraces leading to a canal and a fish pond.

House of Burgesses. Eventually Spotswood was forced to scale down his elaborate garden plans.

The gardens were never completed to Spotswood's total satisfaction, but they were nonetheless developed into extensive, beautiful grounds that echoed the formal beauty of the house. In 1724, the Reverend Hugh Jones wrote in his *Present State of Virginia*, "The Palace, or governor's house, is a magnificent structure, finished and beautified with gates, fine gardens, offices, walks, a fine canal, orchards…"

Today the Governor's Palace grounds only cover approximately ten acres. During the early eighteenth century, however, the total acreage was close to 370. Much of this land was probably used to grow fruit (for both the table and livestock), as pastureland, and to grow trees for firewood. Although the gardens were undoubtedly beautiful, little documentation is now available showing what the original landscape actually looked like. The best piece of evidence is a copper plate dating from about 1740, which was discovered in the

Bodleian Library at Oxford University in 1929. This plate shows the forecourt garden, composed of oval planting beds and paved walkways, and the ballroom garden, laid out in a number of diamond-shaped parterres.

A document known as the Act of 1705 refers to plans for the grounds incorporating what are now known as the ballroom and north gardens. The Act of 1705 made stipulation for "a Garden of the length of two hundred fifty-four foot and of the breadth of one hundred forty-four from out to out, adjoining to the said house, to be laid out and levelled and enclosed with a brick wall, four feet high, with balustrades of wood upon the said wall, and that handsome gates be made to the said court-yard and garden." Using these dimensions as a guide, archeologists in the early 1930s did excavation work that confirmed the garden's width and length.

The reconstituted grounds of the Governor's Palace at Colonial Williamsburg closely resemble those of an early eighteenth-century English country estate, complete with formal geometric parterres, topiary, a mount, a water garden, pleached arbors, decorative lead urns, and a maze.

The forecourt garden, as represented in the Bodleian plate, is planted with four oval parterres. The hedges are of yaupon holly, and the ground cover English ivy. The ballroom garden is laid out symmetrically along a central north-south center line. There are eight diamond-shaped parterres and six yaupon holly topiaries on either side of the central walk. The twelve topiaries are said to represent the twelve apostles of Christ.

The north garden, too, is formally laid out, and the central path is bordered by American beech trees. To each side of the path are formal planting beds filled with bulbs and pansies in spring and with summer annuals later in the year. Dark, shady tunnels, created by the intertwining branches of the beech trees, run alongside the garden.

Left. *Based on an early drawing, the ballroom garden at the Governor's Palace was reconstructed to include a series of diamond-shaped parterres and closely clipped boxwood columns.*

Below. *The English monarchs William and Mary both had a passion for gardening. William was fascinated by topiary and had gardens of boxwood clipped into unusual shapes, a fashion Williamsburg gardeners were quick to imitate.*

The mount at the Governor's Palace is atop the icehouse. Traditionally, a mount was used to survey the surrounding countryside or to enjoy the vista of the formal gardens. From the top of the mount here, the visitor has a splendid view of the maze below.

Although there is no documentary evidence that a maze garden was ever a part of the original garden at the Governor's Palace, it very well may have been—for mazes were often included in seventeenth-century English country estates. The maze now found at Williamsburg was loosely patterned after one at Hampton Court Palace, near London.

Food and entertaining were of the utmost importance to the early governors at Williamsburg—proof of this fact is that the cook was reportedly the highest-paid servant on the staff. The kitchen gardens were accordingly quite significant. In the restoration, the kitchen garden is slightly less prominent. Located to the west behind the kitchen, today's smaller, representative kitchen garden features vegetables, herbs, and fruits. This space would not have accommodated the needs of the colonial governor's kitchen; probably terraces along the canal and additional land across the canal were also used to grow food for the table.

George Wythe House

George Wythe was the first professor of law at the College of William and Mary, a post he retained for twenty-three years. He had the distinction of instructing such notable men as Henry Clay, James Monroe, Thomas Jefferson, and John Marshall. Wythe lived in Williamsburg from 1755 to 1791, in a large, spacious house on the west side of Palace Green. The property had been purchased in 1748 for the royal sum of five shillings by Colonel Richard Taliaferro. He built a large brick house on a lot on Palace Green and purchased additional property to the west. Taliaferro gave the house and property to his daughter Elizabeth when she married Wythe. From 1781 to 1782, during the Yorktown Campaign, generals Washington and Rochambeau used the house as their military headquarters.

Figs were often grown by planters and gardeners in the Colonies. The fig is actually not a fruit but a cluster of closed flowers.

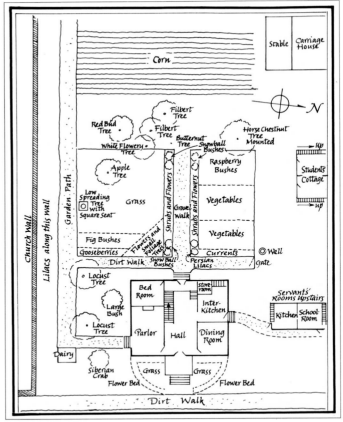

Left. The grounds at George Wythe House are thought to be a close representation of the garden as it looked in the mid-nineteenth century. Reconstruction was aided by a map drawn by Kate Millington sometime between 1837 and 1848.

Opposite. The reconstruction in 1940 of the Wythe House grounds was designed to include a formal landscape with a long central walk, clipped hedges, and an arbor.

In 1791, Wythe moved to Richmond and the property, which had reverted back to the Taliaferro estate, was sold in 1791 and again in 1793. Elizabeth and Henry Skipwith, who owned the house during the late eighteenth and early nineteenth centuries, took out several insurance policies on the property. These policies gave historians the decided benefit of having rather detailed descriptions of the property as it existed at that time. The last of these policies was written in 1815.

Several outbuildings were built on the property some time before 1772, and by 1815 a dairy had been added. Today's reconstruction includes the kitchen, wellhead, laundry, smokehouse, lumber house, and stable, all on their original foundations.

Little is known about the garden on the Wythe property. Archeologists did find rubble behind the house, showing where garden walks might have been.

Historians have found indications that Wythe was interested in fruit culture. Elizabeth, from whose family the property derived, took charge of the kitchen garden.

Arthur Shurcliff, the Colonial Williamsburg Foundation's first landscape architect, imagined the Wythe garden as a formal, ornamental expanse extending the entire length of the property. Since Shurcliff's 1940 reconstruction, additional research has shown that the garden was probably much less formal and less extensive than Shurcliff believed. Pastures and service yards including few plants—and typically covered with a mixture of shell and marl— probably accounted for one of the three large lots that the property comprised. Plots for vegetables, herbs, and fruit were probably originally grown here, and they are now displayed in this way. A very large sycamore tree on the property is believed to be almost two hundred years old, indicating that it was planted soon after George Wythe sold the property.

In the mid-nineteenth century the house was owned by John Millington, whose daughter Kate drew

a map of the site sometime between 1837 and 1848. Her map shows a long central path made of gravel lined with flowers and shrubs on either side. The map also indicates the presence of many fruit trees.

Much of the plant material used in this garden today is of a formal nature. A hornbeam arbor, origi-nally found at the end of Shurcliff's extensive formal garden, was moved to the midpoint of the central walkway when the garden was reworked in the early 1960s. Clipped hedges of American and English box-wood are also present, as well as other shrubs such as Osage-orange, silky dogwood, and yaupon holly.

Benjamin Waller House

Although George Wythe was the first law professor at the College of William and Mary, it was another Williamsburg resident, Benjamin Waller, who taught George Wythe about the law. In addition to private teaching, Waller, an affluent and important citizen, also served as burgess, city recorder, judge of the court of admiralty, and vestryman of Bruton Parish.

Benjamin Waller lived in an L-shaped colonial house on Francis Street from 1742 to 1770. Although the house is lovely, it is the garden that holds the greatest importance, for it was recreated according to a sketch drawn in the early 1880s by Waller's great-great-granddaughter, Luty Blow. The sketch has given invaluable help in reconstructing the garden.

During the first part of the nineteenth century, Benjamin Waller's granddaughter, Eliza, married George Blow and moved to Tower Hill plantation in Sussex County. Eliza had such happy memories of her grandfather's garden in Williamsburg that she recreated this garden at her new home.

This love of gardening passed through two more generations until Luty Blow, Eliza's granddaughter, created a drawing of the garden at Tower Hill. This sketch, taken from the garden that was patterned after Benjamin Waller's Williamsburg garden, proved to be an astoundingly accurate representation of Benjamin Waller's garden. When archeologists uncovered the

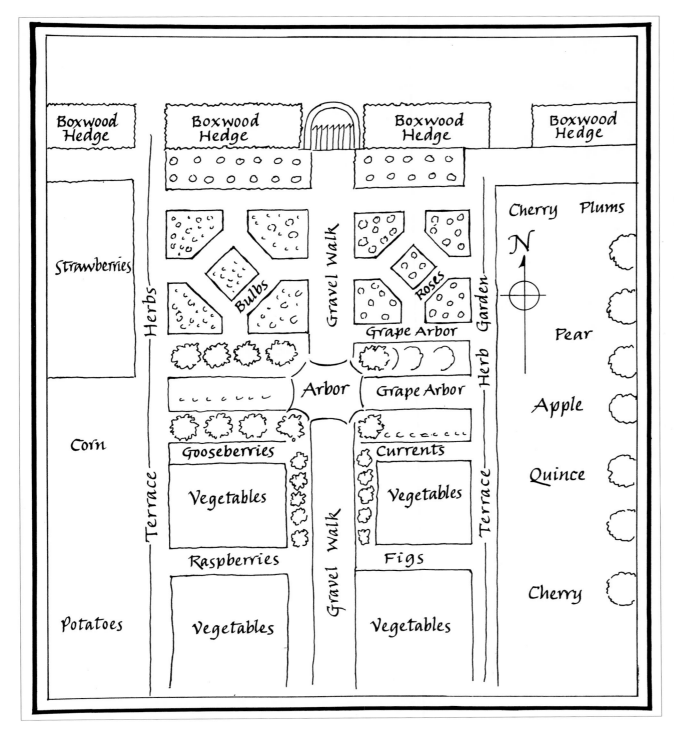

Boxwood Hedge

Boxwood Hedge

Boxwood Hedge

Boxwood Hedge

Strawberries

Herbs

Bulbs

Gravel Walk

Roses

Corn

Terrace

Gooseberries

Vegetables

Arbor

Grape Arbor

Grape Arbor

Currents

Vegetables

Herb Garden

Terrace

N

Cherry   Plums

Pear

Apple

Quince

Cherry

Raspberries

Gravel Walk

Figs

Vegetables

Potatoes

Vegetables

Vegetables

Williamsburg houses form the perfect backdrop for a long perennial border. Bright summer colors come from yellow and red daylilies. Yellow yarrow hovers at the feet of old-fashioned hollyhocks.

surviving central path of the garden at the Waller house in Williamsburg, they superimposed Luty's sketch over it. It matched almost perfectly.

Luty's sketch shows a relatively formal, symmetrical garden, composed of four parts, roughly the same size. According to the sketch, these four components were planted with flowers, fruit, vegetables, and crops (such as corn and potatoes). A long central gravel walk led from the yard directly behind the house, through a small gate, to the family graveyard in the southwest corner of the lot. In addition to the central path, archeological work has uncovered fence lines and the foundations for outbuildings in the back of the house.

The garden was recreated in 1953–54, based on a plan drawn by Alden Hopkins, Colonial Williamsburg's resident landscape architect. Hopkins consulted closely with Arthur Shurcliff, who had by that time retired. Their design included much more decorative vegetation than was indicated in Luty's plan, and included a gazebo rather than an arbor. Perhaps their changes were a reflection of Colonial Revival philosophy, which placed visual beauty before function.

Luty's sketch showed a picket fence separating the yard behind the house from the garden beyond, and this fence has been reconstructed, based on a sample of the original fence material found in the house. The fence, now as then, was lined with box-

wood—standard specimens on the yard side, dwarf box on the garden side. The location of the reconstructed fence is known to be correct, matching the original fence line.

The eastern part of the property was an orchard with cherries, plums, pears, apples, and quince. A grape arbor was also included. A more decorative arbor was found in the center of the garden where the two axes intersect. The vegetables were placed in the bottom or southernmost portion of the garden, beyond the arbor, making them less noticeable from the house and yard. Little of this garden has been restored today. The present garden is lovely, adorned with rich boxwood and clean paths, but lacks most of the original details.

Correspondence between the Blow and Waller families indicates a great active interest in gardening from all members of the families. The families frequently exchanged plants and seeds, or purchased them from sources in America. There were nurseries at this time in Charleston, Boston, Philadelphia, New York, and even in Williamsburg. In 1812 George Blow wrote to his grandfather-in-law, Benjamin Waller:

Make Hercules [the gardener] send as many scions of Privy [privet] as can be spared without injuring the main Bushes. If he has any young Box scions with Roots I would be glad of as many as he can possibly Beg, as well as what can be spared from the garden. Make him also sett out (my mother says) a trench of young Twigs of Box for the purpose of taking

Root to sett out next year.... Eliza begs from the garden some currant Bushes... English Raspberries, ditto a few bunches of Sweet Violet, and my mother wishes some of each Kind of the Garden Seed from New York.

TRYON PALACE

In 1767, the British colony of North Carolina began building a fine and grand palace for its royal governor, William Tryon, in the city of New Bern, at that time one of the largest towns in North Carolina. Tryon himself took a leading role in the planning of this royal palace, which was, not surprisingly, constructed in purely English style: Designed by a British architect, it was planned as a British government house and residence in what was then a British colony.

When it was completed, this thoroughly English edifice was considered by some to be the most beautiful building in North America. It served as residence for two North Carolina royal governors, William Tryon and Josiah Martin, and the State of North Carolina inaugurated its first four governors here.

The state capital was moved from New Bern to Raleigh in 1794. A few years later, in February of 1798, the main building of Tryon Palace was destroyed by fire. The palace and grounds soon deteriorated. A street was cut through the center square, and lots on both sides were sold by the state. The east wing disappeared in the nineteenth century, and the west wing served as an apartment house for many years.

*Brick walls intersect the gardens and provide support for extensive plantings of espaliered fruit. Grapes (**above**), apples, and pears are all trained to grow along the walls.*

In 1945 the Tryon Palace Commission was formed with a view to restoring the magnificent building. Thanks to a generous gift from the late Mrs. James Edwin Latham of Greensboro, North Carolina, the palace was restored and rebuilt on its original foundations in the 1950s. Tryon Palace is today an unexpected pleasure. Encompassing six acres, the restored and reconstructed buildings and grounds of the palace bring a bit of eighteenth-century England to this small town.

A long drive and marl walk grace the front of the palace. The symmetry is impossible to ignore, for the main building is flanked by two wings, and the entire complex is situated neatly on an oval marl walk, centered on a grassy green lawn.

The restoration carefully follows the original drawings of John Hawks, the English master builder; an authentic reconstruction of the east wing and restoration of the west wing were completed.

In order to remain true to the restoration of the grounds as well as the house, the Tryon Palace Commission decided to develop the grounds into the sort of garden found on English estates between 1760 and 1770. The reconstructed grounds were intended to reflect the style and grace evident in the house.

No records of the original Tryon Palace gardens were ever found, but the design of the gardens here was influenced by landscape projects drawn for prominent families of the time. A 1769 drawing by C. J. Sauthier depicts the town of New Bern, including Tryon Palace. According to this drawing, formal gardens flanked a broad expanse of lawn to the north of the palace buildings.

No other records or actual documents have been found indicating the existence of extensive formal gardens, but the possibility remains that they were part of the original palace grounds. An entry in the guestbook dating from June 1783 makes it clear that the original gardens echoed the loveliness of the house, alluding to "ornamentation extremely simple and placed with considerable taste and intelligence."

At the time of the restoration, archeological excavations unearthed evidence of several garden elements, including a well, a marl drive, and the palace courtyard wall. It is known that there was a kitchen garden, because Royal Governor Josiah Martin noted in his diary that he had buried arms and ammunition in a cabbage patch.

During the mid-eighteenth century, and in particular between 1760 and 1770, professional landscapers in England emphasized a return to nature and highly formalized naturalism. "Wilderness areas" were very popular—dense plantings of shrubs and trees interspersed with winding walks and flanked by open expanses of lawn. They are here represented by the plantings close to the south lawn between the mansion and the Trent River.

Several parts of the Tryon Palace gardens were designed to be seen primarily from the palace windows. The first of these, the green garden, is laid out in formal geometric beds. It contains plants that feature different shades of green, and it is the subtle shades and textures of the plants that bring great interest. Clipped hedges contrast with low-growing, shiny-leaved vinca. New growth of English ivy shows a tender pale green against the brick walls.

Farther around the west wing of the mansion stands the Maude Moore Latham Memorial Garden, planted in honor and memory of Maude Moore Latham who gave so much of her time and resources to make the restoration of Tryon Palace a possibility. Here the richness of the palace is duplicated in scrolls of clipped holly. Bricks and clipped hedges provide a framework for color from spring-blooming bulbs and summer annuals.

Evergreen shrubs such as gardenia, oleander, bay, and holly provide a deep background for the seasonal color. Ornate stone baskets of fruit add to the air of opulence that clings to this part of the garden.

At the end of the Latham Memorial Garden stand large, ornate iron gates that lead from one garden to another, just like doors might lead from room to room.

Left. The scroll garden is composed of intricately shaped small shrub borders. Inside these green frames grow colorful bedding plants that change with the seasons. An ivy-covered archway leads from one garden room to the next.

Above. An eighteenth-century brick dovecote was reconstructed on the Palace grounds. Documents show that the royal governor Josiah Martin (Governor Tryon's successor) contracted for a poultry house, smoke house, and dovecote.

Past these gates is a small alcove, called Hawks's Allee. (An allee is a walkway lined with clipped trees or shrubs.) Hawks's Allee was named for John Hawks, the original builder and architect of the palace.

Next to Hawks's Allee is another, the Pleached Allee. (To pleach is to train shrubs and vines over an arched support.) Here, the plant material is yaupon holly.

The end of this allee leads the visitor to the wilderness walk, where trees, shrubs, and vines give one the feeling of wilderness controlled. Winding paths lead to the Trent River; looking back, the visitor has a magnificent view of the south lawn and the palace.

The gardens surrounding the east wing of the palace are principally fruit and vegetable gardens. One exception is the Kellenberger Garden, another private garden that is best viewed from Governor Tryon's bedroom on the second floor.

Perhaps the most outstanding feature of the grounds is the kitchen garden with its espaliered fruit trees. (To espalier is to train trees or shrubs to grow flat along walls or fences.) In the kitchen garden grew the fruits, herbs, and vegetables used at the palace. Several plants of tobacco and cotton are now grown here for display, but these plants were originally grown in outlying fields. Old brick walls hold trained pears, apples, quinces, and figs, and the collection is one of

the largest orchards of espaliered fruit in the East. Particularly noteworthy are the massive grapevines, which have been trained along the old brick walls.

The Tryon Palace gardens' designers have made great efforts to include trees, shrubs, and plants that were known to have been in America before 1771. The gardens thus offer excellent illustrations of how early Americans embraced and duplicated the best of what England had to offer. The British influence on the history of American landscape design is undeniable. We are fortunate in having the gardens of Tryon Palace as example and inspiration for many of our own estate gardens.

HEYWARD-WASHINGTON HOUSE

One of the best-known and best-loved Charleston gardens is located behind the Heyward-Washington House. This house was built in 1770 by Daniel Heyward, whose son, Thomas, was a delegate to the Continental Congress and a signer of the Declaration of Independence. In May of 1791 President George Washington visited Charleston and stayed with Thomas Heyward for about ten days. Ever since, the house has been referred to as the Heyward-Washington House.

In 1931 Mrs. Emma B. Richardson and the Charleston Museum recreated a garden on the back plot behind the house. The plans they used for this eighteenth-century garden were probably those drawn for a garden found close to this house, that of Judge Elijau Hall Bayes.

The garden at Heyward-Washington house in Charleston was reconstructed in 1931. This 1940 photograph shows the garden in the early stages of development.

The garden at the Heyward-Washington House is rectangular with a circular bed at the center that is surrounded by additional geometrically shaped beds. The entire garden is surrounded by an old brick wall. A long central path leads to the back of the garden where an inviting garden bench beckons.

Along the back wall is a wide flower bed planted with a ground cover, many species of native ferns, and flowering shrubs. The presence of the pre-Revolutionary War garden-tool shed, the kitchen, the laundry, and the necessary house give the garden an additional air of authenticity.

During the 1960s the maintenance of the garden was entrusted to the Garden Club of Charleston. A real effort has been made to use only plant species that were actually grown in Charleston before Washington's 1791 visit. Outstanding among these are eight tea olive plants. In spite of these efforts, however, a few modern plants remain; they are gradually being replaced with eighteenth-century plants.

In 1990 the city of Charleston was ravaged by Hurricane Hugo. The damage was extensive, and the gardens and buildings of the Heyward-Washington House suffered greatly. Part of the garden was lost in the hurricane; the Garden Club of Charleston replanted it as an eighteenth-century knot garden. A small tangerine tree is now surrounded by "knots" of green and silver germander and sweet allysa. Other herbs planted in this part of the garden include calendula, digitalis (foxglove), santolina, rue, valerian, and various old-fashioned roses such as gallica and old blush.

*A knot garden (**far left**) intertwines small aromatic shrubs in the herb garden. The presence of several outbuildings— a toolshed, kitchen, laundry, and necessary house—adds an air of authenticity. Perennials (**left**) surround a small statue toward the rear of the garden.*

Opposite. *In 1791 George Washington spent ten days here. It takes little imagination to envision early statesmen strolling the clean walks and enjoying a quiet garden similar to this one.*

{3}
Early Plantation Gardens, 1600-1750

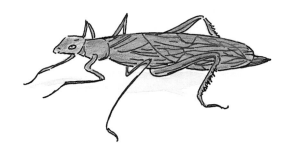

The tragedy at Roanoke Island did not long dampen the enthusiasm of the English for colonizing the New World.

The colony at Jamestown was soon successfully established, and the southern coast was not forgotten. In 1663, Charles II granted all the land between Virginia and the Spanish settlements to a group of his personal favorites including the Earl of Clarendon, the Duke of Albemarle, and Lord Berkeley.

Farther south, the colony of Georgia was founded as an asylum for debtors and to serve as a buffer between Carolina and the Spanish settlements. In the spring of 1733 General James Oglethorpe laid out a ten-acre garden at Savannah. His plan and that of his trustees was to do experimental work in botany and agriculture and to plant fruit trees, tea plants, coconut, and cotton.

Seventeenth-century American gardens were primarily utilitarian rather than ornamental, but settlers gradually began to expand their gardens to include the pleasures of flowers grown for color and fragrance. Rice and indigo were both cultivated on large plantations, and a genteel and wealthy class of citizens arose. Before long, the plantation owners began to move beyond commercial success to the more indulgent and genteel pleasures of gardening.

These rich plantation owners spent much time, effort, and money in creating beautiful gardens. In the mid-1700s, John Brickell, a physician from Edenton, North Carolina, wrote: "Most of the plantations have a very noble and beautiful prospect…. Here are in several places large savannahs to behold which at certain seasons appear at a distance like so many pleasure gardens being intermixt with variety of spontaneous flowers of various colours, such as tulip, trumpet flower and Princess feather."

The slow, lazy-flowing rivers of the South were home to some of the most beautiful and exciting gardens in this country. Along South Carolina's Ashley River, plantations such as Middleton Place, Magnolia Gardens, and Crowfield prospered. In Virginia, the James River Plantations were home to some of the country's most wealthy and prestigious men. Designed to impress visitors traveling by water, many plantation gardens were planted close to the riverbanks.

Page 48. A venerable old oak tree casts long shadows on the lawn at Middleton Place. A gracefully arched bridge beckons the visitor to explore the history and beauty of this early plantation.

Left. *In the early days, visitors to Middleton Place most often came by boat up the Ashley River. The grounds were carefully terraced and beautifully maintained from the plantation house to the river.*

Bottom left. *The lower level of the old springhouse was originally used to store dairy foods, and the upper level was used as a Sunday school for slave children. Today the building houses a history of the plantation.*

Bottom right. *Landscape design at Middleton Place reflects not only French but also English influences. The plantation is considered by many to be a link between seventeenth- and eighteenth-century schools of design.*

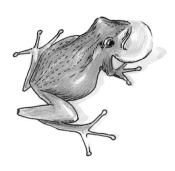

Perhaps one of the most beautiful plantations created during the eighteenth century in America was Crowfield, which was built some time after 1729 near Charleston, South Carolina. Sadly, little remains of Crowfield today. We are fortunate in having a description, written in 1740 by a visitor to the plantation, Eliza Lucas:

The house stands a mile from but in sight of the road and makes a very handsome appearance; as you draw near it new beauties discover themselves; first the fruitful vine manteling the wall loaded with delicious clusters. Next a spacious Basin in the midst of a large Green presents itself as you enter the gate that leads to the House....

From the back door is a spacious walk a thousand feet long, each side of which nearest the house is a grass plat ornamented in a Serpentine manner with Flowers; next to that on the right hand is what immediately struck my rural taste, a thicket of young, tall live oaks...Opposite on the left hand is a large square bowling green, sunk a little below the level of the rest of the garden, with a walk quite around composed of a double row of fine, large flowering Laurel and Catalpas which afford both shade and beauty.

Today, several plantation gardens still exist that show the kind of beauty exhibited by Crowfield.

Eighteenth-century plantation gardens included flowers, bulbs, and shrubs imported from England and other parts of the world, as well as new and exciting plants found growing naturally in surrounding fields and forests. In 1709 John Lawson said, in a description of the Carolinas, "But as for the wild spontaneous Flowers of this Country, Nature has been so liberal, that I cannot name one tenth part of the valuable ones."

Discovering valuable new plants became the obsession of many eighteenth-century botanists, and acquiring new garden plants was a passion on both sides of the Atlantic. Among the most important plant explorers and collectors during this century were John and William Bartram and a Frenchman, André Michaux. Dedicated and untiring in their search for new plants, these men changed the face of gardening around the world by exporting many beautiful plants from the wilds of North America to Europe and beyond. They also introduced many beautiful foreign plants to American gardens.

The descriptions of the native plants of North America must have inspired gardeners around the world, for these accounts were enthusiastic and sometimes even poetic. Toward the end of the eighteenth century, William Bartram wrote:

In these cool, sequestered, rocky vales, we behold the following celebrated beauties of the hills,...delicate *Philadelphus inodorus*, which displays the white wavy mantle, with the sky robed Delphinium, perfumed *Convallaria* and fiery *Azalea*, flaming on the ascending hills or wavy surface of the gliding brooks. The epithet fiery, I annex to this most celebrated species of Azalea, as being expressive of the appearance of its flowers, which are in general of the colour of the finest red lead, orange and bright gold, as well as yellow and cream colour...This is certainly the most gay and brilliant flowering shrub yet known.

After the French Revolution, the French government could no longer financially support Michaux and the work he was doing in North America. To help support his travels and collecting, in 1746 André Michaux bought 222 acres and established a nursery on the Ashley River near Charleston. Here he grew and sold exotic plants obtained from Chinese traders—including the Chinese silk tree, *Camellia japonica*, and ginkgo.

Many of the plants from Michaux's nursery made their way north to Virginia, where they were eagerly bought by enthusiastic gardeners, who planted them among the multitude of colorful and interesting native plants.

Another vivid description comes to us from the Reverend Andrew Burnaby, who wrote a book entitled *Travels through the Middle Settlements in North America in the Years 1759–1760*. Here he lists many of the trees and shrubs found in these woods.

> Besides trees and flowers of an ordinary nature, the woods produce myrtles, cedars, cypresses, sugar trees, firs of different sorts, and no less than seven or eight kinds of oak; they are likewise adorned and beautified with red flowering maples, sassafrass trees, dogwoods, acacias, red buds, scarlet-flowering chestnuts, fringetrees, flowering poplars, umbrellas, magnolias, yellow jasamines, pacoons, atamusco lillies, May-apples, and innumerable other sorts, so that one may reasonably assert that no other country ever appeared with greater elegance or beauty.

It was the dream of men such as George Washington and Thomas Jefferson to make the most of this "elegance and beauty" in their native land and to work with nature to create gardens and vistas of great beauty. Eighteenth-century plantation owners were strongly influenced by English principles of landscape design. They also, however, needed to include practical elements within the landscape. When Jefferson returned to Monticello in 1789, after a five-year diplomatic mission to France, he began to combine English ideas of landscape design with the more necessary parts of plantation life, including areas for livestock and crops.

Such a task was not always easy. The landscape of England differed greatly from that of Virginia. In 1806, Jefferson wrote to William Hamilton, "The ground which I destine to improve in the style of English gardens are in a form very difficult to be managed."

Plantation owners found both beauty and pleasure in their gardens. Accounts of the gardens at Monticello and Mount Vernon, as well as of those found farther south in the Carolinas, prove that these working and thriving plantations were also places of beauty and grandeur.

These early planters left us a legacy of landscapes that were the true beginnings of uniquely American garden design. Combining the best of European thought with the best of American imagination and creativity, the gardens of Monticello, Mount Vernon, Middleton Place, Orton Plantation, and Magnolia Gardens became true showplaces of American beauty.

MIDDLETON PLACE

> Here Drayton's seat and Middleton is found
> Delightful villas! Be they long renowned.
> —*London Gentlemen's Magazine*, July 1753

The author of this 1753 couplet would be pleased. Today, both Drayton Hall and Middleton Place are still renowned.

Fourteen miles northwest of Charleston, South Carolina, nestled into a bend of the Ashley River, lies Middleton Place, America's oldest formal landscaped garden. The first few steps onto the grounds of this estate give the visitor a sense of grandeur and elegance, and a tantalizing glimpse of the sumptuous affluence that this southern plantation must have known. In *The Century Magazine* in 1910, Frances Duncan wrote that Middleton Place "represents a phase of colonial life which has vanished completely, and belongs to the days when South Carolina was a royal province and, like the mother-country, had its hereditary and wealthy aristocracy."

The Middletons were wealthy and important citizens in the early days of our country. Henry Middleton (1717–1784) was president of the first Continental Congress, and his son, Arthur (1742–1787), was a signer of the Declaration of Independence.

Henry Middleton acquired the property when he married Mary Williams; the estate was part of her dowry. The young couple moved into the house in

1741, but it wasn't until twenty-three years had passed that Henry began extensive landscaping. Unfortunately, the original house was burned during the Civil War, and with it, the Middletons' library, including most records and family papers.

Little is known about the plans for the garden, but Middleton is typical of many European gardens from that time period. Many landscape architecture historians today consider the style embraced by Middleton Place to be a missing link between the seventeenth and eighteenth centuries in landscape design—between the geometrically precise French and the free and romantic English landscape doctrines. At Middleton both styles are represented. Loutrel Briggs, in his 1951 book Charleston Gardens, suggested that it is "essentially English, [but] has a distinct French flavor." Many European gardens (and possibly Middleton as well) were influenced by André Le Nôtre, the seventeenth-century French designer whose most famous work was the gardens at Versailles.

The formal influence can be seen in the remains of the mount, bowling green, reflecting pool, and formally laid out flower beds. The scale and the feeling of the plantation as a whole, however, is not confined and restricted, but free and all–encompassing, indicative of the English influence.

Family legend says that it took Henry Middleton and his huge numbers of slaves nearly ten years to lay out and construct the gardens. The first priority was to excavate, mold, and shape terraces from the high bluff on which the house was built down to the Ashley River. Between the river and the terraces, two adjoining "butterfly lakes" were built. These lakes are made up of two small triangles of land that form the inner butterfly wings, and two larger lakes that make the outer wings. Today these terraces and beautifully formed lakes are considered the symbol of Middleton Place.

Although each subsequent generation of Middletons left its mark on the landscape of the estate, the grounds are thought to be remarkably close to the original gardening philosophy of the first

Henry Middleton. The estate has been called an "organic historical document."

English landscape design in the late eighteenth century was greatly influenced by Capability Brown. Under his tutelage, designers in England soon opted for sweeping vistas and wide open spaces and the elimination of formal beds and avenues. Because of this influence, many English and American eighteenth-century gardens were drastically altered—but not so the formal gardens at Middleton Place. It has been suggested that they were left intact because Henry Middleton disliked the idea of "keeping up with the British."

Henry Middleton died the year before the arrival of the French botanist André Michaux. Michaux is said to have had unprecedented influence on southern gardens, for he introduced plants such as evergreen azaleas and camellias, which changed the gardens of the South forever.

Henry Middleton II (1770–1846) was greatly influenced by Michaux; it is thought that the two men became friends. Among the few surviving family papers are excerpts from Henry's gardening diary and an order form requesting plants from England. In this one order the younger Henry requested fifty-two types of flower seeds, fifty-four kinds of bulbs, seventy-one hardy herbaceous plants, forty-one different greenhouse plants, and thirty-five vegetable seeds.

Henry's son, Williams (1809–1883), began the vast azalea plantings that were so popular before the Civil War. Evidence of this influence can be seen on "azalea hill" overlooking the rice pond. This planting was enlarged in the 1930s.

Middleton Place exudes a sense of dignity and grace that only comes with the passage of time. The ancient live oak at the entrance to the grounds gracefully beckons, promising a glimpse of a place secure in the annals of history.

Visitors enter on the west grounds, along the reflecting pool. The long, narrow pool gives back the image of live oaks, azaleas, and magnolias; swans show up starkly white against the waters.

White gardenias (top) fill the late winter garden with an overpowering sweet scent while camellias (above), first brought to Middleton by André Michaux, begin blooming in November, peaking during January and February.

Opposite the pool is the camellia allee. In 1786 André Michaux brought four *Camellia japonicas* to Middleton Place. These were planted at each corner of the parterre. One of these original camellias is still living and is called the Reine des Fleurs (Queen of Flowers). In addition to the camellias, Michaux introduced mimosa, ginkgo, varnish tree, and candleberry tree.

The camellia collection at Middleton begins blooming in November, and generally peaks during January and February. Amy Lowell wrote of the camellias during her visit, "Their blossoms drop on paths, and you walk softly upon the colors of the rainbow."

The camellia allee leads to the ruins of the first house, and to the reconstruction of the "gentleman's wing," first built in 1755. From the steps of the original dwelling the visitor has the first clear view of the size and grandeur of the estate. (Because the grounds were all designed in line with the original mansion, it is important for the visitor to orient himself at the site of the ruins, and not in front of the remaining structure, which is off-center.) To the west, behind the house, is a horseshoe-shaped greensward originating from the gates on the road. Middleton Place was accessible both from the Ashley River and from the Ashley River Road, with the house half a mile from each.

From where the house stood one sees the breathtaking vista of the Ashley River, the terraces, and the butterfly lakes. The formal gardens run parallel to the river, on an axis from one end of the reflecting pool to the top of the terraces. Along this axis is the sundial garden—with separate beds radiating out like petals of a flower—as well as the octagonal sunken garden, a rose garden, and the secret garden, which may have at one time been a tennis court.

Directly in front of the house are long parterres. These contain unusual and interesting botanical specimens, including *Camellia sinensis* (tea) and several different species of magnolias.

It is here that the visitor is keenly reminded that Middleton Place began as a rice plantation. The old, flooded rice fields are clearly visible from the house

Classic statuary and clean-swept walks help give Middleton an aura of timeless beauty. Each vista presents an exciting view, each turn brings to the eye a garden of delight.

site. Rice cultivation in America reached its peak during the eighteenth and nineteenth centuries and began to decline after the Civil War. After a severe hurricane in 1911, rice was no longer grown on a large scale in the low country of South Carolina.

The rice mill was once housed in a small structure close to the butterfly lakes. Today the building contains an exhibit about rice cultivation and displays lovely watercolors by Alice R. H. Smith that depict life on a rice plantation.

The old springhouse is also visible from the house site. The lower level was used to store dairy foods, and the upper level was used as a Sunday school for slave children. Today the upper level of this quaint little building houses a pictorial history of the gardens.

West of the house a series of formal gardens leads back to the reflecting pool. The sundial and rose gardens hold both China and tea roses from the eighteenth and nineteenth centuries.

The Middleton Oak, one of the original trees on the property, is found along one of the walks by the river. The tree is eighty-five feet tall and thirty-seven feet in circumference, and has a limb spread of 145 feet. Gazing at this venerable tree provides one with a sense of both present and past. This live oak has seen fires and hurricanes and earthquakes and yet still spreads its limbs providing a bit of shade, a bit of history to all those who pass beneath.

A landscaping masterpiece, Middleton Place lies quietly along the banks of the Ashley River; the solitude of the place makes it easy to imagine the life of splendor and excitement enjoyed by the plantation owners. This garden has attained a dignity and beauty made possible only by the passage of time.

MAGNOLIA GARDENS

Gertrude Jekyll, grande dame of English garden design, said that a garden must fit its master, just as his clothes do. Much can be told of the master by what his garden looks like. Middleton Place is sedate, cultured, and aristocratic. Magnolia Gardens, on the other hand, is feisty and free, in touch with the times, and illustrative of the unusual family that has proudly owned this magnificent garden since the late 1600s.

Magnolia Gardens today is a place that reflects the personality of present owner J. Drayton Hastie. Hastie takes an intensely personal interest in the gardens, as well he might. It was his ancestor, Thomas Drayton, Jr., who first established the gardens. J. Drayton Hastie is the ninth-generation owner of Magnolia Gardens.

The gardens are composed of five hundred acres adjacent to the Ashley River, only a few miles from Middleton Place. While the Middletons resisted change, the Draytons of Magnolia Gardens embraced it enthusiastically. In 1820 the plantation was passed to Thomas Drayton's grandson, John Drayton, who was at that time recovering from tuberculosis. The new owner immediately set about to change the French-influenced formal beds and walks to reflect the new English flair for a romantic, pastoral landscape. Today only a very small portion of the 1680s formal gardens can be seen. The remainder of the clipped and manicured gardens were converted to informal, romantic paths through "wilderness" settings.

Through the years, each owner of Magnolia Gardens continued to keep pace with the times and did what was necessary to keep the gardens intact.

Like many southerners, John Grimke Drayton suffered great losses during the Civil War. However, he was luckier than most. Although the plantation house was burned, the grounds were left surprisingly untouched. Roses, azaleas, and camellias bloomed profusely, softening the blow of the loss of the mansion.

John Drayton came out of the war nearly destitute. He sold a house in Charleston, an estate at Hilton Head, and 1,500 acres at Magnolia to finance rebuilding the plantation house.

But even these funds were not enough to keep up the garden as he wished. In 1870, at the urging of friends and relatives, John Drayton opened up the gardens to tourists who came by paddle steamer from Charleston. As a result, Magnolia became the first man-made tourist attraction in the United States. By liquidating his assets and opening the gardens to the public, John Drayton was able to maintain and increase the beauty of the gardens.

The gardens soon gained international acclaim for their beauty. In 1900 the Baedeker tourist guide listed Magnolia Gardens as one of the three most important sights in America, along with Niagara Falls and the Grand Canyon.

Magnolia Gardens today is a cornucopia of delights. The present owner, J. Drayton Hastie, is an enthusiastic and determined man. When Magnolia Gardens faced increased competition from other tourist attractions in the area, Hastie decided to open it year-round and to make it horticulturally attractive twelve months of the year—a difficult task.

Spring displays of azaleas and camellias continue to draw the greatest crowds, but tourists now also visit in summer to see grand displays of various bedding plants, roses, and such low-country favorites as bougainvillea, magnolias, gardenias, lilies, and tea

Opposite.
J. Drayton Hastie, ninth-generation owner of Magnolia Gardens, has developed it into a year-round horticultural delight. Thousands of bedding plants are used each year to enhance the natural beauty of the gardens.

Right. *Nature, unadorned and undisturbed, is perhaps the loveliest and most exciting landscape of all. Long board walks allow the visitor a closer look at this eerily beautiful spot.*

Bottom left. *An 1885 advertisement includes the price of a boat excursion up the Ashley River to Magnolia Gardens. Magnolia was considered America's first tourist attraction and is still considered one of the most beautiful.*

Bottom right. *After the Civil War, much of the house staff remained at Magnolia Plantation, evidenced by this postwar photograph.*

Bottom center. *Chinese Holly (Ilex cornuta)*

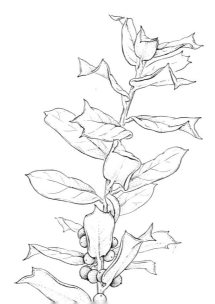

olive. Fall brings color from bright yellow cassia, aucuba, hibiscus, and lantana.

Winter is also an exciting time to visit Magnolia Gardens because the profusion of berries and winter fruits attracts so many different kinds of birds. Beauty-berry, cherries, hollies, nandina, plums, and pyracantha all add vibrant color to the winter landscape. Since 1975, the entire five hundred acres of Magnolia Plantation has been managed as a wildlife refuge. The tremendous horticultural diversity of the gardens attracts a wide range of wildlife.

More than nine hundred varieties of camellias start the flowering show over again in late winter and early spring, introducing the season with blossoms of pink, red, and white.

In a garden of this magnitude, bulbs and flowers are planted by the thousands, or even by the ten thousands. Though he admits to being more of a businessman than a gardener, J. Drayton Hastie oversees the ordering and installation of plants. He prefers sweeping swaths of color, and believes that big, bold flowers go a lot further in coloring this garden than small ephemeral blossoms.

In addition to the kaleidoscope of color created by the flowering plants, Magnolia boasts many unique kinds of horticultural displays. A biblical garden was patterned after the garden at the Cathedral of St. John the Divine in New York City. The garden is divided into two sections. In the New Testament section, flowers are planted around a cross; in the Old Testament, the central point is the Star of David. The cross is made up of twelve small squares, for the twelve disciples. The star is made up of twelve sections commemorating the twelve tribes of Israel.

A colonial herb garden represents the kind of garden probably found at Magnolia Plantation during the late seventeenth century. Herbs from this garden were used to flavor and preserve food, and for medicines. The design of this garden is based on a seventeenth-century English design, where the herbs are enclosed within a framework of a boxwood knot garden.

The horticultural maze was patterned after one designed by Henry VIII for his country estate, Hampton Court. Instead of the traditional boxwood, however, the maze at Magnolia Plantation was planted with over five hundred camellias, which add color, fragrance, and beauty to this horticultural puzzle.

A topiary garden adds a feeling of fun and frivolity, nicely balanced by the eerie mystique of the Audubon Swamp Garden. Long boardwalks lead the visitor into the mystical swamp, where time seems to stand still. A quiet stillness pervades, broken only by the shrill cry of a bird. Here one is abruptly reminded that formal gardens can only imitate the beauty that nature lavishly displays. Balance, grace, color, texture—all the elements of a good garden are here naturally, without the help of humankind.

Even in the swamp garden, however, the visitor is reminded of the long and difficult history of this plantation. Signs and a path lead from the swamp to the plantation cemetery, where dozens of small headstones are all that remain of the slave culture. Before the Civil War, there were more than three hundred slaves at Magnolia. Several of these people remained and worked at the plantation after the war. A photo from the early 1900s shows the plantation gardening staff, most of whom were descendants of slaves who lived and worked at the plantation during the Civil War.

Today the plantation is still a busy, bustling place. A petting zoo was added where children of all ages can come face to face and hand to hoof with sheep, miniature ponies, ducks, pygmy goats, and peacocks.

The original plantation house was built in 1670 but burned forty years later. The second house, a mansion of some note, was also burned, torched by victorious Northern troops. The house that stands at Magnolia Gardens today is a pre–Revolutionary War summer house owned by John Grimke Drayton. After the plantation mansion was burned, Reverend Drayton disassembled the summer house, located in Summerville, fourteen miles up the Ashley River. He loaded it on barges, floated it

Winter in the gardens is colored by shrubs that bear brightly hued fruit and berries. Nandina is one of the most common— and most beautiful—of these.

down the river, and had it reassembled at the site of the ruins of the original house.

Looking around at the many innovative additions that have come to Magnolia Gardens through the centuries, one leaves with the secure sense that Magnolia Gardens will continue to keep pace with the times. In this garden the roots of the past give a firm foundation to the budding promise of the future.

ORTON PLANTATION GARDENS

Unlike many of the other early coastal plantations, Orton Plantation has not had the luxury of ownership by a single family, or even two or three families. Instead, Orton Plantation has been bought and sold numerous times, the residence of a variety of interesting and wealthy families.

The land on which Orton lies is found close to Cape Fear, North Carolina—a name given to this coastal area because of the nearby treacherous Frying Pan Shoals, which extend many miles out into the Atlantic Ocean.

The first settlers to the Cape Fear area were led by Colonel Maurice Moore, son of the first governor of South Carolina, James Moore. Colonel Moore and his brothers, Roger and Nathaniel, together with several other enterprising men, established several plantations in the region.

The main crop of these plantations was rice. Although the plantations could not compete with the volume of rice being produced in South Carolina, the coastal North Carolina rice was of superior quality. It came to be used as seed rice for plantations all over the South.

Colonel Moore owned vast lands in the area and soon sold Orton Plantation to his brother Roger, who built a home there. Roger Moore had a strong and masterful personality and was soon known in the community as "King Roger." The first house he built at Orton was destroyed by Indians; he rebuilt it in 1735.

After Roger Moore's death in 1751, Orton had a series of different owners, one of whom was Benjamin

Left. Orton Plantation's first house was constructed by Roger Moore but was burned down by Indians. The present house was begun in 1735 and was altered and remodeled by several successive owners.

Smith, grandson of Maurice Moore. A prominent citizen, Smith was elected governor of North Carolina in 1810. His public services were somewhat marred by his fiery temper, however, which led him into three different duels.

A later owner, Dr. Frederick Jones Hill, increased the value and beauty of the house by remodeling. In 1840 he added another story and the four fluted Doric columns that were examples of the Greek Revival style popular at that time. In 1854 Hill sold the plantation to Thomas Calezance Miller. His daughter wrote of the plantation, "I remember the last time I saw the place, it was beautiful beyond imagination.

Below. Although today the house is not open to the public, the Sprunt family has been very generous in sharing the expansive grounds with all who wish to come to visit.

Opposite. Native pines and oaks create a soft frame around "Luola's chapel" built in 1915 by Dr. James Sprunt in honor of his wife.

The family having spent the winter there my mother and father took great pleasure and pains in adding to the beauties of nature without destroying."

The modern history of Orton Plantation and the beginning of Orton Plantation Gardens occurred in 1910, when the house and grounds were purchased by Dr. James Sprunt, grandfather of the present owners.

In 1910 Dr. Sprunt added two wings to the Orton House and in 1915 built a small chapter in honor of his wife, Luola. He enlarged the gardens, which were begun in 1910, to their present size of about twenty acres between 1935 and 1950.

At Orton Plantation Gardens today, the beauties of nature are indeed enhanced without being destroyed. The woodland paths are muted by softly falling blossoms from thousands of azaleas. The trees overhead drip Spanish moss and create an ambiance of sedate beauty.

Hushed and awed by the grandeur of the oaks, the visitor is taken by surprise when the vista is suddenly interrupted by an expanse of formal gardens. A stark white belvedere on one side overlooks the old rice fields, today maintained as a wildfowl refuge. On the other side the view is startlingly different, a formal landscape showing a scroll garden complete with clipped hedges and bedding plants.

The beautifully curved hedges are a dark evergreen called podocarpus. These were nearly killed by freak cold weather in the winter of 1983, but although they were cut back nearly to the ground, these outstanding hedges have slowly regained much of their original beauty.

Across the scroll garden is another belvedere—a bridgelike landing overlooking the water, which juts out over the lagoon. Alligators are known to swim in the murky waters. Other wildlife also inhabits the quiet haven of Orton Plantation. The footprints of deer, opossums, and raccoons can often be found.

The floral display of Orton Plantation is best seen in spring when camellias, azaleas, and flowering peach,

In 1854 a young girl wrote of Orton Plantation that it was "beautiful beyond imagination" and that the family "added to the beauties of nature without destroying." These words are still descriptive of the gardens today.

Laura C. Martin's
Southern Gardens

cherry, and apple trees put on a spectacular show. The visitor can find special plants by scent as well as by sight, for several trees and shrubs give off a fragrance that creates unusual delight. Winter daphne emits an enticingly sweet fragrance, while banana shrub adds a peculiar but pleasant scent to these southern woods.

Orton Gardens are now the pride and pleasure of the present owners, Kenneth Murchison, Samuel Nash, and Laurence Gray Sprunt, who take a personal interest in the planting and maintenance of their ancestral home.

Although it is a modern garden by many standards, the present owners have certainly not forgotten their past. A colonial cemetery is the final resting place for many of the past owners and offers a tantalizing glimpse into the rich history of the plantation. "King" Roger Moore is buried here under the epitaph

Here rests King Roger Moore (ca. 1694–1751)
Granted 8,000 acres by Lords Proprietors in 1720.
He built older part of Orton Mansion in 1725.

Here also is buried John Hill, M.D., the brother of Dr. Frederick J. Hill, who once owned Orton.

The gardens strongly reflect the personalities and whims of the present owners. A Chinese bridge zigzags across the lagoon. Cypresses, irises, and fringe trees add a distinctly Eastern flavor to this part of the garden. A circular sun garden is planted with pansies in late winter and spring. As the weather warms and summer approaches, these are dug up to make room for a variety of summer annuals.

The white circle garden is surrounded by live oak trees interspersed with white camellias and azaleas that bloom from late winter into spring. During summer and fall the bed is filled with white petunias and vinca. Farther down the trail, the blue mound is planted all in blue with pansies in spring, blue ageratum in summer.

Close to the scroll garden, overlooking the lagoon and rice fields, a small tree house—its platform covered with a climbing yellow rose—commands a grand view of the Cape Fear River, the gardens, and the house.

Right. Bright, bold hibiscus blossoms bring a tropical air to this North Carolina coastal garden. The grounds are studded with blossoms from native and exotic plants.

Far right. The grounds today reflect the tastes of the present owners. Bedding plants add seasonal color to many parts of the garden, including the white circle garden and the blue mound.

Winter Daphne (Daphne odora)

George Washington always referred to Mount Vernon as the "home farm." As a boy he fell in love with this property nestled on the banks of the Potomac River, a love affair that was to last his lifetime.

The house at Orton still stands today, but it is not open to the public. However, Orton's owners have been most generous in opening up their gardens and allowing us to share in their beauty and their history.

MOUNT VERNON

More richly steeped in American history than almost any other house in the nation, Mount Vernon is also wealthy in horticultural history. George Washington was not only the leading statesman of his day, he was also knowledgeable and greatly interested in agriculture and horticulture.

The property of Mount Vernon was originally owned by Washington's half-brother, Lawrence. In 1752 George inherited the house and property, in which Lawrence's widow, Anne, had a life interest. Anne soon remarried and moved away, and George Washington leased it from her until her death in 1761.

Washington always referred to Mount Vernon as the "Home Farm," for even as a boy he came here for long visits and became intimately familiar with this beautiful land along the banks of the Potomac River.

In 1759 Washington married the wealthy widow Martha Custis and set up housekeeping at Mount Vernon. At this time there was only a small house and a few nearby outbuildings on the extensive property. But Washington was a young and ambitious man, proud of

his inheritance and anxious to create a house and grounds that would reflect his important standing in the colonies. He began to enlarge the house and greatly increase his holdings on each side of the property. The original house was one and a half stories. By 1787 he had doubled the length, increased it to two and a half stories, and added a cupola. In spite of the alterations to the house, its original position has never changed.

Trained as a surveyor, Washington had a keen eye and quick mind for measurements and distances. Thanks to his intense interest in all types of plants, Washington was in an enviable position: he had an outstanding piece of property and the talent to embellish and enhance it.

Washington did not hire a landscape architect to help design the grounds at Mount Vernon. He began, instead, to develop ideas based on the land itself. The house stood on a small plateau, with the ground gently sloping away from it in all directions, most steeply to the east, toward the Potomac River.

Tulip-poplar (Liriodendron tulipfera)

Right.
Washington had the trained eye of a surveyor, but also brought a surprisingly sensitive artistic touch to landscape design as well. The design of the grounds was greatly influenced by eighteenth-century horticulturists such as Batty Langley.

Above. Open lawns roll gently toward the Potomac River, interrupted only by gracious trees and a ha-ha, a stone wall designed to keep wildlife out of the garden.

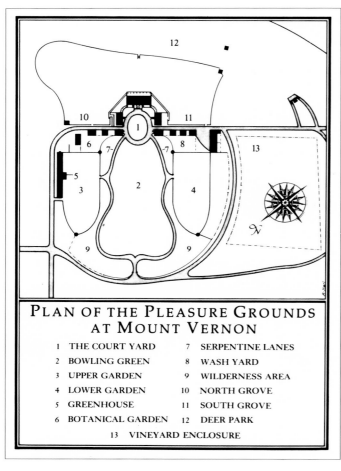

12
10
11
1
6 7
7 8
13
5
3
2
4
N
9
9

PLAN OF THE PLEASURE GROUNDS AT MOUNT VERNON

1	THE COURT YARD	7	SERPENTINE LANES
2	BOWLING GREEN	8	WASH YARD
3	UPPER GARDEN	9	WILDERNESS AREA
4	LOWER GARDEN	10	NORTH GROVE
5	GREENHOUSE	11	SOUTH GROVE
6	BOTANICAL GARDEN	12	DEER PARK
	13	VINEYARD ENCLOSURE	

Washington was greatly influenced by other colonial plantations that he had visited. Adjacent to Washington's property was Belvoir, the estate of George William Fairfax. Gunston Hall, home of George Manson, was just down the river. Washington was also a frequent visitor to Williamsburg, where he may have picked up horticultural ideas from John Custis, Martha Washington's father-in-law by her first marriage. Custis was a noted botanist who regularly corresponded with plant collectors and horticulturists from England. His garden was thought to be of particular beauty, and Washington visited there often. Undoubtedly both these plantations had great influence on Washington as he began to design his own estate.

In addition to these nearby acquaintances, Washington was also influenced by the writing of several English horticulturists of the day. In 1758 he sent to England for a copy of Batty Langley's *New Principles of Gardening*, first published in 1728. Langley was one of the first to encourage a turning away from the rigid formality of the French and Italian garden styles toward a more naturalistic design. It was Langley who called the curve "nature's gift," a phrase that Washington took to heart.

It is obvious that Washington studied Langley and included many of his design ideas in his own estate. Serpentine walks, groves, wildernesses, and shrubberies, all popular in England at the time, became a part of Mount Vernon.

Washington was also attracted to the neat and symmetrical. In partial defiance of the prevailing fashions, Washington developed Mount Vernon into a beautiful blend of English naturalistic landscape design and orderly symmetry. He established groves at the north and south ends of the mansion and placed a round courtyard in front of the house. The original entrance to the house was by means of a straight drive, which came directly to the courtyard; in 1786 Washington moved this road so as to have an uninterrupted vista in front of the mansion. A long bowling green was laid out in front of the courtyard, the inspiration for which may have come from the beautiful bowling green at nearby Nomini Hall, home of Robert Carter.

On each side of the bowling green, gently curving roads—mirror images of each other—lead to the house. On each side of the roads there were walled gardens, shrubberies, and small garden houses. Twin mounds at the foot of the bowling green were each planted with a weeping willow tree.

After taking possession of Mount Vernon, Washington postponed the planting for many years, as he fulfilled the obligations of his busy life. When he and Martha had first moved to Mount Vernon in 1759, he wrote, "I am now I believe fixd at this seat

Opposite.
Gardeners and horticulturists at Mount Vernon today carry on the tradition of planting started by Washington nearly 250 years ago. Preservation of garden design and horticultural education are important parts of Monticello.

Tiny hedges make a miniature scroll garden. In Washington's time an entire section of the garden was enclosed and used as a nursery plot to grow plants from seeds and cuttings sent to Washington from around the world.

with an agreeable Consort for Life and hope to find more happiness in retirement than I ever experienc'd amidst a wide and bustling World." This "retirement" was to be short-lived; Washington was away from Mount Vernon a full twenty of the forty years he had left to live.

In 1785, Washington finally turned his attention to the planting at Mount Vernon. Much work had been accomplished in his absence, including the building of a ha-ha (a low, sunken fence), and the completion of brick walls enclosing the upper and lower gardens, which were planted with fruits and vegetables.

Washington himself instigated the major plantings of the estate. His diary in early 1785 reflects the time and effort that he put into the job. He was particularly interested and fond of using the native plants that surrounded his land. In January he wrote that he rode into the woods "in search of the sort of trees I shall want for my walks, groves, and Wildernesses.... In the Branch of Hell hole betwn. the Gate and its mouth are a number of very fine young Poplars-

Locusts-Sassafrass and Dogwood. Some Maple Trees on high ground & 2 or 3 Shrubs (in wet ground) which I take to be of the Fringe tree."

Washington did not limit his collection of plants to those that grew close to home. He became intensely interested in collecting new plants and was the happy recipient of many different types of plants sent to him by friends and admirers. Some of these, such as the greater magnolia sent to him from South Carolina by his nephew George Augustine Washington, flourished beautifully. Others, such as the royal palmetto tree sent to him by William Blake of Charleston, South Carolina, did not survive the colder Virginia winters.

The first boxwood at Mount Vernon came in 1785 from Colonel Henry Lee, Jr. ("Lighthorse Harry"), of Stratford, Virginia. He wrote to Washington on March 12, 1785, that he was sending "twelve horse chestnuts, twelve box cuttings and twelve dwarf box cuttings."

So great was Washington's interest in growing new and unusual plants that he set aside a small enclosed plot as a nursery for the seeds and cuttings that he accumulated from around the world. This spot, between the salt house and the spinning house, was sheltered on the west side by the wall of the upper garden and was protected from wandering animals on the remaining sides by a paling fence.

In his "Botanick Garden" Washington experienced both success and failure. His successes included the Pride of China trees, which he started here from seed; Lombardy poplars, grown from cuttings that he rooted there; and many kinds of hollies and cedars.

Today very few of Washington's original trees remain at Mount Vernon. The most outstanding examples of these are the two tulip-poplar trees on the south side of the bowling green.

Washington was keenly interested in the fruits, nuts, and vegetables planted within the enclosed upper and lower gardens. Mount Vernon was known far and wide for its outstanding hospitality, and Martha Washington was famous for laying a fine table. To meet her needs, a large and successful kitchen garden was an undeniable necessity.

Martha Washington was a keen plantswoman, and whenever she left Mount Vernon she would write back instructing her servant "Old Doll" how to deal with the garden in her absence. Many of the plants (such as roses) she grew in her kitchen garden were plants that we consider today to be merely ornamental. In a letter to Anthony Whiting on May 12, 1793, George Washington wrote, "Mrs. Washington desires you will direct Old Doll to distill a good deal of rose and mint water." At that time, rosewater was used extensively as flavoring, much as we use vanilla extract today. Rose petals were used for making rosewater, and the hips were used medicinally and for teas. These utilitarian roses were probably not laid out in a formal or symmetrical pattern but were stuck in here and there among the vegetables and fruits.

From this letter and from other references, we know that Martha Washington took an important and active role in managing the walled gardens at Mount Vernon. George Washington, also, was active in these gardens. A June 1788 entry in his diary states that he "Planted in the No. Garden, between the Green house & quarters 10 grains of early Corn; given to me (from So. Carolina) by Gen Spotswood." In 1787 Samuel Vaughan, an English friend and admirer of Washington's, paid a visit to Mount Vernon. Washington was away in Philadelphia at the time, but Vaughan examined the estate in great detail, measuring, taking notes, and finally drawing the estate in perspective to the Potomac River and the Maryland shore. He later rendered this drawing to scale and presented it to Washington.

Vaughan's records and drawing must have been quite accurate, for Washington acknowledged the gift by writing on November 12, 1787, that the plan "described with accuracy the house, walk and shrubs except in front of the Lawn, west of the Ct. Yard. There the plan differs from the original; in the former you have closed the prospect with trees along the

*Left.
Washington loved all plants but seemed to hold a special place in his heart for trees. He was constantly searching for native trees, such as the tulip-poplar, to include in his garden.*

*Below.
Although Washington's greatest horticultural interests involved trees, fruits, and vegetables, historic documents indicate that flowers, too, were grown at Mount Vernon.*

walk to the gate, wheras in the latter the trees terminate with the two mounds of earth on each side of which grow Weeping Willows leaving an open and full view of the distant woods. I mention this because it is the only departure from the original."

In his drawing, Vaughan labeled both walled gardens "Kitchen Gardens" and showed that each garden was divided into six plots.

It is unlikely that the gardens contained purely ornamental flowers until the 1790s, and no direct record exists of the ornamental plants that grew here, but their presence toward the end of the century is evident.

Nearly a decade after Vaughan's visit, the architect Benjamin Latrobe came to Mount Vernon. He noted in his journal, "On one side of the lawn is a plain Kitchen garden, on the other side a neat flower garden laid out in squares, and boxed with great precision."

Washington apparently had little interest in herbaceous flowers, for his records of these ornamental plants is quite sparse. Although he listed with great detail the vegetables and fruits grown in the enclosed gardens, his references to flowers are limited to "sundrie flower seed bought for Mrs. Washington."

At least one of Washington's gardeners, however, showed great interest in the flowers grown at Mount Vernon. While Washington served as President, his nephew wrote from Mount Vernon that "he [the gardener] seems fond of Flower but says he will pay strict attention to the necessary parts of Gardening by furnishing a good supply of everything for the Kitchen."

The gardens today reflect the kinds of flowering plants that might have been available for cultivation during Washington's lifetime. These plants, some native and others introduced, were sold by nursery owners such as John Bartram in Philadelphia. They include plants such as heliotrope, foxglove, pansies, peony, canterbury bells, cornflowers, hollyhock, tulips, daffodils, lilies, and iris. Some of the wildflowers popular in gardens were bloodroot, cardinal flowers, larkspur, violets, and asters.

After Washington's death in 1799, Mount Vernon was kept in the family for nearly sixty years. In 1853 the Mount Vernon Ladies' Association was formed. The original members raised funds and in 1858 bought the mansion, outbuildings, and two hundred acres from a descendant of Washington's, John Augustine Washington III. When the association purchased the estate, the grounds and gardens were overgrown and had suffered much neglect.

It has always been the goal of the association to restore Mount Vernon to its state at Washington's death in 1799. In doing so, the association has been guided by Washington's letters and diaries and his written instructions to managers and superintendents, as well as by letters to Washington and the written accounts from many visitors who stayed at Mount Vernon.

Centuries before environmental problems were even considered, and years before words like "ecology" and "recycle" were ever used, George Washington had a strong sense of stewardship with the earth. On December 4, 1788, he wrote to Arthur Young, "I am led to reflect how much more delightful…is the task of making improvements on the earth, than all the vain glory which can be acquired from ravaging it."

George Washington loved Mount Vernon and loved working with the trees and shrubs that adorned it. To visit Mount Vernon today is to stroll through history. To touch the tulip-poplar trees that Washington himself planted is to touch the life of a man who is known to us only through history books. As we delight in his gardening successes and commiserate with his failures, we span time and space.

MONTICELLO

In 1811 Thomas Jefferson wrote to Charles W. Peale: "I have often thought that if heaven had given me choice of my position and calling, it should have been on a rich spot of earth, well watered, and near a good market for the productions of the garden. No occupation is so

Opposite.
Thomas Jefferson inspired generations of gardeners with his exciting horticultural work at Monticello. Not only did Jefferson create a place of beauty, he was also instrumental in introducing hundreds of new plants to American gardens.

Right.
Jefferson's 1807 drawing shows plans for including flowers in oval and round beds near the house. He kept detailed records of what was planted, the time of year, and the growing conditions.

Far right. *Tulips were a favorite spring flower in Jefferson's time. These are shown planted along the winding walk in front of the house—an area that Jefferson designed while on holiday away from the White House in May 1808.*

Below. *English Pea (Pisum sativum)*

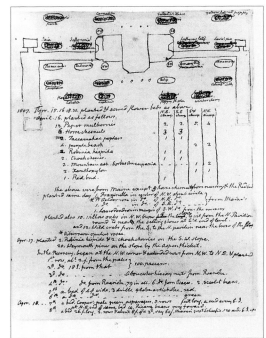

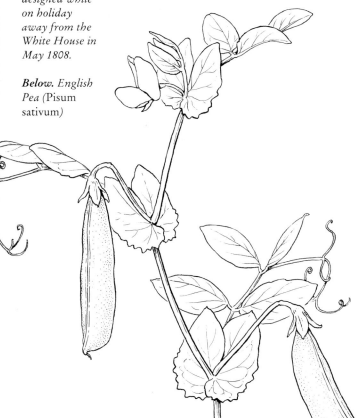

delightful to me as the culture of the earth, and no culture comparable to that of the garden....I am still devoted to the garden. But though an old man, I am but a young gardener."

Heaven showed favor to Jefferson, for his "little mountain" in Virginia—Monticello—was indeed a rich spot of earth, and here Jefferson enjoyed a lifetime of gardening. Although he served as statesman, ambassador, governor, vice president, representative, and finally president of the United States, Thomas Jefferson seemed never too busy or preoccupied to take careful notice of his beloved gardens. Even on July 4, 1776, Jefferson found time to record the temperature three times.

From an early age, Jefferson showed great interest in nature. Born at Shadwell, Virginia, on April 13, 1743, Thomas Jefferson was the son of a wealthy Virginia planter. His father was a pioneer, his mother an aristocrat. The diversity of his parents' backgrounds was to play a major role in his life, for he combined aristocratic grace and taste with the unabashed enthusiasm and fortitude of his pioneer father.

Even as a boy, Jefferson kept a record of the flowers that were found at Shadwell. He noted when they bloomed and when they disappeared. By the time he was twenty-three, Jefferson formalized these notes and began his "garden book," in which he kept careful records from 1766 to 1824.

Two years after he began his garden book, in 1768, Jefferson began clearing land at Monticello. He moved there in 1770. South of Monticello lies another, taller mountain, which Jefferson also purchased. He called it Montalto, meaning "high mountain."

Jefferson had grandiose plans for both properties. He sketched plans for a series of cascading waterfalls on Montalto, which he would be able to see from his home on Monticello. Because he inherited much debt and added to this debt during his lifetime, Jefferson was unable to realize these plans, but they remain a testament to his grand visions.

Jefferson's concept of landscape design was influenced by several different factors. While serving as ambassador to France, he visited many English estates and gardens. These exhibited the naturalistic style popular at the time, which included long, open vistas, groves of trees, and gently curving lines.

Jefferson was also influenced by the publication in 1806 of Bernard McMahon's book, *The American Gardener's Calendar*. This book was one of the first publications to address American, rather than European, conditions of gardening.

Jefferson included many of the new English design concepts in the landscape at Monticello. His primary goal in landscaping his estate was to combine the useful and the beautiful, or, as he phrased it, to create an ornamental farm where "the articles of husbandry" were combined with "the attributes of a garden."

The plan for Monticello unfolded slowly. Before 1786 the landscape work consisted of clearing land, building roads, and planting trees and shrubs. A plan drawn before he went to France indicates that he planted trees parallel to the terraces of the house, but it is not known what types of trees he planted. By 1772, however, plans were drawn that had trees and shrubs alternating in an unusual pattern in the semioval on the eastern side of the house.

A memorandum Jefferson left for his overseer indicated that the following shrubs were to be planted to implement this plan: weeping willows, European (Italian) larch, Chinese arborvitae, "Newfoundland spruce," and balsam-fir.

Jefferson was demanding and persistent in his interests in nature and the garden. Letters to his children and in-laws suggest that he was sometimes irritated by their lack of enthusiasm in keeping records and corresponding about the minute details of what was happening in his garden during his many absences.

In 1791 he wrote to his daughter Maria from Philadelphia:

My dear Maria
...I hope our correspondence will now be more regular, that you will be no more lazy,

Pages 74–75. Monticello, "little mountain," is aptly named, for it does indeed perch on top of a small mountain. At its peak, Jefferson's magnificent vegetable garden was a thousand feet long, eighty feet wide, and was composed of twenty-four separate beds.

and I no more in the growls on that account. On the 27th of February I saw blackbirds and Robinredbreasts, and on the 7th. of this month I heard frogs for the first time this year. Have you noted the first appearance of these things at Monticello? I hope you have, and will continue to note every appearance animal and vegetable which indicates the approach of Spring, and will communicate them to me....Tell me when you shall have peas &c. up, when every thing comes to table, when you shall have the first chickens hatched, when every kind of tree blossoms, or puts forth leaves, when each kind of flower blooms.

Jefferson's vision of a grand landscape was not limited to the flower and vegetable beds close to the house. In 1806 he drew a sketch of a grove that he envisioned as a pleasure ground. Here he dreamed of having an "ornamental" forest where the larger trees were pruned and thinned and underbrush was carefully removed so that it would give the appearance of an open forest.

In the upper part of his grove Jefferson planted trees such as chinaberry, deciduous magnolia, Carolina silverbell, and catalpa. The lower grove represented Jefferson's ideal of the American garden. The concept was to create a garden by opening up the forest and planting groups of particular shrubs and trees. In his own words, the grove was to be a place where "gardens may be made without expense. We have only to cut out the superabundant plants."

Early in 1807, Jefferson seemed to have been inspired to design and plan more formal gardens. In January he wrote to Bernard McMahon, "The tulip roots you were so kind as to send me, I planted at Monticello last autumn. I intend to go there the first week in March in order to commence planting out some things to be in readiness for my kitchen & flower gardens two years hence." At the end of this letter Jefferson added a list of plants he wanted:

best Globe artichoke	Auricula
Antwerp raspberry	Ranunculus
Alpine strawberry	Hyacinths
Lillies of a few of the best kinds	Sweet William (Dianthus)
Tuberose	Wall flower
Crown Imperials	Marigold
Anemone	Saffron

Jefferson arrived from Washington for his annual spring visit to Monticello in the mid-April of 1807. He spent this time working on the design and the planting of his flower and kitchen garden. Between April 11 and 15, he laid out the circular and oval flower beds near the house, and by the end of the month these had been planted.

After he returned to Washington the flower gardens at Monticello still seemed to occupy his time and attention. In June he wrote to his granddaughter Ann Randolph that he had developed the idea of a "winding walk surrounding the lawn...with a narrow border of flowers on each side."

During his visit the following spring, in May 1808, Jefferson laid out this winding walk and flower borders in the lawn on the west side of the house and promptly planted these with a variety of roots and seeds.

All during his presidency Jefferson showed an extraordinarily active interest in the gardens at Monticello. He visited at least twice a year, staying several weeks during each visit. Even while not actually there, though, Jefferson was kept abreast of the activities in the garden.

His overseer, Edmund Bacon, wrote, "He always knew all about everything in every part of his grounds and garden. He knew the name of every tree, and just where one was dead or missing."

Years after Bacon had left Monticello, he still remembered it fondly. He wrote, "The grounds around the house were most beautifully ornamented with flowers and shrubbery. There were walks and borders, and flowers, that I have never seen or heard of anywhere else. Some of them were in bloom from early in the spring until late in the winter. A good many of them were foreign. Back of the house was a beautiful lawn of two or three acres, where his grandchildren used to play a great deal."

Many of the "foreign" plants were sent to Jefferson by friends and admirers from all over the world. Mimosa and golden-rain tree were introduced from China. Upland rice was brought by Captain William Bligh from the South Seas. Native American plants brought back by Lewis and Clark during their famous expeditions also made their way into the flower and vegetable gardens at Monticello. Among these were Mandan corn, salsify, and Arikara beans, brought from the plains of the American West.

Monticello was not only beautiful—it was also a thriving, working plantation. In 1796 it comprised five thousand acres. Although Thomas Jefferson considered slavery an "abominable crime," he had 110 slaves living at Monticello—most of whom he had inherited.

In his lifetime Jefferson tried many moneymaking schemes at Monticello. "Mulberry Row" was a long avenue of various buildings and shops found on the grounds. Among others, the blacksmith, joinery, and woodworking shops were found here. Jefferson said that "to be independent for the comforts of life we must fabricate them ourselves." In the shops at Monticello furniture, carts, carriages, and farm implements were made.

It took a tremendous amount of food to feed the people of this thriving plantation. Here, as on most other plantations, the vegetable garden was of considerable importance.

At the peak of its glory, Jefferson's vegetable garden was a thousand feet long and eighty feet wide and was composed of twenty-four separate beds. A stone wall ran the length of the garden, rising to twelve feet at some points. This wall not only served to terrace the garden but also retained heat, allowing Jefferson to plant tender species by taking advantage of the extra warmth radiating from the wall. Jefferson was able to grow figs successfully in this manner.

Below the stone wall, Jefferson put in an extensive orchard. Here there were more than four hundred fruit trees, as well as two terraced vineyards and berry squares.

A ten-foot-tall wooden fence surrounded the entire garden complex, stretching for nearly three-fourths of a mile. Few southern vegetable gardens displayed the tremendous variety and international flavor that was shown at Monticello. Because of his interest in gardening and his many friends throughout the world, Jefferson was able to experiment. He not only cultivated hundreds of unusual and exotic plants (such as Italian broccoli, French grapes, and Mexican peppers), but also grew 450 varieties of ninety-five different kinds of fruits, nuts, and herbs.

The primary purpose of the vegetable bed was to provide food, but Jefferson was not one to neglect aesthetics. He planted an arbor with different shades of scarlet runner bean, and placed purple and white broccoli alongside the green.

Jefferson used many new and innovative gardening methods. He was one of the first plantation owners to use contour plowing, to interplant various crops, and to use manure to enrich the soil. In 1793 his daughter Martha Randolph wrote to him complaining some of the vegetables were suffering damage from insects. He replied: "We will try this winter to cover our garden with a heavy coating of manure. When the earth is rich it bids defiance to droughts, yields in abundance, and of the best quality. I suspect that the insects which have harassed you have been encouraged by the feebleness of your plants; and that has been produced by the lean state of the soil. We will attack them another year with joint efforts."

Like all gardeners, Jefferson suffered his share of setbacks and losses. He had, however, a holistic approach to gardening and often said that the "failure of one thing was repaired by the success of another."

Jefferson's failures did not deter him from continuing to plant and work in his garden. In 1813 he wrote to Dr. Samuel Brown, saying, "Planting is one of my great amusements, and even of those things which can only be for posterity, for a Septuagenary has no right to count on any thing beyond annuals."

Because Jefferson was so prominent, his interest in gardening greatly influenced the world of American horticulture during the early nineteenth century. Through his own work at Monticello and his official capacities in sending Lewis and Clark to explore the wilds of America and collect plants from across the continent, Jefferson enforced and strengthened the interest of gardeners and nature lovers throughout the country.

Perhaps Jefferson's best lesson was in the enthusiasm that he showed for his garden. He was a relentless record-keeper and an enthusiastic experimenter, a legacy we are fortunate to have. The garden served Thomas Jefferson just as it serves gardeners today— as a refuge and a retreat from the stress and pressure of everyday life.

After Jefferson's death in 1826, the grounds at Monticello quickly fell into a state of disrepair. Jefferson had inherited much debt from his father and

had himself added to this burden. At his death, therefore, Monticello had to be sold. The lawn was reportedly plowed and planted in corn, and many of the choice trees were cut and replaced with mulberry trees to supply leaves for the silkworm industry.

A visitor in 1839 wrote of the appearance of Monticello, "Around me I beheld nothing but ruin and change, rotting terraces, broken cabins, the lawn, ploughed up and cattle wandering among Italian mouldering vases, and the place seemed the true representation of the fallen fortunes of the great man and his family."

The Thomas Jefferson Memorial Foundation was formed in 1923. Between 1939 and 1941, the Garden Club of Virginia restored the flower garden at Monticello. Much of the original landscape, including the garden, garden wall, pavilion, orchard, and vineyard, have been restored to their original state. Jefferson left copious garden records, which have helped the efforts to be historically accurate.

Monticello today is an exciting and beautiful testimony to a brilliant and inspiring man. The roundabout flower border spills over with the same kinds of flowers grown when Jefferson lived here. The expansive vegetable garden produces the same types of fruits and vegetables that were grown in the eighteenth and early nineteenth centuries; the harvest finds its way to the tables of Monticello's employees.

There is no question that Monticello was, and is again, a place of beauty. Jefferson's artistic eye, mixed with the natural grandeur of the land, resulted in a place of rare loveliness. Jefferson was justifiably proud of Monticello and of his own endeavors to enhance its beauty. To Jefferson, gardening was an important and pleasurable enterprise. In 1805 he wrote to Ellen Randolph about the fine arts: "Many reckon but five: Painting, sculpture, architecture, music and poetry. To these some have added Oratory…Others again add Gardening as a 7th fine art. Not horticulture, but the art of embellishing grounds by fancy."

Opposite. The vegetable garden supplied much-needed food for Jefferson's thriving, working plantation. Crops grown here included those commonly found in colonial gardens, as well as more unusual crops such as arkara beans and Mandan corn.

Jefferson was innovative with his gardening methods. He experimented with contour plowing, using manure to enrich the soil, and tried rotating crops to "rest" the soil.

{4}

Far From The Coast: Inland Gardens, 1750-1825

lthough the first and most prosperous settlements in America were found along the Atlantic coast, adventuresome men and women soon began to penetrate the vast forests of America and settle parts of this land far from coastal waters.

The frontier and the lure of the unknown inspired some; others picked up and moved because of the attraction of vast amounts of untamed land. Some groups, though, moved to this huge wilderness of the southeastern United States for more idealistic reasons. Such a group were the Moravians, a Protestant sect who bought a 100,000-acre tract of land in what is now North Carolina. They called their land Wachovia. Here they hoped to establish a town where Moravian ideals would be the guiding force in the settlement, and where they could help convert the local tribes to Christianity.

The Moravians' land was beautiful, rolling country. Forests of oak, hickory, and chestnut grew on the slopes, and beside the rivers beech, sycamore, walnut, and sweet-gum trees grew to towering heights.

The Moravians became careful stewards of their land. They timbered the wood carefully and appointed a forester to supervise its cutting. Skilled gardeners, the Moravians developed beautiful and useful gardens, but they did not ignore the natural bounty supplied by the woods and fields.

Page 80. The Moravians were highly skilled craftsmen who moved to the wilderness of America during the eighteenth century. They quickly became good stewards of their land, carefully cutting trees from the forest and developing neat, productive gardens.

In 1761, notes from a Moravian diary said, "During the month [May] careful survey was made of the native herbs with an eye to their medicinal value, and several useful ones were found, for instance, 'Squashweed' for rheumatism, 'Milk-weed' for pleurisy, 'Indian Physic' for preventing fevers, 'Robert Plantin,' a valuable antidote, as is also 'Snake Root,' and much 'Holly.'"

The Moravians were organized and disciplined. When they first settled Bethabara, the original town in Wachovia, in 1753, it took them just three weeks to prepare land and sow wheat. By the spring of 1754 they had planted turnips, corn, pumpkins, and beans, and had begun a small orchard.

The town of Bethabara was set up under the *Oeconomie*, a system of communal living that included a community garden. Original plans for this garden dating from July 1754 show a large garden laid out in two series of rectangular beds, with small work paths

Left. *Herbs were important to the Moravians, not only for flavoring food, but also as key ingredients to essential medicines. From treating coughs and colds to healing broken bones, these herbs were crucial to the health of the small town.*

Bottom left. *A 1787 drawing shows a view of Salem, and another illustration (**bottom right**) depicts a small garden in the corner of the boys' school yard. The residents of the town lived together in groups (called choirs) based on age, gender, and married status.*

Right. The Moravians were extremely disciplined and well organized. Within three weeks of moving to their wilderness home, they had planted herb and vegetable gardens and had begun construction of their houses.

Far right. Although each family was responsible for putting in their own vegetable garden, common lots and vacant grounds were often used to grow fruit for the community.

between the beds and a large central path. Within this garden, vegetables and herbs also grew.

In Moravian communities, women had an important role in gardening. In Salem, the Single Sisters (a group made up of the unmarried women) were responsible for their own extensive garden. In 1772 records indicate that as soon as the Single Sisters were situated, "they began to dig their garden, so that it might be ready for planting." So successful was their garden that in 1839 they were granted extra land behind the Congregation House as an extension of their kitchen garden.

By the 1800s, only older Single Sisters still cared for this garden, which by this point was mostly filled with flowers. One of the Sisters spent so much time in the garden that she was affectionately known as "Miss Flowers."

The large eighteenth-century gardens were considered primarily the domain of the male. The Moravian settlements were unusual in that women were given such important roles in the garden. Another place where a woman had a leading role in the garden was the Hermitage, Andrew and Rachel Jackson's estate.

Although separated from the Moravians by hundreds of miles, and created for very different reasons, the garden at the Jacksons' Hermitage is laid out in a remarkably similar design to the community garden at Bethabara.

"Rachel's Garden" at the Hermitage remains a tribute to a lovely woman and serves as a reminder of the turning point of women's role in the garden. In 1827 a visitor wrote of Rachel Jackson, "I never saw any one more enthusiastically fond of flowers."

The enthusiasm of Rachel Jackson and the diligent and loving work of the Moravian women have been an inspiration to generations of women who have a passion for the natural beauty of the earth.

OLD SALEM

In the mid-eighteenth century, most of the New World remained an uncharted wilderness. In 1753 the Moravian church of Germany bought a 100,000-acre plot of land in this wilderness and sent 15 of its brethren into the Piedmont of North Carolina to establish a community.

The Moravians had originally come to America from Germany in 1735, first settling in Savannah, Georgia, and establishing a second settlement in Bethlehem, Pennsylvania, in 1740. In 1753 the Moravian brethren decided to establish a third settlement in the South. They called this land Wachovia, and proposed that the purpose of this community was to create a town where Moravian ideals of Christian living might be realized and where Moravians could preach the Gospel to native Americans.

In 1766 the small town of Salem was begun and quickly became the center of trade and commerce in Wachovia. Salem was established as a congregation town, meaning that all aspects of settlement life, both economic and spiritual, were governed by the church. The residents were divided into groups, called choirs, based on natural groupings of age, sex, and married status. These choirs included Single Brothers, Single Sisters, Married People, Widows, Widowers, Older Boys, Older Girls, and Children.

Married People lived in individual houses with their children. Single Brothers and Single Sisters lived and worked in separate large buildings called choir houses.

The residents of Salem were primarily craftspeople, not farmers, but each home and choir house was responsible for its own food. In the preliminary plans for Salem, written in July 1765, it was noted, "This town is not designed for farmers but for those with trades, but until the town has so grown that each resident can support his family with the money earned by his handicraft or profession, it will be necessary.... for each to have an out-lot and a meadow where he can raise his bread, flax, etc. and winter a cow."

In addition to the large communal plots just outside town, each house also had a garden plot. Based on the current German style, houses were built close together on the street. To the rear of the houses were service yards, and behind these the garden plots. All these elements, taken together, created a neat and orderly township.

In 1791 a visitor described the town. "The antique appearance of the houses, built in the German style, and the trees among which they are placed have a singular and pleasing effect; the whole resembles a beautiful village, and forms a pastoral scene... Every house has its garden."

The service yard served as an extension of the working portion of the house. It was here that the baking ovens were found, the wood was chopped, and children played. Because the yard received constant use and heavy traffic, it was generally a "swept yard," with no grass, only hard-packed earth swept clean daily with a broom. Close to the yard was the "bleaching green," a grassy square used to sun bleach clothes after they had been washed.

The gardens were of crucial importance to the Salem settlers, for here were grown vegetables and fruit for the table, and herbs used for seasoning and for medicines. The design of these gardens followed a pattern used in Europe for many centuries. The garden was divided into rectangular or square beds of equal size, called "squares," with a long central walk and several side walkways between the squares. These walks were generally made of grass, but they were sometimes covered with tan bark or were made of packed dirt and fine gravel.

According to individual tastes, fruits were also sometimes included in the garden plot. Empty lots and common grounds in the town were often planted as orchards. The church records of March 1767 noted that "This spring several apple and peach trees are to be planted in Salem around the Square, along the street and the two lanes."

Church records also indicate that the Single Brothers set out peach trees on the south line of their property and maintained an orchard near the creek. Although none of these trees still exist in Old Salem

today, the town looks very similar to the way it did when it was first established.

Old Salem is unique in that it is, and always has been, a working, lived-in town with shops and residences sprinkled throughout. When the town of Winston was established in 1849, a mile north of Salem, the major industries settled and businesses developed there. This fact helped save the old town of Salem from the altering influences of the twentieth century.

In the early days, "every house had its garden." None of these gardens exist today, but many have been authentically recreated. Along Salt Street, as well as in other areas of this small town, a series of gardens is open to the public, showing the kinds of gardens found in Salem in the eighteenth and early nineteenth centuries.

Perhaps most outstanding of the Salt Street gardens is the one behind the John Henry Leinbach House, which was established in 1822. Mr. Leinbach was a shoemaker and obviously took great pride in his garden. Excerpts from his diary indicate that gardeners in early Salem faced the same challenges and pleasures that gardeners today do.

> Myself and T. Fetter went to my plantation to dig out green-briar roots....Went to view the bottom along the mill branch, so called, to see whether it would be practicable or profitable to make a meadow there as I contemplate....
>
> One of my bee stands began to swarm, it settled on my apple tree in the yard....I was mending my garden fence along Salt Street....
>
> Rain plenty these days; in the fields and gardens everything grows wonderfully; we get plenty of all kinds of vegetables this summer out of my garden....I sent all my hands out this morning to finish digging potatoes, they have a warm time of it.

The lot behind the Leinbach house gently slopes down toward the creek. The slope was carefully terraced with rock walls. On the top terrace stands a rosebush originally planted by Mrs. Leinbach in 1823, according to family history. Mr. Leinbach's diary also notes that his "bees settled on the widow's snowball bush in the next yard over." Peering across the fence, the visitor can see a snowball bush and can easily imagine one of Leinbach's prized bees slipping over for a sip of nectar.

It is just these human touches that make a visit to Old Salem extraordinarily appealing. There is nothing contrived, nothing fake about this town. The same carefully simple philosophy that the Moravians brought here two hundred years ago still prevails.

Farther down Salt Street, a cherry orchard turns the neighborhood into a cloud of pink when the spring weather warms. Next to the orchard, a hops garden is planted, the vines trailing on a series of posts. Used in brewing beer, hops were an important crop in Salem. Individual families used hops-water like yeast, to start bread.

Next to the hops, but closer to the house, an area patterned after the medical garden in nearby Bethabara displays herbs that might have supplied the occupants with plants for cooking and for medicine. Salsify stands tall with startling bright pink flowers. A square of feverfew looks like a miniature meadow, and the soft feathery leaves of fennel seem to beg to be touched. The exuberant growth of tansy is contained within the brick squares that compose the planting bed.

As the brethren became more settled in Salem, many of them depended less and less on the garden plot as a major source of food and medicine. With a bit of leisure time and the luxury of being able to purchase fresh produce and medicinal herbs, more gardeners began growing flowers for pleasure as well as for their usefulness. The Salem residents grew roses, larkspur, daffodils, amaranthus, clove pinks, cockscomb, China or Indian pinks, hollyhocks, hyacinths, lilacs, lilies, daisies, lavender, and sweet peas.

Fences were an important part of the landscape in the old village of Salem. Church records dating from

June 1772 read, "The family houses are to fence in their yards, in order better to keep the children at home and not let them run around the streets." The record in 1788 read, "Since experience has taught us that so many complaints and quarrels and damage can derive from the connections between the different lots, so that it often happens that one cannot enjoy one's own piece of land and work on it, it is determined that every lot is going to be fenced in all around."

Fences in Old Salem today are similar to those used when the town was begun. Stark white picket fences surround many of the gardens; board or plank fences enclose others, while still others are fenced with post-and-rail. The kind of fencing used usually reflects the wealth and prominence of the house and garden. Simple, unassuming gardens are generally surrounded by like fencing.

Old Salem boasts many historical buildings now open to the public. In these, costumed guides tell visitors about the early days of this Moravian village. But the residents of Old Salem never allow the visitor to forget that this is an authentic town—nothing contrived or reproduced. People have been living and working here since the very beginning, a fact of which Old Salem residents are justifiably proud.

THE HERMITAGE

Andrew Jackson was a man of fierce passions. He was strong and independent, and he portrayed enormous strength of will. He also showed uncommon gentleness and love for his wife Rachel. When Rachel died in December of 1828, Jackson was devastated. His devotion to her caused him to put particular emphasis on the gardens and grounds at their home, the Hermitage.

Left. The heavy, sweet fragrance of the magnolia tree at the Hermitage stands guard over Rachel Jackson's tombstone.

Jackson referred to the garden as her monument, and he wrote, "Her memory will remain fresh there as long as life lasts." Her tomb was situated in her favorite part of the garden, where Jackson spent many hours after her death. The gardens today are maintained as they were in Rachel Jackson's time.

Andrew Jackson's early life was marked by hardship and tragedy. His father died before he was even born and his two brothers died during the Revolutionary War. By the time Jackson was fourteen, his mother had died as well, leaving the boy orphaned and forced to make his own way. After teaching school and pursuing the saddlery trade, he decided to study law and was licensed in 1788. Three years later, he married Rachel Donelson and gained not only a wife but a network of relatives whose successes he applauded and whose problems Jackson embraced as his own. Perhaps because he had been orphaned at such an early age, Jackson's sense of family responsibility was enormous.

In 1804 the Jacksons bought a 425-acre farm called the Hermitage. Here they lived in a small cabin with three rooms, one on the ground floor and two upstairs. The large downstairs room was used as kitchen, dining room, sitting room, and parlor.

Andrew Jackson was enormously successful as a social and political leader, and gained national recognition for his outstanding performance in the military.

Below. It was Rachel's love of flowers such as the rose and the rhododendron that caused the Hermitage grounds to include such a large garden. These plants added an elegant grace to the Tennessee wilderness.

Below left. Southern Magnolia (Magnolia grandiflorum)

Left. *Even after Jackson's death, the Hermitage was used to host political gatherings. This 1910 photograph shows a barbecue held in honor of Jacob McGavok Dickinson, Secretary of War.*

Opposite. *A one-acre plot next to the mansion was set aside for Rachel's garden. Although a white picket fence surrounds the garden today, historical documents indicate that the original fence was made of different kinds of materials.*

Because of his national prominence, Jackson naturally associated with the leading statesmen of the day, many of whom had beautiful plantations and estates. These, undoubtedly, had an effect on Jackson and on the development of his own estate.

Although the garden at the Hermitage was much grander than those of the surrounding farmsteads, it still lacked much of the sophistication found on the estates and plantations of the mid-Atlantic coast.

The general plan of the Hermitage garden, like that of the original Moravian garden at Bethabara, calls for a large, central bed intersected by crosswalks.

Rachel Jackson's direct influence on the design and maintenance of the garden at the Hermitage was instrumental in changing a cultural perspective about women in the garden. Society began to see that women had not only a permissible, but also a desirable, role in the development of home gardens. As southern plantations grew in size and grandeur, the garden became the select dominion of the mistress of the plantation.

Adjacent to the house were two or three smaller buildings, used for lodging by family or guests. Guests at this first Hermitage home were numerous and included Jefferson Davis (who visited as a nine-year-old boy), Aaron Burr, and President James Monroe.

In spite of the fact that they never had children of their own, Rachel and Andrew Jackson assumed responsibility for many children during their lifetimes. Their adopted son, Andrew Jackson, Jr., and their ward, Andrew Jackson Hutchings, were raised in the first small Hermitage cabin and the first brick house. In 1804 an Indian boy named Lyncoya, orphaned by the Creek Wars, was also brought here to live.

Jackson had a passion for horses and thoroughbred racing. In a duel over a horse race, Jackson killed his opponent and was subsequently shunned and ostracized by Nashville society for many years.

In spite of this unfortunate incident, Jackson continued to gain popularity and political power. In 1815 he led the U.S. forces that defeated the British at the Battle of New Orleans. He instantly gained national attention. As his powers and ambitions grew, Jackson realized that he needed a larger, more refined dwelling, and he and Rachel began building a new large brick house. They contracted the services of an accomplished landscape designer from Philadelphia, William Frost, to design the garden.

A large one-acre plot adjacent to the site for the house was set aside for the garden. It is assumed that it was Rachel's love of flowers that caused the Jacksons to include the garden within the initial plans for the estate. Documents make it clear that the garden was always intended to be an integral part of the estate and was not simply tacked on as an afterthought.

Jackson's visit to Mount Vernon in 1815 may have greatly influenced his desire to create a large and beautiful garden. Formal and manicured landscapes had become somewhat of a status symbol for the wealthy and learned men of the times. In this new, raw wilderness of America, it was a statement of control and power.

The original version of the mansion was built in 1819–21, and the garden was begun at the same time. Although Jackson may have been influenced by the elaborate houses and gardens of Virginia, his own garden was initially quite unpretentious.

The large, four-square design was a version of the English kitchen garden. During the 1820s, Rachel Jackson exerted great influence over the garden. Her interest may have stemmed from her responsibilities in seeing that ample food was placed on the table. During this time the garden included essential herbs and vegetables as well as more ornamental plants.

A visitor to the Hermitage wrote in 1827: "After I rested, she [Rachel] proposed walking into the garden, which is very large and quite her hobby. I never saw any one more enthusiastically fond of flowers. She culled for me the only rose which was in bloom and made up a pretty nosegay; after an agreeable stroll we returned to the drawing room...Mrs.

Jackson would not permit me to go without a bouquet, which she arranged very tastily."

In 1828 Jackson was elected president of the United States after a long and bitter campaign. During the campaign, Rachel's character and reputation were questioned, but she never lived long enough to face her opponents. In December 1828, only a few months before Jackson took office, his wife died.

After his wife's death, Andrew Jackson showed much interest and enthusiasm for the garden. In 1829 he wrote to his son from Washington asking about the garden. "Still you have not informed me of its situation, and whether the weeping willows that we planted around it, are growing, or whether the flowers reared by her industrious, and beloved hands, have been set around the grave as I had requested."

In 1830 he wrote to one of his wife's nephews, "That garden is now to me a consecrated plot, and I wish it carefully attended to, particularly the square around the sacred tomb."

At the time of Jackson's death in 1845 the total acreage of the Hermitage was 1,050; today the grounds comprise 625 acres. Jackson himself often found these grounds too large for easy control. He wrote to his son in 1836: "We must seed well or we never can reap well and I discover all oats, hemp and millet has been badly

Left. Neat, geometric beds are filled with roses and bedding plants in the center of the garden. The surrounding area was divided into four large squares.

Below. After Jackson's death, the grounds were allowed to deteriorate. It was not until the Ladies Hermitage Association was formed and they bought the property that restoration work was begun.

and slovenly sowed. We must plow better and cultivate less (acres), and we will produce more."

In 1837, after his second presidential term, Jackson retired to Tennessee to enjoy the beauty and peace of the Hermitage. Jackson spent his last years in relative peace and solitude and devoted much time in the garden around Rachel's tomb. His granddaughter, Rachel Jackson Lawrence, wrote: "No one ever went to the

tomb with him. Every evening, just about the time the sun would be nearly down, he went to the tomb. I always went to the gate and saw him in. He would stay there a half hour, I suppose, and then return."

When Jackson died in 1845, he was buried next to Rachel in the garden.

Located on the east side of the mansion, Rachel's garden covers approximately an acre and is laid out in a large square. At the present time it is completely surrounded by a white picket fence. Documentary research indicates that several different types of fencing were originally used to surround the garden. A low brick footer occurs along the west side, and twenty feet along the south side. Walkways divide this into four equal quadrants with a large circle of planting beds in the center.

Midway down the north side of the garden is a small brick structure originally used as a privy. The center beds are circular or geometric and are edged with unusual bricks, which are longer than standard bricks of today and beveled at one end.

The tombs of Rachel and Andrew Jackson as well as many other family members are located in the southeastern corner of the garden. Near the tombs are numerous hickory trees planted in Jackson's time.

Archeological work has given some insight into the original garden site. Today's garden is probably a bit fancier than that enjoyed by Rachel and Andrew Jackson.

Apparently there was a major reorganization of the garden in 1835 or 1836, when the house—gutted by fire in 1834—was being altered. The basic four-square design was left intact, but the fence along the side of the garden nearest the house was probably changed to tall, thin pickets set close together and painted white, footed with a low brick wall like the one in the garden today. Today the paths are edged with a wide assortment of bricks from a number of different time periods.

The Jacksons grew both vegetables and flowers. In 1837, Jackson wrote to his nephew, "I cannot be with-out a good vegetable garden." It is assumed that his wishes for a "good vegetable garden" were seen to. After his death, other family members continued to use the garden as a source of both pleasure and produce.

In 1852 a letter (now in the collection of the Tennessee Historical Society) was written between family members, stating, "We have also had very cold weather here…all our early flowers are destroyed, also all the first plantings of vegetables….We have about fifty varieties of roses."

Soon after that, in 1856, the state of Tennessee bought the Hermitage from Andrew Jackson, Jr. Lack of funds caused much decay and deterioration during the next few years. In 1859 James Parton, biographer of Andrew Jackson, wrote in his journal: "House locked and empty. Went into garden, close behind. 1½ acre. Beds bordered with upright bricks, all of which were loose and many gone—some lying about beds. Paths were pebbled, but not well. A large, mean, ill-kept garden."

It was this "large, mean, ill-kept garden" that the Ladies' Hermitage Association faced when it was formed as a private organization in 1889. Its purpose was to administer the Hermitage property for the state of Tennessee. The association placed great emphasis on the restoration of the garden. In their zeal to make it a beautiful and exciting place to visit, association members formalized and changed much of the garden, creating a space that was probably neater and more beautiful than it ever was during the Jacksons' lifetimes. As a result of this restoration, all of the plants found in the garden today are purely ornamental, with the exception of a few herbs.

With the information gained from archeological digs and greater knowledge and understanding of historical landscapes, the tone and message of the Hermitage garden is being constantly reviewed and revised. While the Ladies' Hermitage Association presented a beautiful garden, in time it may become a more accurate and equally lovely, but less manicured representation of Rachel's garden.

Opposite.
Rachel's Garden is all greenery and color, fragrance and texture, warmth and grace— everything a southern garden ought to be.

{5}

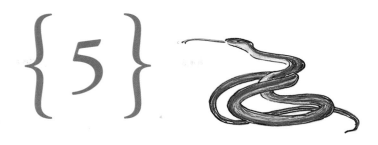

Antebellum Plantation Gardens, 1800–1865

*I*n the years before the Civil War, the American South knew tremendous prosperity. In the magical land of Louisiana, in an area with the lilting name of Feliciana, lie antebellum plantations that exemplify and glorify the spirit of the Old South. With names like Rosedown and Afton Villa, these vast and magnificent plantations were once showplaces of unparalleled beauty and the backdrop for a way of life never to be duplicated after its disappearance.

Nearby Natchez, Mississippi, was a city of millionaires, and the town's splendid history has been beautifully preserved. More than five hundred pre–Civil War homes and buildings still stand in this unusual place.

Antebellum homes and plantations today show the effects of time and the inevitable changes brought on by the decline of an opulent and ostentatious way of life. The grace and beauty of the gardens at such homes, however, can still be seen today. A visit to Natchez, or to Afton Villa or Rosedown, offers a chance to stroll through paths perfumed by the rich scent of camellias and bejeweled by the bold colors of azaleas.

The parish of West Feliciana is an area blessed with great natural beauty. To the north lie the gentle slopes of the Tunica hills. In the south and west, white chalk cliffs tower over the wide brown waters of the Mississippi River. For thousands of years the Mississippi has carried vast deposits of nutrients to this area, enriching the land. This fertile soil and an abundance of rainfall has made the area of West Feliciana a place most desirable for gardeners and farmers for many generations.

In 1681 the French explorers LaSalle and Tonty left Canada to explore and claim Louisiana and the Mississippi River. Before they reached the Gulf of Mexico they met with the Natchez Indians and established friendly relations with them. Although both men had planned a return to Natchez territory, circumstances prevented it.

The first Europeans to settle in this area were the French. Here they created a small settlement at the village of St. Francis. After the French and Indian War, West Feliciana, including the village of St. Francis, was deeded to the English. Retired British soldiers were offered vast amounts of land here as payment for their service to the Crown. During the American Revolution, many Tories sought refuge in this area, which remained staunchly British.

Opposite.
The live oaks leading to Rosedown are nearly 200 years old and give the plantation a studied grace impossible to duplicate. Rosedown today has a rare collection of old, mature horticultural specimens.

Page 94. The ravages of war took their toll on the grand plantations of the South, but the roots of beauty run deep and much of the grace of these plantations can again be seen today.

Page 95. Sarah Turnbull Bowman and James P. Bowman are shown here at Rosedown. After the war and the death of Martha Turnbull, the gardens at Rosedown deteriorated quickly. On her death in 1914, Sarah left Rosedown to her four unmarried daughters.

Rosedown provides us with a window in time. Clipped boxwood hedges and venerable old live oak trees paint a rich portrait of history and beauty.

West Feliciana, part of what was then called West Florida, was brought under Spanish control in 1779 by Bernardo de Galvez. As acting governor of Louisiana at New Orleans, he captured the entire region.

The new Spanish rulers tried diligently to grow crops of economic value here. Tobacco proved inferior, however, and indigo was valuable but difficult and expensive to process. Cotton grew well, but removing the seeds was a tedious and expensive procedure. With the invention of the cotton gin in 1793, however, the search for a cash crop ended. Cotton became king.

When word spread of the fresh new lands capable of growing cotton, many settlers left their worn-out acres in the Southeast and moved westward to Louisiana and Mississippi. Among these early settlers was the widow Olivia Ruffin Barrow, who left her home in Halifax County, North Carolina, and—after a two-year stop in Tennessee—continued westward with her children and her slaves. Her thirty covered wagons, filled with household items, gold, and agricultural implements, arrived in Natchez in the latter part of 1800. The Barrows were soon enmeshed in the political life of their new home.

In 1803 Thomas Jefferson signed the Louisiana Purchase; West Florida, including the Feliciana area, was excluded and remained under Spanish rule. In 1810 William Barrow III and other planters revolted against the Spanish rule and set up their own tiny republic. This burst of independence lasted seventy-six days, until President James Madison finally declared that West Florida was part of the Louisiana Purchase and belonged to the United States.

Cotton was an extraordinarily successful cash crop, and the planters in West Feliciana soon enjoyed great prosperity. In 1860 the *New Orleans Crescent* reported that "West Feliciana is one of the richest parishes in the state. Some of the planters of this parish rank among the largest in the state."

Olivia Ruffin Barrow's grandchildren were among the most successful of all the West Feliciana planters. The family soon became well known for their large

and gracious estates and their beautiful gardens. Four of these estates—Greenwood, Ellerslie, Afton Villa, and Rosedown—were considered among the most outstanding country houses in America.

ROSEDOWN

Rosedown is a picture-perfect example of a southern plantation. A long allee of live oaks gracefully frames the large, white-columned house. Spanish moss hangs from the tree limbs, giving the grounds and the house a sense of timelessness and grandeur.

Olivia Ruffin Barrow, the original pioneer from North Carolina, was, by the early nineteenth century, grande dame of a large, brilliant, and prominent family. In 1828 the family was united with another important pioneer family: Olivia's granddaughter Martha married Daniel Turnbull. Martha, who had been educated at Madam Legoin's Institute in Philadelphia, returned to the West Feliciana area a sophisticated young woman with an excellent sense of styling in clothes, manners, and tastes.

Martha and Daniel Turnbull had an extravagant wedding in West Feliciana and immediately left for a "Grand Tour" of Europe. The Turnbulls were impressed with the gardens of Italy and Versailles. Swayed by what they saw—long avenues of trees, formal parterres, and statuary—the young couple began to dream of creating their own grand estate. While in New York they saw a romantic play called *Rosedown*. This inspired them to choose the same name for the plantation that they planned to create in West Feliciana.

Cotton was in enormous demand. A successful planter who had good crops several years in a row could make millions of dollars in a very short time. Daniel Turnbull was such a planter. Both Daniel and Martha had inherited land from their families, but even this was not enough acreage for the grand estate that they dreamed of. Daniel began buying land and continued until he had acquired massive acreage. Included in this was "The Flower Tract," 217 acres of land that Daniel purchased for $6,333.36 from former owners of the St. Francisville Jockey Club.

Work on the house and grounds was begun on November 3, 1834. Daniel's journal entry was succinct: "Commenced hauling timber cypress for house." His journal also suggests that work on the house was completed on May 1, 1835, at a final cost of $13,109.20.

While Daniel oversaw the cotton, Martha turned her time and efforts to directing the work of household servants and to the gardens. The gardens at Rosedown were the passion of her life; she devoted sixty years to cultivating and maintaining them. She faithfully kept a garden diary, beginning when she first moved into the mansion, and ending with her death in 1896. In the diary she recorded the work done in the garden and both the successes and the failures she experienced.

Often the day's entry would end with the words: "My gardens are in perfect order." These were wonderful words to be able to say over and over again. As early as 1836 the Turnbulls imported exotic azaleas, camellias, and other trees and shrubs from nurseries in New York and Philadelphia.

Like other plantation owners of the time, the Turnbulls began their gardens as small formal areas close to the house. But Martha was not content with this small garden; with every trip to Europe, she came home inspired to add more acreage to the garden and to decorate it with imported statuary and ornaments. Rosedown was considered the most expansive garden of its time. Middleton Place and Magnolia Gardens in Charleston did not attain such size and grandeur until the 1860s, and Mount Vernon and the James River Plantations were on a much smaller scale.

Margaret McDonald wrote of southern life in the 1850s that it was a time "when the song of the mockingbird sounded more clearly than the death knell of a way of life." The last decade before the outbreak of war was marked by extravagant gaiety in the Deep South. The Turnbulls took their daughter Sarah to Europe to show her classical landscape designs and

bought more Italian statuary to install in their own growing garden. The last cotton season of the antebellum South was the largest that the nation had ever seen but plantation owners continued to ignore the growing threat of war.

Daniel Turnbull died on October 30, 1861, and Martha was left to face war and its aftermath alone. These were turbulent times at Rosedown, but throughout it all, Martha continued to make entries in her garden journal, many of which show the difficulties she was facing and her sorrow at not being able to maintain the gardens. In January 1864 she wrote: "Up to this time, since the Federals landed in May, neither field or garden has been worked. The garden is a wilderness, sedgegrass. It looks melancholly." In January 1869 she wrote, "No hands in Garden but John and John Prenter—not one speck of ground yet plowed." And on February 10th: "I feel perfectly discouraged—not one thing toward making a garden done—garden looks deplorable. I see no seed coming up—the repeated and heavy rains since Christmas."

The decline of her gardens must have been heartbreaking to this gentle and proud woman who so loved her trees and flowers. Although Union soldiers never burned her home, never destroyed the plants in her garden, the war nevertheless took its toll. Martha had to sit by and watch the ineluctable tide of nature overtake her garden, even though the Union Army had not done so.

Martha never lived to see her gardens restored to their former beauty. At her death, Rosedown Plantation was inherited by her daughter Sarah Turnbull Bowman, who in turn left it to her four daughters, none of whom ever married.

Through the years the descendants and relatives of the Turnbulls kept the house and grounds intact, but it was not until Rosedown was purchased by Catherine Fondren Underwood in 1956 that the plantation began to see a real renaissance. Mrs. Underwood was a wealthy and enthusiastic garden lover, and in Rosedown she saw an opportunity to

reinstate the grandeur and beauty of one of America's most exciting plantations.

The garden restoration was a long-range plan. As Mrs. Underwood put it, "A garden is never finished anyway." The restoration of the gardens was a unique project. Unlike other historical gardens that were excavated and pieced back together, Rosedown's gardens were still intact, but were practically invisible because they were so overgrown.

Many huge shrubs and trees dating back to the mid-1800s still exist on the grounds and are living proof of Martha Turnbull's enthusiastic gardening experience. Her diary provided invaluable help in reclaiming the gardens and restoring them to their original grandeur.

Some of the plants that originally grew here were no longer available through the horticultural trade. In their dedication to remain as authentic as possible in both the house and grounds, the Underwoods encouraged Larry Marshman, head gardener for the estate, to obtain new plants of these old species by taking cuttings from specimens that could still be found on the grounds.

Some of the more important plants that were propagated in this way included the hip gardenia (*Gardenia thunbergia*) and the lace cap hydrangea (*Hydrangea macrophylla tricolor*). Others were various species of old roses and begonias.

The influence of Rosedown is strong enough to bring out the romantic in us all. The elongated walks look as if they are still swept clean by the long, full hoop skirts of southern belles. Each tree casting a shadow on the sun-dappled lawn looks as if it holds secret stories of love and adventure.

The live oak trees that create such a dramatic setting for the plantation house are nearly two hundred years old, having been planted in the early 1800s. On each side of the central walk, and behind the oaks, lie vast gardens of camellias and azaleas, intersected by narrow white paths. The Turnbulls were thought to be among the first of all the plantation owners to import camellias, and many different species of camellias and azaleas still grace the grounds of Rosedown. Nestled in this forest of flowering shrubs are small secluded summer houses. Between the camellia gardens and the house is the

original garden-tool house, which is now filled with examples of old-fashioned tools.

Close to the front entrance of the grounds, a statue of St. Francis of Assisi stands starkly white against a backdrop of dark green leaves. The statue honors the patron saint of animals and birds, and the namesake of the small village of St. Francis, now known as St. Francisville.

Closest to the house are the formal gardens showing geometric shapes and clean white walks. Although the rose garden still boasts many different kinds of old-fashioned roses, many of the trellised roses have now been replaced by confederate jasmine. A formal flower garden lies closest to the house. Behind the house is a long lawn leading down to a wooded area filled with hydrangeas, azaleas, and small wildflowers.

Adjacent to the outbuilding that housed the old kitchen lies the kitchen garden. Here Martha Turnbull grew vegetables and herbs that were used to feed the family and the slaves who lived on the plantation. Today ornamental cabbages have taken the place of edible ones, and although parsley and spring greens are still grown, other herbs and flowers are now grown more for their beauty than for their culinary value.

Not far from the kitchen garden lies the old doctor's office and a garden where medicinal plants were grown. In spite of its great beauty and its capacity to grow good cotton, West Feliciana was not considered a very healthy place to live. The lower Mississippi Valley in the early 1800s was often ravaged by fevers and diseases; and New Orleans during this period was known as the "sickliest city in the world." Although the Turnbulls usually left their home during the summer, spending these hot months in the relative cool of Saratoga in upstate New York, they declined to do so during the summer of 1843. Disease struck the plantation, and their seven-year-old son became ill and died only a few days after his birthday. After this tragic event, Daniel Turnbull built an office and hired a plantation doctor who was responsible for the health and well-being of all those living on the plantation—almost five hundred people.

The medicinal garden shows which plants were useful to the doctor. Many of these are still considered important medicinal plants today. Comfrey, foxglove, fennel, and dill were all used frequently by doctors of the day.

Rosedown is highly regarded in the horticultural world for its work with older plant specimens. Many of the trees and shrubs date back to the early 1800s, and where possible these have been allowed to attain their full height and maturity without being pruned. The results are sometimes surprising. Several camellias are now well over twenty-five feet tall, and a group of sweet olives is over thirty feet tall. Few gardens in North America hold such a large collection of old plantings.

Although today the statues are weathered and the trees and shrubs twisted and gnarled with time, the gardens of Rosedown present a spectacular glimpse of life in the antebellum South. The persistence of the gardeners, both past and present, is beautifully illustrated by the wonderful collection of plants and walks that make up the gardens of Rosedown Plantation.

Martha Turnbull would be pleased and proud to see her gardens now. Once again she could rightly say, "My gardens are in perfect order."

AFTON VILLA

In 1820 Bartholomew Barrow bought a large tract of land close to what is now St. Francisville, Louisiana. This land and a small six-room frame house passed to Bartholomew's son David. In 1847 David Barrow married for the second time, his first wife having died in childbirth. His new wife, a Kentucky widow named Susan Woolfolk Rowan, came to live in the small house but it was not long before the new Mrs. David Barrow began to want something more grand. Luckily, by this time her husband was a very successful planter and had the means to fulfill her desires.

During these opulent and ostentatious days in the South, Gothic Revival architecture was quite in vogue

Left. *Though the house at Afton Villa no longer exists, the gardens remain exciting and inspiring. The home of David and Susan Barrow, the plantation was at one time considered one of the most beautiful in the South.*

Below. *The romance of Afton Villa and the beauty of Susan Barrow inspired Robert Meyer to write a waltz which he named after the plantation and dedicated to her.*

Far left. *Poet's Narcissus (Narcissus poeticus)*

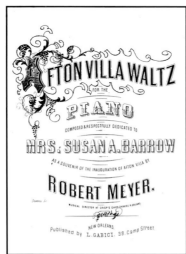

Daffodils fill the landscape at Afton Villa, turning green vales yellow and white in spring.

Opposite. The ruins garden is located at the site of the original plantation house, which burned in 1963. Instead of a sad reminder of the past, these colorful gardens are now a testament to the triumph of beauty.

prime the landscape of Afton Villa included a top terrace composed of a formal garden, a second level made up of colorful perennials, and a bottom level planted with a field of roses. Smaller terraces were planted with flowering fruit trees, azaleas, camellias, and cape jessamine bushes. In the ravine there was a series of hothouses that supplied the plantation with exotic fruits and flowers.

Perhaps it is because there is no house to distract one from the garden itself that the landscape appears so beautiful. Perhaps it is because the ruins of the old mansion are brought alive by the cascading beauty of tumbling flowers that it so captures the imagination of the visitor. Perhaps it is the combination of formal boxwood mazes and sweeping grassy terraces that is so tantalizing. Perhaps it is a combination of all of these factors. Whatever the reason, the grounds of Afton Villa cast a spell on anyone lucky enough to visit these gardens.

At first one looks for a grand mansion, for such lavish and extravagant gardens have always been used to adorn fine homes. But once in the garden, one begins to think that a house would simply block the view of such beautifully maintained and scrupulously neat botanical displays.

The ruins of the house are not reminders of a tragic past but seem to signal a triumph of the present blaze of living color. Magnificent statues stand guard at the entrance to the ruins, and neat gravel paths beckon one to enter. The foundation and broken brick walls suggest the size and opulence of the house that once stood here. Steps leading nowhere are softened by ivy, beautified by small fragrant narcissus. Mounds of bricks do not appear as desolate signs of destruction; planted with sweet-smelling phlox, they are reminders of the glorious and rejuvenating powers of nature.

The "ruins garden," as this area is affectionately called, is bounded by partial brick walls, foundation stones, and steps. The overall feeling is one of a marvelously rich sunken garden. Tall stately trees droop graceful branches, creating a high ceiling. Outdoor

with many of the wealthy plantation owners. Susan Barrow enthusiastically embraced this new fashion and began to plan her mansion based on a château that she and David had seen near Tours, France. Construction on the house and gardens began in 1849 and was not completed until 1857. During this time it is believed that a French architect and landscape designer lived at the estate to supervise all construction.

The only guideline that David gave to his extravagant and enthusiastic wife was that the original house had to remain intact and be included within the new structure. The result was a house within a house, the original six-room home being completely surrounded and engulfed by the new forty-room mansion.

The plantation house at Afton Villa burned in 1963, but the expansive gardens are meticulously maintained and are astoundingly beautiful. At the entrance to the estate sits a Gothic gatehouse and a wrought-iron gate. This opens up to a long half-mile oak allee, leading the visitor to the ruins of the house and the beginnings of one of the South's most magnificent and haunting gardens.

The original gardens included more than twenty acres of walks, terraces, and formal beds, and much of the original landscape design can still be seen today. The landscape, showing the influence of French park design, was divided into a series of terraces. At its

furniture is scattered throughout this portion of the garden, the tables decorated with large pots of flowering plants. The scene gives one the feeling of being in an enormous outdoor room, where tea might be served at any moment.

To the west of the ruins garden is the beginning of the formal garden. A clipped and manicured low hedge creates a maze garden. Like a living tapestry, the green maze weaves in and out and around, forming a background for vibrantly colored tulips and petunias. At the center of the maze stand four standard cherry laurel trees and a small white statue. Finding this peaceful, tranquil spot is well worth the effort it takes.

Next to the maze is another formal garden. Here mounds of white pansies fill geometric beds, sliced into neat pieces by clean brick walks. The orderly symmetry of the garden is soothing; one can imagine that in times of trouble, both visitors and owners of the estate might have escaped to these walks to stroll and meditate.

The Civil War brought troubled times to Afton Villa. Union soldiers swept through the area, causing great damage to homes and property. Afton Villa was miraculously spared. Some people speculate that the house was spared because the soldiers believed that the severe wrought-iron gates at the entrance to the estate could only lead to a cemetery.

Family history suggests that during the Civil War the family silver was hidden in the raised box tombs found in the small family cemetery. Today this cemetery is still secluded, surrounded by sweet olive trees and gnarled and twisted camellias, rising ten to fifteen feet. The graves are planted with white tulips and pansies; the beauty of the blossoms pays solemn tribute to past owners and relatives, while giving a joyful note to the present.

In this cemetery are buried David Barrow, his first wife, Sarah, and two of their children. David's uncle Alexander Barrow is also buried here; a senator from Louisiana at the time of his death in 1846, he was at one time considered the "most handsome man in Washington."

Grand old live oak trees and huge mounded azaleas bear testimony to the age of the garden. The oldest azalea bush, known as the "Pride of Afton," was the particular joy of Dr. Robert E. Lewis of Illinois, who bought the plantation in 1915. Dr. Lewis took cuttings from this shrub and used them to establish this variety all over the grounds at Afton Villa.

Below the formal gardens are broad grassy terraces, interrupted only by gracefully placed azalea hedges, occasional circles of bright bedding plants, or lovely, stark white statues. A series of statues of Cupid reminds visitors that a garden is for delight.

The terraces lead down to a large valley where in spring fifty thousand daffodils proclaim the joy of the season. From a distance they look like a piece of yellow-and-white calico laid upon a carpet of green. If the visitor wanders in among them, each takes on an individual beauty and charm. Native yellow senecios mix proudly with their imported cousins, adding a bit of natural grace to this scene of springtime delight. White leucothoe blossoms nod gracefully and add a different texture, and shy little purple phlox—almost hidden from view—contribute a bit of contrasting color to this sea of white and gold.

Afton Villa may be without a house, but every visitor who strolls the walks and enjoys the rich beauty of this garden will feel very much at home.

MONMOUTH

One of the most prominent citizens of nineteenth-century Natchez was John A. Quitman, owner of Monmouth Plantation. Born in New York in 1799, Quitman was the son of a poor and frugal Lutheran minister. From an early age he showed great promise and ambition and desired not only to amass a fortune but also, in his own words, to "live genteelly."

When he attained his law degree, Quitman left New York for the Mississippi River town of Natchez where he quickly established himself as a successful lawyer and gradually acquired several cotton and sugar plantations. Among these was Monmouth, a beautiful, two-story, Federal-style brick mansion. He bought the house and thirty-one acres for $12,000 in 1826.

Quitman was also drawn into public service. In 1836 he led a group of volunteers to Texas to assist in their fight for independence. This military duty made a hero of the poor preacher's son from New York.

Although Quitman held numerous political offices, including that of U.S. representative, governor of Mississippi, and chairman of the House Committee on Military Affairs, he is perhaps best known as the father of secession. Quitman was a staunch supporter of the South and worked diligently in his attempts to help the region secede from the Union.

With the purchase of Monmouth and his marriage to Eliza Turner, one of Mississippi's most beautiful and socially prominent young women, John Quitman did indeed begin to live "genteelly." John and Eliza were at the top of the social ladder in Natchez. They had wealth and happiness and were eventually to have ten children.

*Work on restoring the house and gardens at Monmouth Plantation was begun by Ron and Lani Riches in 1977. They were aided by historical documents such as letters, diaries, and maps. Included in these documents was a reference to violets (**above**), which were grown in a separate formal bed.*

***Below left.** White Violet (Viola blanda)*

In 1855 Daniel Barringer, former U.S. ambassador to Spain, wrote of his visit to Monmouth: "My friend who is an acquaintance of General Quitman, proposed a ride to visit him—and see the neighborhood of the richest men in the whole South—and I assure you, in all Europe. I never saw anything which impressed me more. The General's place is very striking—very much improved, yet left so as to give the most natural effect and the beautiful ground and splendid oaks, with long hanging moss, to their branches."

Quitman died in 1858. But his mansion and grounds at Monmouth nonetheless suffered greatly during the Civil War, for his aid to the secessionist cause was widely known. The mansion was ransacked, the gardens were raided, and many of the ancient oaks were cut for firewood. After the war, the family lived at Monmouth sporadically. The estate went into a severe decline and finally passed out of the family's hands in 1925.

In 1977 the mansion was in poor condition and the grounds were overgrown and unsightly. It was this ghost of an antebellum belle that Ron Riches, a California developer, saw and dreamed of restoring. He and his wife Lani moved to Natchez in 1977, bought Monmouth, and began the monumental

Far left. The original owner of Monmouth, John Quitman (left), was called the Father of Secession. Although he died in 1858, his estate still suffered greatly during the war because his political views were so well known. The gardens at Monmouth were ransacked and many large oak trees cut for firewood.

task of restoring both the mansion and the grounds, converting them to an inn.

The grounds at Monmouth, nearly a century and a half after Daniel Barringer's visit, are once again very striking—improved, yet with the most natural effect. The gently sloping lawn leading to the front entrance of the mansion is covered with grass interspersed with tiny colorful wildflowers.

It is in the rear of the house, however, that the true grace and charm of the grounds can be experienced. Landscape architect William Garbo suggested opening up the broad lawns that now drift down to the woods and the still waters of a peaceful pond. Brick walks and graceful statuary lend an air of formal elegance. Small fountains add the delightful sound of trickling water. A formal rose garden is hidden from view below the second terrace. A distant pergola draws the visitor into the garden.

Restoration work at Monmouth Plantation was greatly aided by two maps dating back to the mid-nineteenth century. The Sanbourn Insurance Company maps (1850–1900) and a Union Army defense map for Natchez (1864) helped in the accurate placement of the carriage house, barn, and other buildings, now reconstructed as part of the inn.

Horticulture was important to John and Eliza Quitman. He was always on the lookout for new and unusual plants, whether they were imported from the corners of the world, or from his own woods and fields. In 1833 he wrote to Eliza: "My ride as usual thro' the piney woods was dreary, and only diversified upon passing small streams, the banks of which are at this season literally festooned with the yellow jasmine in full bloom. On my return I will endeavor to take up and bring with me a few roots as well as some wild strawberry plants." Today visitors to Monmouth can see both yellow jasmine and wild strawberries growing on the grounds.

Quitman's diary provides evidence that Henry Clay, who visited Monmouth in 1830, was presented with several magnolia plants from the plantation. Clay penned a graceful note, thanking Quitman for the trees and inviting him to visit his own estate of Ashland some day so he could "witness their prosperous growth."

Albert Quitman, John's brother, sent him over forty trees and vines from France, including a peach tree. In his orchard Quitman grew peaches, pears, plums, nectarines, olives, figs, persimmons, and apples. Among the flowering plants were hyacinths, geraniums, azaleas, and violets—all of them grown in separate formal beds.

Although Eliza seemed to share John's love of flowers and plants, she did not always love the work that the orchard demanded. In August 1855 she wrote in her diary: "For the last seven days past we have been busily engaged in making brandy peaches and preserving figs. Cooking is a terrible siege which one is destined to undergo every summer."

So important were John Quitman's garden and orchard to him that he brought one of his gardening staff all the way from England.

Among the most beautiful of all flowering plants at Monmouth were the camellias. In 1857 Rose Quitman, John's daughter, wrote in her diary that she wandered into the gardens after a bad storm and was rewarded for her "muddy adventure" with the sight of a "large, beautiful white camellia, each leaf was perfect and looked as if nature had taken no little pains in fringing them."

Today Rose could still see large, beautiful camellias without having to track through the mud. Now, neat brick walks criss-cross the grounds at Monmouth, leading to the small gazebo or the white bridge over the stream that feeds the pond.

One advantage that visitors today have that Rose could not have dreamed of are electric lights that magically illuminate the garden at night. With the reflection of the moon in the still waters, and the fragrance of the sweet olive, ginger, and banana shrub mixing with the distant cry of a night-flying bird, Monmouth still offers an adventure of the most delightful kind.

ELMS COURT

Legend says that Natchez once had a mansion on every hill, a millionaire on every corner. Certainly Natchez, which boasts over five hundred pre–Civil War buildings, occupies an unusual place in the history of our country.

On top of one of the most beautiful hills in Natchez stands a gracious antebellum home decorated with white cast iron, surrounded by graceful, well-kept grounds. The house itself, seemingly untouched by the passage of time, blends beautifully with the garden, which has been done and redone over the years.

The present owner, Mrs. Grace MacNeil, is an accomplished and talented gardener. Like plantation ladies of the past, Mrs. MacNeil has kept a garden journal every day for many, many years. In this she includes records of what is blooming, the weather, what's been planted, what has been taken out. Her diary serves as a guide and a source of information, and the gardens show the benefits of keeping such careful records.

The house and gardens have always been in Mrs. MacNeil's family. Her great-grandfather, James Surget II, built the main part of the house in 1830. The outstanding grillwork and the one-story sections of the house were added in 1850.

The house was given to Mrs. MacNeil's parents in 1901 as a wedding present, and Mrs. MacNeil grew up here. She has wonderful memories of the beauty of the gardens during her childhood years and has particularly fond thoughts of the showy wisteria vine growing on an arbor just off the back gallery. The vine still graces the gallery, lending continuity to the house and grounds.

The most recent garden restoration work began in 1975 when landscape architect William Garbo fell in love with Elms Court. He first saw this garden in 1949, when he came to Natchez as a student; but it wasn't until many years later that he was able to work closely with Mrs. MacNeil and develop the gardens.

Opposite. Gently curving grapevines give Elms Court garden a gentle elegance. The family home of Mrs. Grace MacNeil, the garden has been a source of pleasure for many generations.

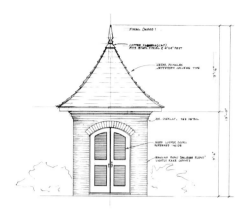

Far left.
Wisteria (Wisteria floribunda)

Center left.
Viewed from the swimming pool back toward the house, several different terrace levels are apparent. The modern pool house (an architectural drawing is at left) blends beautifully with the older structures such as the barn, laundry, and coach house.

Opposite. *Old letters written about the MacNeil garden describe them as being a "rainbow of colors," a description that is still accurate today. A long central brick walk intersects the perennial border.*

Today the garden is a union of the wild and the cultivated, of old and new, of annuals and perennials. "This country is so rich in natives I wanted to include them in the garden," Mrs. MacNeil said. And evidence of her wishes is found throughout the garden.

The entrance to the house has been left as an open wood. Understory plants include both native and imported plants. Wild blue phlox grows side by side with hostas beneath towering trees. Small woodland wildflowers show up brightly between narcissus, lycoris, hyacinth, and tulips. Senecio, sometimes called high-water weed, stands tall and clear in a simple sort of beauty. In addition to offering a splash of color outdoors, this plant is also good for cutting and lasts indefinitely indoors.

Behind the house are found many old structures. The slaves' quarters, laundry, coach house, stable, and barn are still standing in good repair. A long brick walk leads directly from the back gallery down several terraces to the swimming pool. The terraces are curved to follow the natural contour of the ground; family letters, newspaper articles, journals, diaries, and photographs indicate that these terraces were once spectacularly beautiful. One visitor wrote of the "rainbow of colors" found here. Then, as now, the terraces served also to channel the flow of water toward the bayou.

Until recently, the woods encroached, and the first and second terraces were separated by a barbed-wire fence. Today the woods have been kept at bay, and the barbed wire has been replaced with a cedar split-rail fence.

Graceful curves play a big part in the design of this garden. The walks curve gently around the terraces, and circular beds, grouped around a small sundial, hold a host of bedding plants. A big iron pot, once used to boil down sugar cane to make syrup, bursts to overflowing with water lilies and hyacinths. The beds around the pot are planted seasonally with various annuals and perennials.

The true form of the garden can be seen in the magnificent twists and turns of the huge grapevines growing in the back garden. The vines growing close to the ground are as big around as a man's arm, and grow high up in the trees until they are only a sliver, not even as thick as a fingernail. These naturalized vines add a touch of the wild to this sedate old garden.

A visitor standing by the modern swimming pool and looking back at the house might feel that he is looking back in time. Romantic imaginings about old plantation days seem to have found the perfect setting; Elms Court allows you to combine romance with realism. The magnificent splendor this plantation must once have had is mingled with the perseverance and single-mindedness of the owners, who have been at such pains to restore the beauty of their homes and gardens.

{6}

The Great Estates,
1875-1925

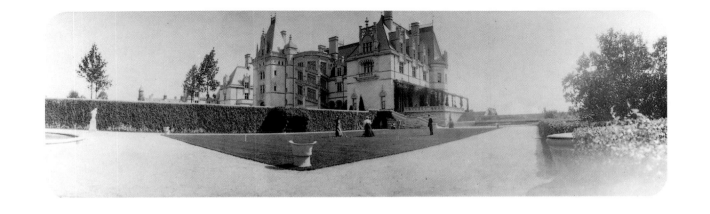

In the new century nothing must be impossible.
—*The Saturday Evening Post*, April 26, 1902

T he beginning of the new century in America was characterized by change and spirit. With the death of Queen Victoria in England, rigid social mores became more relaxed on both sides of the Atlantic, and Americans became bolder and more aggressive in their attitudes.

For many this was a time of tremendous economic growth. Names like Carnegie, Vanderbilt, and Morgan became household words, symbolizing the realization of the great American dream.

The turn of the century was also a time of great economic disparity. With the development of an industrialized nation and the need for moving products quickly, many men made vast fortunes, but rarely were profits passed on to the common laborer. While families like the Vanderbilts lived in fantastic mansions in New York City, the workers who made it possible lived in tenement slums in the same city.

In the South, too, there were a select few who had great wealth. Coca-Cola and the railroads brought fortune to some, cotton mills and machinery earned riches for others. The rigors of the business world often created tremendous stress for these millionaires, who were lucky enough to have the means to create beautiful homes and gardens in which to seek peace and tranquility. It is our fortune today to be able to visit many of these estates and to share in the beauty that money could buy in the early years of the twentieth century.

Because these men and women wanted only the best of the best, they hired professionals to help them who were considered the brightest in their field. Among American landscape architects, one name stands out far above the rest. Frederick Law Olmsted (1822–1903) is considered the father of landscape architecture in America. With his partners, Olmsted designed Central Park in New York City, Prospect Park in Brooklyn, and the campuses of Amherst College and Stanford and Cornell universities. Olmsted's fifty or so other projects included the Biltmore Estate in Asheville, North Carolina.

Page 114. The Biltmore mansion rises in the background while the formal pleasure gardens take center stage. Perennials and colorful annuals mix to create a tapestry of color.

Page 115. George Vanderbilt, grandson of "Commodore" Cornelius Vanderbilt, wanted to build an estate large enough to entertain as many guests as he could ever desire. Playing croquet on the lawn was a favorite pastime of many of these guests.

Left. A gilded fence is proof of the elegance of the landscape. According to Olmsted's design, formal areas close to the house gradually give way to more naturalistic areas.

Below. Within the walled English garden are found the greenhouse (**far left**), conservatory (**center**), and rose garden (**left**). Just as it did at the turn of the century, the conservatory supplies the house with greenery and exotic flowers throughout the cold months. Today unusual plant collections make the greenhouse a favorite spot for visitors. Horticulturists at the Biltmore Estate prefer to grow roses that were popular at the turn of the century.

Right. George Vanderbilt began buying land for the estate in 1888. Eventually his holdings would include 125,000 acres of North Carolina land.

Below. In the early 1900s Edith Vanderbilt and her daughter Cornelia led a springtime parade from a flower-bedecked carriage.

Bottom left. Edith Vanderbilt and daughter Cornelia.

Bottom right. Frederick Law Olmsted.

Far right. The "English garden" was begun in the early 1890s. The wall that surrounds this formal garden provided privacy and protected tender young plants from chilling winds and low temperatures.

Coastal Azalea (Rhododendron atlanticum)

*A beautiful structure on its own, the greenhouse (**top**) was built to supply the grounds with huge numbers of bedding plants, a purpose for which it is still used today. Azaleas (**above**) of every sort and description fill the beds at the estate.*

The design he developed for the rural estate of George Vanderbilt was masterly. Olmsted considered it to be the pinnacle of his career.

By the middle of the nineteenth century, unprecedented growth in this country had already severely reduced the amount of natural wilderness. This fact, coupled with the fact that many American cities at the time were unpleasant and unhealthy places to live, created a great need for a naturalistic landscape, particularly within the cities. Olmsted considered the social and psychological aspects of a landscape to be more important than the decorative elements. He believed firmly that a rural setting could help relieve the stress of urban life, and he felt that such a setting would promote tranquility, or at the very least give city workers a few moments of quiet peace. Olmsted wrote, "The park of any great city [should be] an antithesis to its bustling, paved, rectangular, walled-in streets."

At the turn of the century, landscape architecture was still a male-dominated field; as the new century began more and more women entered the profession. Ellen Biddle Shipman (1870–1950) was not only a talented and successful garden designer herself, she was also untiring in her efforts to help other women become professional landscape architects. Shipman worked extensively with Charles A. Platt, and through this close association she developed great skill in designing houses as well as landscapes.

Among her most important works are the New York Botanical Garden, the Sarah P. Duke Gardens in Durham, North Carolina, and Lakeshore Boulevard in Grosse Pointe, Michigan. Today she is probably best remembered for her designs of estate gardens. Longue Vue Gardens, which she designed in the 1930s, remains one of her most important works.

Beatrix Jones Farrand (1872–1959) was a contemporary of Ellen Shipman. She was one of ten founding members (and the only woman founder) of the American Society of Landscape Architects. Although Farrand studied landscape design in Europe and was inspired by William Robinson, the English author of

The Wild Garden, and Gertrude Jekyll, she was probably most strongly influenced by Charles Sprague Sargent, founder of the Arnold Arboretum at Harvard University.

Farrand's work has been described as being a combination of horticultural impressionism and formal English landscape design. Robert Patterson, a close friend and associate, wrote that her work had "a freedom of scale, a subtle softness of line and an unobtrusive asymmetry."

It was this masterly use of asymmetry that is shown so beautifully at Dumbarton Oaks, which is considered Farrand's finest surviving work. Her design here, as well as in many of her other landscapes, is marked by a diverse and imaginative selection of plant material as well as a gentle subtlety.

Many different factors influenced American landscape design during the early years of the twentieth century. European influences are undeniable—English formal design was frequently used, as well as innovative designs from Italy and Spain. But at the turn of the century Americans also began to develop their own style and flair for design. Vast resources of talent, material, and money went toward the creation of some of the most beautiful gardens in this country.

BILTMORE

In 1894, Sarah Whitman, a visitor to the Biltmore Estate, wrote, "Not even all that has been said prepared me for this place, its beauty, its splendor, its amazing possessions! I have walked about it and measured the towers thereof and it is one long tale of delight."

The story of the Biltmore Estate is a never-ending tale, for the grandeur of the gardens and the opulence of the house have only increased and matured with the passing years.

Calling the grounds of the Biltmore Estate a mere garden is like calling the Biltmore mansion a mere house. A new vocabulary with bigger and grander adjectives is needed to describe this magnificent estate, for it not only contains the finest objects that money could buy, but also represents the collective genius of many gifted people.

George Vanderbilt brought together the talents and skills of Richard Morris Hunt, who designed the mansion, and Frederick Law Olmsted, who designed the grounds. For both of these men, outstanding in their respective fields, Biltmore became the culminating project of their careers. So ensconced was Olmsted in the project he spent the rest of his life working on it, and he was succeeded by his sons.

George Vanderbilt was the grandson of the famous "Commodore" Cornelius Vanderbilt, the phenomenally successful railroad magnate who began his ventures by borrowing $100 from his mother to purchase a small sailing ship. This one small ship was soon profitable enough for the Commodore to buy more ships, and eventually to buy railroads. By 1867 he controlled the major railroad lines between New York and the Great Lakes.

The Commodore's grandson was the youngest of eight children and was always rather thin and quiet. Interested more in art and antiques than the business world, George sought refuge from the clamor of the big city and decided to build a home in Asheville, North Carolina, a fashionable resort town during the 1880s.

George Vanderbilt began buying land for the estate in 1888. Eventually the estate encompassed 125,000 acres of land. Included in this acreage was Mount Pisgah, for Vanderbilt wanted to make sure that nothing interfered with his view of this lofty mountain.

During his childhood, George Vanderbilt had made frequent trips to Europe and had become fascinated with the idea of a grand country estate. As an adult, Vanderbilt decided to build an estate large enough to entertain as many guests as he could ever desire, and a place to showcase his collections of books, antiques, and art. To this end he hired Hunt and Olmsted. The three men worked closely together, creating the estate as a working, living entity.

Even before formal plans of the estate were completed, Olmsted realized that he would need an unprecedented number of plants to complete the design. In late 1889 he established a nursery on the grounds of the estate. The nursery was a necessity, for at that time there were no commercial nurseries within five hundred miles of the estate. Shipping the plants by rail would have been prohibitively expensive, as well as dangerous to the health of the plants.

A section of the estate near the French Broad River was chosen as a site for the nursery. Thousands of plants were collected and propagated, then planted in nursery rows. In 1890 Chauncey Delos Beadle, a Canadian horticulturist, was hired to run the nursery; he became superintendent of the Biltmore Estate, a post he held for sixty years. Beadle is known to have said that he came to the Biltmore Estate for a month and stayed a lifetime.

Although Beadle stocked the nursery with plants from all over the world, his first love was azaleas. He and his friends earned the nickname of the "azalea hunters," for they traveled throughout the southeastern United States collecting native azalea species.

When work on the grounds began, Olmsted wrote to Beadle from his Massachusetts office, asking for a list of plants available in the nursery. It was from this list that Olmsted based his decisions on plant material to be used in the formal gardens, the approach drive, and the surrounding grounds. By the late 1890s the nursery had gone commercial and had produced four million plants of hundreds of different kinds. The nursery was tragically destroyed by a flood in 1916.

The land that Vanderbilt had purchased and which Olmsted transformed was originally eroded, overworked farm land. Olmsted's initial recommendation was that only the area immediately surrounding the house be formally landscaped and that the remainder of the land be left as managed forest and farmland. It was from this recommendation that a vital and important part of the estate was established. In working to rehabilitate the forest, the Biltmore Estate set a prece-

Canna lilies and dusty miller create an interesting combination of colors and textures in the walled garden. Thousands of bedding plants are used in this area to make outstanding floral displays during the year.

dent; in connection with these efforts, the Biltmore School of Forestry was started as a place to train scientists in forest management. In 1914 a newspaper article said of this forestry school that "it formed an object lesson that forest conservation was not only sane within itself, but also profitable."

The forest operations were not the only "sane and profitable" ventures on the estate, for farm operations here included both horticulture and animal husbandry. The estate was essentially self-sufficient.

In keeping with the European tradition, the estate was to include a village as well. In 1889 George Vanderbilt purchased the small nearby village of Best and renamed it Biltmore Village.

The grounds of the Biltmore Estate are composed of five main elements: the approach drive to the house; the deerpark; the forest; a series of pleasure, or formal gardens; and the farm.

Olmsted's grand plan called for a gradual transition from formal areas close to the house to more natural landscapes farther away, until finally the landscaped areas blended almost imperceptibly into the forest. Thus the manicured pleasure gardens sur-

round the mansion, while the more naturalistic shrub garden and bass pond are found farther away.

By far the most popular and most visited parts of the grounds are the pleasure gardens, which are on the same scale as the house. When they were planted in 1890, these gardens were state-of-the-art horticulture. During an age when plant exploration enjoyed unprecedented popularity, many new and exotic varieties were included within the pleasure gardens.

In front of the house is a three-and-a-half-acre lawn. Starkly simple and lacking in ornamentation, it is intended not to distract from the elaborate design of the house. From the house, a large retaining wall, with a ramp and grand vista, is visible at the end of the lawn. Atop the wall is a statue of Diana, goddess of the hunt.

The library terrace connects to the south wing of the house and is shaded by a vine-covered arbor. Wisteria and trumpet creeper add beauty and fragrance to the arbor in late spring and summer. In the early days of the estate, this terrace provided an excellent spot for watching lawn bowling. Today the bowling green holds an outdoor swimming pool, surrounded by a clipped boxwood hedge. The view from the terrace is magnificent, and it includes the deerpark and the nearby Blue Ridge Mountains.

Adjacent to the terrace is the area called the Italian garden. It was here that visitors to the estate gathered on a Sunday afternoon to play croquet. To this day the Italian garden has not been changed and still contains three original geometric pools, each displaying different water plants. The pool closest to the house contains lotus, a plant sacred to the Egyptians. The next pool holds a variety of aquatic plants, and the third, a collection of water lilies.

A rather steep, hilly area separates the Italian garden from the formal, walled English garden. It took the genius of Olmsted to create a "ramble," or shrub garden, in this area. The winding paths are laid out to make the decline to the English garden almost unnoticed.

Some of the finest horticultural specimens of the estate are found in this shrub garden. Flowering dogwoods, azaleas, Japanese cut-leaf maple, forsythia, spirea, magnolias, and Japanese cherry put on a floral display that lasts from early spring through fall.

The English garden is surrounded by a stone wall built in the early 1890s. Its purpose was to provide boundaries for the garden and to create protection from the chilling mountain winds. Olmsted originally envisioned this garden as an old-fashioned English kitchen garden, complete with fruits, vegetables, herbs, and flowers.

Vanderbilt vetoed this idea, saying that the surrounding farms could give him all the food he needed. He wanted this area to be resplendent with flowers and, not surprisingly, Vanderbilt's vote was carried. Although fruit trees such as apple, peach, pear, plum, and apricot are espaliered on the outer walls of the garden, and herbs are found in several of the beds, it is the flowers that take center stage here.

In spring, Dutch tulips turn these four acres into a brilliant wave of color. Summer finds thousands of annual bedding plants such as marigolds, zinnias, impatiens, and begonias. Pockets of perennials are found also, showing such old-fashioned favorites as iris, peonies, daylilies, and phlox.

The lower half of the garden is taken up by the rose garden where over two thousand bushes represent eighty different kinds of roses. There is tremendous variety here, but a great effort is currently being made to use more of the old-fashioned roses.

The conservatory and greenhouses were originally built to supply the estate with massive numbers of bedding plants and hundreds of plants used in the indoor winter garden. Today the remaining conservatory is used for similar purposes. In addition, the conservatory also features collections of cacti, orchids, and ferns.

Farther from the house—following Olmsted's plan for a more naturalistic landscape—is the azalea garden, which used to be called "the Glen." Here Chauncey Beadle's original azalea collection has a setting worthy of its value. A small brook runs through the property and occasional spots of wildflowers add

to the beauty of the area. In early spring, when the azaleas are in full bloom, it is truly a fairyland of color and fragrance.

A bass pond, complete with a gaggle of geese, a wooden boathouse and a gazebo, provides an isolated spot to observe the beauty of the estate. Between the glory of the formal gardens and the quiet splendor of the forests, the bass pond provided Vanderbilt's visitors a spot for fishing and boating as well as garden viewing.

The vast fields and meadows surrounding the Biltmore mansion are collectively known as the "deerpark." This area is composed of 250 acres of pastoral scenery and was based on the European idea of an estate parkland. Although Vanderbilt originally wanted to create a larger park from these lands, Olmsted convinced him that the land was too hilly and poor, suggesting instead that much of it be left as forest, with a smaller portion made into a park. The original plans for the estate included fencing the deerpark, but the cost—even for a Vanderbilt—was prohibitive.

The approach drive to the house was and is an important component of the grounds. It is here that the visitor receives his first impression of the estate and experiences a pastoral, picturesque landscape.

Olmsted wanted the three-mile approach drive to maintain an aura of mystery. He wrote that the drive should have "a natural and comparatively wild and secluded character; its borders rich with the varied forms of vegetation, and with…springs and streams and pools, steep banks and rocks, all consistent with the sensation of passing through the remote depths of a natural forest."

Along the approach road, Olmsted was able to combine the native flora with plant introductions from all over the world. Rather than follow the ridges, the road follows the ravines, allowing the visitor to view the deep pools, springs, and rich vegetation of the forest.

Today the vision and genius of both Vanderbilt and Olmsted are firmly secured for history and for the future in the Biltmore Estate. Most of the original

Pages 124–125. The Italian garden is found adjacent to the library terrace. A series of geometrically shaped pools hold different kinds of water plants, such as lotus and water lilies.

***Right.** James Deering served as vice-president of the International Harvester Company until 1919, when his doctors suggested he move to a warmer climate. He purchased land just south of Miami and built Vizcaya.*

***Far right.** This 1922 aerial view shows the mansion, extensive gardens, and the small house he called the Casino.*

***Below.** Maidenhair Fern (Adiatum pedatum)*

***Opposite.** The grounds at Vizcaya are composed of many small garden rooms that lead into one another. These rooms had different purposes. Some were used for entertaining, others for intimate conversations.*

125,000 acres was given to create the Pisgah National Forest, and today the estate comprises eight thousand acres. Within these grounds there exists a living legacy of grandeur and elegance. At the Biltmore Estate, the visitor does not have the feeling of being in a museum or a monument to the past. Instead, one has the sensation of being a part of a bustling, vibrant working estate. It is an exciting present, tempered and matured by an exciting past.

VIZCAYA

On seeing the gardens of Vizcaya in Miami, Florida, it is possible to understand why the Italians have words like *Bravo! Bravissimo!* and *Encore!*

This is a garden that needs more than subtle adjectives. This is a real "Wow!" garden, sure to impress and delight even the most sated and sophisticated visitor. "Bravo!" for sure. But "Encore!"—probably not. The house and gardens of Vizcaya are of such magnificent proportions that it would be virtually impossible to duplicate them today.

The formal grounds of Vizcaya include twelve acres of clipped hedges, pebble walks, stone fountains, dark pools, and greenery. The gardens at Vizcaya are not flower gardens. Color is used as an accent rather than as the central theme. Italian garden design traditionally included three major elements: greenery, water, and stone. Vizcaya is a glowing

example of how these elements can be combined into an unforgettable experience.

Vizcaya was built by James Deering in 1919. Deering was the son of William Deering, developer of the Deering harvester machine. In time the Deering family business merged with the McCormick Harvester Company and other companies to form International Harvester Company. James Deering served as vice president of this company until 1919.

Deering suffered from pernicious anemia, which at that time was little understood. His doctors suggested that Deering spend the cold months of the year in a warm climate, and Deering set out to find the perfect winter home. After much consideration, he decided to build his winter home on a tract of land just south of the city limits of Miami, Florida.

In 1912 he purchased land from Mrs. William Brickell, a member of a prominent Miami family. This land included 180 acres of shoreline, hammock, and pineland.

Although the best house site on this tract was the natural limestone ridge above the tidal shoreline,

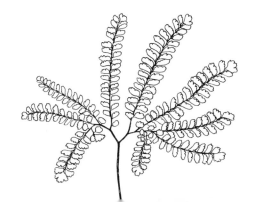

Deering decided against building the mansion here. An early conservationist, James Deering had great concerns about preserving the native hammock growth. It was of great importance to him to retain as much of this native growth as possible. For this reason, he chose to situate the house closer to Biscayne Bay.

Building the house closer to the water was an expensive decision. Extra pilings were necessary to create solid foundations in the marshy land. But Deering spent both the time and money to make sure that his house was on firm ground, all of which paid off in the end. The hurricane of 1926, which devastated much of the coastal area around Miami, left Vizcaya surprisingly intact. The gardens, however, suffered extensive damage.

Despite the strong Spanish influence in Florida, Deering and his advisors finally decided on Italian, rather than Spanish, architecture for his house. It was the influence of the great estates near Venice that swayed Deering to make his final decision.

Deering did not make all the decisions about the estate on his own. Although he was a bachelor and did not have to consult with any family members, he did surround himself with outstanding advisors. Chief among these men was Paul Chalfin, a Harvard graduate who had trained as a painter at the New York Art Students' League and the Ecole des Beaux Arts in Paris. Together, Deering and Chalfin traveled to Europe to observe architectural and garden designs and to buy art and ornaments for the estate.

The scale of this project quickly grew in size and expense. Deering was a quiet and somewhat austere man, but a more lavish and grand side of his personality emerged when he began work on the estate.

Chalfin once wrote, "I think I can say that Vizcaya is as much the result of a game which Mr. Deering and I worked out for ourselves as it was of studying and dreaming and working with an Italian palazzo decided upon."

What a grand and glorious game it turned out to be! The house is situated directly on Biscayne Bay. Coming out of the east loggia, one steps onto a magnificent patio that ends in a curved, U-shaped seawall. At one end of this wall is the yacht landing, which, in

Above. True to the Italian style, color is used in the garden only as an accent. The essence of the landscape is greenery, water, and stonework. Small fern grottoes and much statuary help to complete the Italian aura.

Right. The grounds at Vizcaya were designed by a South American landscape architect, Diego Suarez. Opposite the main house is a small Baroque garden house called a casino.

Opposite. Clipped live oak trees create a huge hedge lining the central walk. Farther away from the house on the mount, these are allowed to grow to their full height. Antique urns and statuary are found throughout the garden.

Deering's time, was frequently used. At the other end of the wall lies a small but beautiful latticed teahouse. Here Deering served not only morning tea but also late-afternoon cocktails to his guests.

In between the landing and the teahouse, some forty feet into the water, lies one of Vizcaya's most delightful and fanciful components—a stone barge. Shaped like a large boat, the stone barge was originally ornately decorated with statues sculpted by A. Stirling Calder.

The gardens of Vizcaya were designed by Diego Suarez, a landscape architect born in Bogota, Colombia. Suarez was educated in Florence, Italy, where he later worked as an architect. But it was gardens rather than buildings that captured his heart, and Suarez worked for a time at the historic Villa La Pietra near Florence. It was here that he met Deering and was later hired to design the gardens at Vizcaya. The First World War interrupted the progress of the gardens, and it took Suarez seven years to complete his task.

The extensive grounds are so filled with small gardens and garden spots that the visitor will do best to orient himself by climbing to the top of the south terrace stairs. The view from here is spectacular, and gives the visitor an overview of the gardening treasures that await his exploration. Here, also, is a fountain decorated with lead lizards and frogs designed by the American sculptor Charles Carey Rumsey.

From this vantage point the visitor can most easily see Suarez's master plan. The main garden was developed in a fan shape. The central axis is contiguous with the north-south axis of the house. At the end of this long line lies a baroque garden house, called a casino. This little house is situated on an artificial hill or mount. Beyond this, but hidden from view, was a lagoon garden, a large boathouse with a roof garden, and a smaller, domed garden house called the Casba. Little of the area beyond the mount is still part of the estate today, having been sold off to developers nearly fifty years ago.

The long, central section leading to the mount is lined on both sides with avenues of clipped live oak trees. On the mount, these trees are untrimmed and are allowed to attain their complete height and fullness. The contrast is an inspiring one, and leads one from the precise order of the formal garden to the exciting and unusual casino. The Italian word *casino* today has a different connotation than it did in Deering's time. To Deering and his advisors, it was considered a place to indulge in fantasy. Chalfin wrote:

> What was a Casino for? For one to dream in or perhaps to weep; for two to steal to; for three to sing and for eight to dance in. Or perhaps the footmen—just liveried boys from the farm—had fetched and displayed hampers of cold fowls and sherry and sorbets made from the strawberries that ripened—even in winter. A Casino held itself a household in miniature, was a playhouse for an hour, the great establishment with all its etiquette abbreviated and curtailed, but unbroken. For days perhaps it slept—dawn, noon, and night—awakening for its brief function, and then went to rest again to the sighs and gurglings of its fountains.

Deering himself also loved and appreciated this fanciful house. In 1922, only three years before he died, Deering wrote to Chalfin, "If proportion is the highest expression of beauty, as I believe it is, I do not know where you would go to find anything more beautiful...."

Sensitive to the overwhelming grandeur and excitement of the main garden, Suarez and Deering included many small, enclosed gardens to complement the central grounds.

The first of these, to the left of the south terrace stairs, is a delightful walled secret garden. This was a place of privacy for the family. High walls provided an outdoor room for the family to sit and read, or talk and slowly stroll in the warm winter Florida sun.

Ferns—both native and exotic—are used effectively throughout the garden to impart their greenery and fine texture.

This outdoor room is furnished with interesting and unusual plants. Four small trees with braided trunks stand at the four corners of a central square bed. The walls are decorated with large stone planters, dripping with bright pink impatiens.

At the north end an archway leads to the patio area and the seawall. To the south, a double grotto entrance leads back to the formal gardens. In these miniature grottoes, water drips continuously, providing a rich environment for the multitude of ferns that grow there.

Just beyond the secret garden is another miniature garden of a playful nature. Called a theater garden, it has several small curved terraces, each planted with soft grass. A higher, flat area is reminiscent of a stage, and the entire shape of the garden reminds one of an amphitheater. In Italy, the theater gardens found on small estates were not meant to be used as the setting for plays, but were a fanciful garden accent instead. Large theater gardens, like those found in Florence, were often used for performances.

The original maze garden suffered many major setbacks, including a hurricane and disease. The maze has been replanted with high clipped hedges, and today it offers the fun and challenge of finding your way to the center marble column.

Continuing to wander down the pebbled paths, the visitor will come upon the remains of the "peacock bridge." This bridge originally spanned the lagoon that divided the formal gardens from the south garden area. The bridge is so named because of the spectacular carved peacocks that sit atop tall columns at the entrance.

If the visitor continues his walk, he will find himself directly opposite the south terrace steps and exactly halfway around the gardens. Here, at the mount, is the focal point of the gardens. From the vantage of the elevated ground, one has a wonderful view of the grounds in all directions. Behind the mount is the casino.

The remains of an old Venetian-style boat landing are found at the edge of the lagoon. Painted gondola poles are an indication of the festive spirit that must have greeted guests who arrived by boat.

Behind the mount where there was once a large parterre is a newer garden called the Ellis A. Gimbel Garden for the Blind. Plants in this garden were chosen for delighting all the senses, not just sight. Fragrance and texture, in particular, were of great importance in choosing plants for this area. Orange jasmine, ylang-ylang, rosemary, and mint fill the air with their distinctive aromas. The soft, feathery blossoms of Christmas bush and the thick leathery leaves of many other plants beg for a touch.

The east and west walks leading back to the house are lined with a long row of beautiful seventeenth- and eighteenth-century statues of mythological gods and goddesses and allegorical figures.

Everywhere in this garden there is a feeling of opulence, of a richness rarely experienced in our world today. The size and grandeur of the grounds gives one a sense of royalty and of feeling quite fortunate that we can be a part of such a world, even if only for a short time.

BELLINGRATH GARDENS

Bellingrath Gardens is a carnival of color, a stunning display of the best blossoms of the season. The site of the gardens began as Walter Bellingrath's favorite fishing hole on the Isle-aux-Oies River and grew into a magnificent floral display, attracting visitors from all over the world. But the history of the family's interest in gardens predates their purchase of this beautiful site.

In 1899, two Tennessee businessmen—Walter Bellingrath and his brother, Will—signed a contract with Asa Candler, owner of the Coca-Cola company in Atlanta. This contract allowed them to bottle this phenomenally successful soft drink and distribute it throughout the United States. In 1903 the Bellingraths bought the Coca-Cola bottling franchises in Montgomery, Birmingham, and Mobile, Alabama. Within a short time, the Bellingrath brothers grew rich.

Left. *A kaleidoscope of color appears every season of the year at Bellingrath Gardens. Fall is particularly beautiful, with thousands of chrysanthemums of many different varieties on display.*

Bottom left. *Walter and Bessie Bellingrath devoted much of the latter part of their lives to creating Bellingrath Gardens. In the spring of 1938 a bronze plaque was given to them in appreciation for creating the "charm spot of the Deep South."*

Bottom right. *During the late 1920s the Bellingraths bought huge trees and shrubs from surrounding farmers, not only supplying the gardens with beautiful, mature specimens, but also giving the farmers much-needed financial support.*

Laura C. Martin's
Southern Gardens

133

Right. This 1935 photograph shows an artesian fountain facing the courtyard. It is affectionately known as Rebecca at the Well, commemorating the Biblical verse.

Bottom left. An Eastern influence is apparent in this Alabama garden in the Oriental-American section. Red-lacquered bridges span dark lagoons, and azaleas and camellias color the banks.

Bottom right. In November 60,000 chrysanthemums create a spectacular display. These colorful flowers are found cascading down rock walls, piled high in columns, and carpeting the ground throughout the garden.

In 1906 Walter Bellingrath married his stenographer, Bessie Mae Morse, and the two settled in to enjoy life in Mobile. In 1911 the couple, still childless, moved to a large three-story house on South Ann Street, which Bessie began with great enthusiasm and zeal to furnish. She acquired the most beautiful furniture, silver, and *objets d'art* that she could find.

Once the house was decorated to her satisfaction, she turned her energy and enthusiasm to the grounds. She and her husband eventually developed the property, which stretched from one city street to the next, into a large and beautiful azalea garden. This spot soon was considered one of the most beautiful in town, and many people in Mobile came to visit in spring when the azaleas were at their peak.

While Bessie Bellingrath was busy creating a garden of delight, Walter continued to pour time and energy into his work. As his business ventures made increasing demands on him, Walter escaped more and more frequently to Mobile's nearby marshlands, where he would often spend the day fishing with Frank Woodward, his constant companion, guide, and paddler.

Bessie, meanwhile, continued to acquire objects of beauty for her South Ann Street house and garden. She often bought giant azaleas for her gardens; one Mobile businessman confessed that her generosity in buying these beautiful shrubs from his family paid for his first year of college.

The Bellingraths, however, suffered from poor health. Their physician suggested that they buy a place in the country where they could go often to relax and enjoy the out-of-doors. A friend suggested that they purchase the Lisloy fishing club on the Isle-aux-Oies River, about a mile and a half up the Fowl River from where it entered Mobile Bay. In November 1918, Walter wrote to a friend in Atlanta, "If a trade I am now negotiating goes through, I expect to acquire 25 acres of land on Fowl River near Coden, on which it is my intention to build a comfortable bungalow to be used as a country resort and fishing grounds and a place to entertain our friends when they come to see us."

Bellingrath soon had not only the original twenty-five acres, but had increased his purchase to include sixty and later several hundred acres of land. There, it was his firm intention to make good an old Spanish saying, "The days were made for rest, the nights were made for sleeping."

The property was primarily wilderness with only a few pockets of cleared land adjacent to the rough houses that made up the fishing camp. It was beautiful, exciting land and full of rich history and legend. Locals say that the famous pirate Jean Lafitte cruised quietly along this river and buried his treasures along its shores.

Local legend also suggests that Spanish settlers bred fierce bulls on the property, sent them downriver to Mobile Bay and the Gulf of Mexico, thence to the bullfight rings of Spain and Mexico.

By January 1919 the Bellingraths felt that their wilderness home, Bell Camp, had been tamed enough to entertain guests for the first time. Although Walter Bellingrath loved and appreciated his fine South Ann Street home in Mobile, he was particularly thankful for the easy informality of Bell Camp. He said to a friend that "I built my camp because I wanted a place to lie down with my feet on the sofa."

As for Bessie, she found Bell Camp a ready storehouse for the overflow of treasures from her South Ann Street garden. Azaleas and camellias were planted around the lodge, adding charm and color to the wooded landscape.

Both Walter and Bessie Bellingrath greatly enjoyed traveling, and on their excursions throughout the United States and Europe, they kept their garden in mind. Gardens in South Carolina, Delaware, and Pennsylvania had great influence on the place that eventually would be called Bellingrath Gardens. Perhaps the largest influence, however, came from a trip to Europe in 1927, when the Bellingraths visited English, Italian, and French gardens.

Compiling these influences and experiences, the Bellingraths returned to Bell Camp full of ideas about transforming their modest fishing camp into a world-class garden. They began to create an overall plan for beautification of their private estate.

In attaining these goals, Bessie Bellingrath purchased huge old azalea and camellia bushes, often paying enormous prices for them. The people who sold the Bellingraths these shrubs were always glad to see her coming; few suspected that part of her determination to have these shrubs was also a desire to help those who might be down on their luck.

Throughout the Depression, the Bellingraths were able to continue to transform this bit of Alabama wilderness into a true showplace of the South. On April 7, 1932, they opened the gardens to the public for the first time. Public interest was so great that local sheriff's deputies were called in to handle traffic.

In 1935 the Bellingraths began work on a fifteen-room mansion on a site just north of the lodge at Bell Camp. The brick used in the construction of this house had been salvaged earlier from a Mobile hotel built well before the Civil War. Iron lacework on the balconies and patios pays tribute to the influence of the Gulf Coast area. As she had done at her house in Mobile, Bessie Bellingrath soon began filling this country retreat with beautiful furniture and art.

Today Bellingrath is made up of 905 acres, sixty-five of which are landscaped and open to the public. The entire property is a bird sanctuary.

The most outstanding feature of Bellingrath is the staggering number of flowering plants. Almost without pause, row after row, bank after bank, bed after bed proclaims the colors of the season. The floral displays change dramatically from one season to the next, but each one has its own charm. Walter Bellingrath often referred to his gardens as a beautiful woman with a different dress for every week of the year.

From the entrance the visitor crosses over the rose garden bridge, which offers a stunning view of the symmetrical beds within the rose garden.

Flagstone walks surrounding the house look as if they may have been there for centuries. These stones were once used as ballast for empty sailing ships that came to load cotton at Mobile.

The Eastern influence in the Oriental-American Garden is easy for all to see. The dark waters of a lagoon contrast well with azaleas, camellias, iris, and other plants of oriental origin. Bridges spanning the dark water are accented with red lacquer. It is a garden of the exotic, touched by the familiar. The walks continue to wind over rustic bridges, past rock gardens and shimmering lakes. Everywhere is a plethora of blossoms.

Because Bellingrath Gardens has always been an extremely popular spot for a wedding, a bridal garden was created expressly for this purpose. The round garden surrounded by fragrant white flowers is a setting unsurpassed in beauty, and provides a perfect backdrop for memorable wedding photographs.

Walter Bellingrath loved to show off his garden to visitors and was particularly pleased when they responded with equal enthusiasm. He was especially pleased at the comments of the famous actor Sir Charles Laughton, who visited while in Mobile for a performance of *Don Juan in Hell*. Walter asked him to sign the guest register, and the actor wrote, "How can I play the part of the devil tonight after being in Heaven all afternoon?"

Bellingrath looks heavenly in all seasons. In late winter and early spring the azaleas take center stage and put on an unforgettable show. Based on sheer numbers, this display is probably unmatched anywhere else in the South. Over 250,000 azalea plants can be found here, some of which are over a century old. Tulips, daffodils, and crocuses add to this magnificent show. Later in spring and into summer, tropical plants lend an exotic air. Alamanda roses, coleus, hibiscus, chenille, and copper plants line the walks and surround the fountains.

One of the most popular times to visit Bellingrath Gardens is in November. Then, sixty thousand chrysanthemums create the world's largest outdoor display of these flowers. During the holiday season, banks of poinsettias form massive and colorful arrangements.

Bessie Bellingrath died in 1943, and Walter in 1955. The cadence of life at Bellingrath has not slowed in the decades since their deaths. Although Walter Bellingrath achieved great worldly success and business prominence throughout the country, it was his garden that he held closest to his heart.

DUMBARTON OAKS

At the corner of R and Thirty-first streets in the center of Georgetown in Washington, D.C., lies Dumbarton Oaks—sixteen acres of cool, green delight. Stone paths wind up and down the many hillsides. A multitude of trees offer shade from the hot sun, and flowers are everywhere, subtly peeking from underneath trees and shrubs or joyfully shouting with vibrant colors from the center of an incomparable perennial border.

The property of Dumbarton Oaks has a rich history. It has been home to many different men and women with diverse and exciting backgrounds. The name "Dumbarton" was given to it by Colonel Ninian Beall, a Scot known for his industrious nature, his military skills, and his genius at accumulating land in the new and raw frontier of America. At one time Colonel Beall succeeded in assembling land grants that totaled nearly thirty thousand acres.

In 1703 Beall added the future site of Dumbarton Oaks to his holdings. In a patent granted in November 1703 it was stated: "We doe therefore hereby grant unto him the said Ninian Beale [sic], all that Tract or parcell of land called Rock of Dumbarton—lying in the said County."

This particular parcel of land totaled approximately eight hundred acres and was located opposite the "little falls" of the Potomac. Beall named the land after a Scottish landmark—the Rock of Dumbarton, located on the north bank of the Clyde, below Glasgow, near his birthplace.

Ninian Beall died in 1717 and left his estate to his son George, who moved there soon after his marriage to Elizabeth Brooke. The house that they built still stands at 3033 N Street. During these lifetimes the land surrounding the Rock of Dumbarton, much to their disappointment, quickly developed into an urban area. A little over thirty-three acres of their property was bought (in spite of their protests) by a commission of seven members, who were authorized by the Maryland Assembly to "buy and purchase sixty Acres, Part of the Tracts of Land belonging to Messieurs George Gordon and George Bell."

The commission established this tract of land as a town, which it named George Town, in honor of George II.

The land on which the present Dumbarton Oaks now stands eventually passed out of the hands of the original Beall family and was bought and sold nine times between 1801 and 1920. During this period, the land and houses were called by a variety of interesting names, including Acrolophos House (Greek for "grove on the hill"). It was while the estate was called Monterey, after a famous battle in the Mexican War, that it became known as "the show place of the District." During this golden age the property was described as having "a well-filled greenhouse [the orangery of today], flower gardens to the east, a wooded lawn in front, a grove of forest trees to the west and gently sloping well-sodded hills in the rear, all of which were kept in perfect order."

The next owners of the estate renamed it "The Oaks" and unfortunately did not maintain the "perfect order" of the grounds.

In 1920 Mr. and Mrs. Robert Woods Bliss purchased the estate. They renamed it Dumbarton Oaks, completely rebuilt the house, and set in motion the plans and ideas that were to make the estate not only "the show place of the District" but also a showplace worthy of comparison to any in the country.

Robert Woods Bliss was a successful diplomat who led a somewhat nomadic life. In spite of his

A host of orange day lilies softens the entrance to the Dumbarton Oaks mansion. Though tucked into busy Georgetown only ten minutes from the White House, this estate gives one the sense of being out in the country.

The rose garden with spiraled shrubs and incomparable rose beds was the Bliss's favorite part of the garden. Neat grass walkways intersect these beds of color and fragrance.

Laura C. Martin's
Southern Gardens

wanderings, or perhaps because of them, Bliss had "a dream…of having a country house in the city." The beginning of the realization of that dream occurred in April 1920 when he was assigned to the Department of State as chief of the Division of Western European Affairs. The Blisses, thinking that they could now settle in Washington for several years, purchased The Oaks and began planning the grand estate that they both keenly wanted to create.

It was the joint efforts and skills of Mildred Bliss and her friend Beatrix Jones Farrand that resulted in transforming the neglected grounds of Dumbarton Oaks into the magnificent landscape for which the estate is now famous.

By the early 1920s, Beatrix Jones Farrand had well over forty years' experience in landscape and garden design. She had studied extensively with Professor Charles Sprague Sargent, founder and first director of the Arnold Arboretum at Harvard University. From him she learned important design concepts: "To make the plan fit the ground and not twist the ground to fit a plan, and furthermore to study the tastes of the owner, to look at great landscape paintings, to observe and analyze natural beauty, to travel widely…and learn from all the great arts, as all art is akin."

Armed with this basic philosophy, Mrs. Farrand began looking at Dumbarton Oaks with an eye for how it might become a garden of grace and beauty. It was no easy task. In Mrs. Farrand's words:

> The gardens of Dumbarton Oaks were perhaps one of the most difficult problems presented to me, for I found not only an existing and rather dominating house and an unusually wide variety of grades, but also the very definite personal preferences of the owners with their special interest in design and texture. The gardens were to be for spring and autumn enjoyment and in winter to have perennial green in abundance. A swimming pool, tennis court, and brook completed the illusion of country life, while clever planting bordering the lawn screened the street on the south side and left the birds undisturbed.

Unfortunately Mrs. Bliss was not able to oversee personally the transformation of the gardens according to her plans and dreams. In 1923 Robert Bliss was appointed Minister to Sweden, and he and Mrs. Bliss once again left the United States, this time to spend four years in Stockholm and the next three years in Argentina.

Even in their absence, however, the Blisses were able to continue to work toward the fruition of their dream. Mr. Bliss, passionately interested in Byzantine art, continued to collect objects that would eventually make up the Byzantine Art Museum at Dumbarton Oaks.

Under the careful supervision of Beatrix Farrand, work on the gardens proceeded. Terraces were created, retaining walls and drainage systems installed, and decisions about walls and walks, gates and garden ornaments were carefully made based on close communication between Mrs. Farrand and Mrs. Bliss.

It was 1931 when Mr. and Mrs. Bliss at last came to Dumbarton Oaks to stay. A decade of garden work accomplished during their absence had successfully achieved Mr. Bliss's desire for a "country house in the city," for the road was completely screened by the combination of a wall and shrubbery, and wide expanses of lawn gave the illusion of an isolated country estate.

On the north side of the house were four rectangular lawns, each on a different level. These became more narrow as the distance from the house increased, so that the eye was drawn toward the center of the lawns and to a point above a steep drop-off. From here one could see only trees from across the valley, giving the impression of woods and wilderness in between.

Left. *The herbaceous borders at Dumbarton Oaks attain a rich grandeur during the summer months. Bright yellow black-eyed Susans tumble over heliotrope, while a wide swath of green grass lends an orderly air to the chaos of color.*

Below. *Mr. and Mrs. Robert Woods Bliss purchased this Georgetown property in 1920 and spent the next ten years making it one of the most beautiful and important gardens in the American south.*

Laura C. Martin's
Southern Gardens

Areas on the same terrace level were divided by stone walls to create a series of garden rooms. When Beatrix Farrand first began her work at Dumbarton Oaks, she wrote to Mrs. Bliss, "On the northeast corner of the house two magnificent oak trees inclosed by the low brick wall inevitably suggest the making of a green garden which would in a sense be a part of the rooms looking out on it." She designed this green garden for entertaining and planted it with trees, grass, and ivy.

Another small, intimate garden room is the star garden, named for the large ten-pointed star made of lead and Aquia Creek stone set into the cobbled pavement. An inscription from Chaucer is found under the star: O THOU MAKER OF THE WHELE THAT BERETH THE STERRES AND TORNEST THE HEVENE WITH A RAVISSHING SWEIGH.

An Aquarius fountain and Zodiac circle complete the star garden, which was originally designed as a place for quiet family meals.

From the green garden the visitor can look down on the swimming pool and pebble garden. The steps leading to the pool are divided halfway down, and within the division is a small oval fountain. Leaves of various plants are etched into the stone, and the basin of the fountain is lined with reliefs of bulrushes. The garden ornaments here impart a distinctly French feeling, although Mrs. Farrand derived the basic lines for the fountain from one in the small Italian town of Nervi. The swimming pool was originally surrounded by weeping willows, cherries, wisteria, and Korean azaleas. With the diversity and wealth of plant material used in this small enclosure, it was possible to have color and fragrance many months of the year.

Many visitors consider the pebble garden the most unusual and exciting part of Dumbarton Oaks. The original site of the tennis court, it was transformed in 1960. Shallow pools laid out in intricate and graceful patterns are filled with clear water so that it is easy to see the lovely pebble mosaic on the bottom of the pools.

During spring and summer, the pebble garden becomes a wonderfully elaborate and sophisticated birdbath. Mockingbirds, purple grackles, robins, and catbirds all come to drink and bathe in this beautiful garden. Small islands throughout the garden support various types of bedding plants, adding a splash of color to the cool liquid landscape.

Another garden "room" is the ellipse garden. In 1920 a small house stood on this site. When the house was removed, a garden was created by enclosing a clean, level lawn and fountain with box hedges. The boxwood has since been removed and replaced by hornbeam trees that have been clipped and formed to make an aerial hedge.

As the distance from the house increases, the landscape becomes less formal and more natural until the visitor is finally in a wooded ravine. When planning this part of the garden, Beatrix Farrand wrote, "The whole scheme for the north slopes of the property should properly be studied from the ground itself rather than from any plan, as the contours and expressions of the ground will control the plantings more strongly than any other feature."

As the visitor turns back up the hill and heads toward the house again, other small garden spaces beckon. The terrior garden is named for a small statue, a copy of one which Mrs. Farrand saw in Naples, Italy. The story goes that during the Napoleonic wars, a French admiral fell in love with a beautiful young girl from Naples. Neither could speak the other's language but they communicated just the same and he brought her many gifts. Among these was a small terrier dog, which she mistakenly called a "terrior." When the little dog finally died, his mistress was so distressed that she raised this monument over his grave. It has since been known as the "terrior's tomb." Mrs. Farrand was so taken with the simple statue and the legend of its origin that she suggested to Mrs. Bliss that they include a copy at Dumbarton Oaks.

The gardens now open up and reveal the splendor and glory of the herbaceous borders. During summer

months these long borders are a kaleidoscope of colors. Mexican sunflowers vie for attention with dahlias and snapdragons. Black-eyed Susans and salvia compete with purple coneflower and heliotrope. Perennials, biennials, annuals, flowering vines, and bulbs combine to make this a marvelous mass of color and fragrance. Beatrix Farrand modestly referred to this perennial border as "a sort of generally friendly mixture of color and form."

The terrace below the perennial beds holds fields of cutting flowers and herbs. These are grown almost as crops, and moved to more formal areas of the garden as needed.

The rose garden was supposedly the favorite garden of both Robert and Mildred Bliss. It was patterned after a formal English garden and, in the European tradition, includes the family coat of arms. In the east part of the garden, a stone is set into the wall and above it are two escutcheons. They are crowned by the crest of a sheaf of wheat; below is the family motto: *Quod Severis Metes*—As ye sow, so shall ye reap.

Returning to the house, the visitor finds himself at the orangery, which is part house and part garden. The orangery was originally built by Bradshaw Beverly in 1810 and was fully repaired and furnished by Edward M. Linthicum after he purchased the estate in 1846. According to a letter written by a friend of Linthicum's, "The east parlor opened into a bright, sunny dining room, which in turn looked out upon a well-filled greenhouse." The fig vine that now covers the entire interior of the orangery was first planted in 1860.

The individual gardens at Dumbarton Oaks can be enjoyed and appreciated one at a time. The green garden, the perennial border, the pebble garden, and a dozen other sites—each could stand alone on its merits. Taken together, however, these individual gardens and their beautiful setting constitute an estate of great magnitude, beauty, and importance.

It was the genius of Beatrix Farrand and Mildred Bliss, their keen regard for beauty and grace, and their respect and appreciation of each other that made this garden possible.

In 1907 Beatrix Jones (who married Max Farrand in

1913) wrote for *Scribner's Magazine*: "The two arts of painting and garden design are closely related.... A collection of flowers, no matter how beautiful they may be, does not make a garden, any more than the colors on a painter's palette make in themselves a picture."

"The owner of a garden is like the leader of an orchestra; he must know which of his instruments to encourage and which to restrain." It is our luck and fortune that Mrs. Farrand and the Blisses were masterful conductors. The symphony that they created at Dumbarton Oaks is one not likely to be duplicated again.

LONGUE VUE

The usual marriage of gardens and house develops in such a way that the grounds are done and redone to match the style and scale of the house. Rarely does the house come second. This was the case, however, with Longue Vue House and Gardens—or, perhaps more accurately, Longue Vue Gardens and House.

Edith Rosenwald was the third child of Julius and Augusta Rosenwald. The year that Edith was born, Julius invested in a small firm called Sears, Roebuck

Longue Vue was the home of Edith and Edgar Stern. The original gardens were designed by Ellen Biddle Shipman as formal English with an Italian influence.

and Company. In 1909 Richard Sears retired and Julius became chief executive and led the firm to astounding success.

With the fortune that he made, Julius Rosenwald became a much-loved philanthropist, supporting many different causes and institutions. Philanthropy was a lesson that Edith learned early in life.

Edgar Bloom Stern was born in New Orleans, went to public school there and then on to graduate with honors from Harvard University. When he returned to New Orleans, he applied his energies and genius to several business ventures and accumulated great wealth. He, too, realized the importance of philanthropy. At one time he reflected that "life is a stewardship."

In 1921 Edith Rosenwald married Edgar Stern and settled in New Orleans. They purchased a small lot (250 by 500 feet) adjacent to the golf course of the New Orleans Country Club and on this site they built a large, comfortable, Colonial-style house.

Mrs. Stern became increasingly interested in gardening; over the course of the next few years, the Sterns purchased more and more acreage to allow them more privacy and to begin building the gardens that Mrs. Stern dreamed of.

In 1935 Mrs. Stern engaged the services of landscape architect Ellen Biddle Shipman, from New York. Together they laid out plans for eight acres of flower gardens and walks. The majority of the gardens were located on the south side of the house. As the gardens began to grow and mature, Mrs. Stern became increasingly frustrated: There were few windows on this side of the house, and Mrs. Stern was continually unhappy because she was unable to enjoy her flower gardens from inside. More and more she began to dream of building a large, gracious house to match the brilliance of the gardens. The Sterns finally decided to move their house and make way for a house that would better relate to the gardens.

With the help of winches, cypress logs, and mules, the Sterns moved the house from its original site to a

Opposite. The present house is the second constructed on this site. The forty-five-room mansion was built so that the gardens could be viewed easily from indoors. Small, intimate garden rooms are found close to the house.

spot down the street, at the corner of Metairie Road and Garden Lane, where it still stands today.

The house that was built to take its place is a variation of Neoclassical architecture. Three stories high, it contains forty-five rooms. Longue Vue is considered one of the last great houses in America to be custom-built. The Sterns took possession in December 1942.

Through careful acquisition of adjacent land, the Sterns were able to accumulate enough property to make the grounds a truly expansive and exciting place. One of the more important pieces of land acquired was a lot off Bamboo Road that allowed the Sterns to include a rather grand entrance to the property.

They planted the property with live oaks, creating an avenue that leads from the front courtyard to the front of the house. Although the trees were only planted in 1940, they have today attained great size and maturity, and they look imposing enough to create the feeling that Longue Vue is a grand old estate.

Ellen Biddle Shipman originally designed the grounds as a late eighteenth-century English garden with an Italianate influence. The basic plan included designs for a large main garden (the south vista), a walled kitchen garden (which would include vegetables and herbs), and a wildflower garden—for Mrs. Stern had an avid interest in Louisiana's native flora.

Because the Sterns' interest grew along with the accumulation of more property, Shipman's original design was revised and expanded to include a series of small gardens or "outdoor rooms," each with a different personality and character. Much of the plant material chosen for the estate is indigenous to southern Louisiana's semitropical environment.

The Pan garden is a small, intimate area that extends out from the dining room of the house. The garden contains a small statue of Pan, Greek god of fields and forests. So important was this garden to Mrs. Stern that she had the glass doors in the dining room designed so that they could be lowered into the floor, creating one large room, half indoors, half outdoors.

One of Mrs. Stern's favorite roses, Margo Koster, grows profusely in this garden. On one wall of the garden is found a friendship plaque, dedicated to Ellen Biddle Shipman, whom the Sterns affectionately called the "godmother of the house."

On the other side of the house is the yellow garden, which Mrs. Stern designed herself, using chiefly her favorite color, yellow. Depending on the season, the visitor may find lilies, tulips, pansies, cassia, snapdragons, callendula, compass plant, jasmine, marigolds, coreopsis, or a host of other flowers—all yellow, of course. During spring, the Lady Banksia rose covers the walls. Plants boasting variegated yellow foliage are also found here. The yellow garden dates from about 1965, the time when the Sterns also created their "Spanish court."

Next to the yellow garden is the portico garden, which has a distinctly English flair. This garden was adjacent to the original house and has remained intact throughout the years. The neatly clipped boxwood and pink camellias offer a strong contrast to the yellow garden. The portico garden is a perfect place to view one of the most outstanding features of the Longue Vue gardens, the Spanish court.

Originally called the south lawn, the Spanish court was first planted according to Ellen Biddle Shipman's plan, which included an elaborate garden with geometrically shaped beds, a lattice-pattern brick wall, and a reflecting pool at the south end. An outstanding feature of this area is the camellia allee, featuring hundred-year-old camellias and hedges of azaleas.

In 1965, following damage to the gardens by Hurricane Betsy, Mrs. Stern decided to change her gardens to reflect more of the Spanish influence so important to the development of Louisiana. She and the architect William Platt transformed the south lawn into the Spanish court, which now offers a striking example of Moorish-Spanish landscape design. Mrs. Stern and William Platt toured the gardens of Europe extensively, looking for ideas and creating a clear picture of the new addition to the estate gardens. William Platt's modification of the south lawn is based on designs in the Generalife Gardens of the Alhambra in Granada, Spain.

The result of their European brainstorming was the incomparable Spanish court. Platt and Mrs. Stern installed fantastic fountains, mosaic walks, and geometrically cut boxwood hedges. The largest fountain in the Spanish court is also the most outstanding fountain at Longue Vue. It is composed of ten pairs of graceful water arches, making a beautiful entrance to a semicircular loggia. French tiles laid out in a herringbone pattern surround the fountains; they alternate with sections of black-and-beige-pebbled mosaic, inspired by a street in Barcelona.

The vegetation within the Spanish court includes blue plumbago, planted against the south-facing wall, Oriental magnolia, and lilies-of-the-Nile. Large pots are planted with the best that each season has to offer. Daffodils and tulips provide color in spring. Summer annuals fill the pots during the hottest months of the year, and chrysanthemums add colorful accents in autumn.

Longue Vue boasts twenty-two other fountains to please and tantalize the visitor. Most in the Spanish court are copies of Moorish fountains in the Generalife Gardens, but there are modern fountains as well. One of the most beautiful is Lyn Emery's aquamobile of white bronze, called *Arabesque* (1974), whose gracefully curved dolphins seem to swim and dive in the water continuously. At the other extreme is the sixteenth-century dolphin fountain, carved from Seville marble, adding a touch of ageless beauty to the garden. The fountains contribute the soothing sound of running water and provide a cooling effect for visitors in the hot, humid Louisiana summers.

The canal garden is narrow, with a long, brick-lined pool that looks very much like a small canal. Patterned after Portuguese canal gardens, it contains Japanese yew, sansanqua, loquat, and azaleas. Planted at the edge of the property, these large shrubs and trees effectively screen the garden from the nearby street.

Long before the days that wildflowers were in vogue, Mrs. Stern voiced her love of native plants and her desire to preserve them for future generations. Thus the wild garden—designed to display some of Louisiana's most beautiful and important native plants—was part of Ellen Shipman's original 1942 site plan. To help select plants, Mrs. Stern enlisted the help of naturalist Caroline Dormon. In this shady area grow southern pine, red oak, live oak, dogwood, bald-cypress (the state tree of Louisiana), and southern magnolia (Louisiana's state flower). Native flowering shrubs include buckeye, wild azaleas, sweet shrub, and starbush. The many different kinds of native ferns here include Louisiana shield, holly-leaf, leatherleaf and royal ferns. Although camellias are not native, they have been included here, bringing welcome winter color. More than 150 varieties of camellias are grown here. The central point of the garden is a small pool; a nearby pigeon house is an attractive brick structure copied from one that stood at Uncle Sam Plantation near Convent, Louisiana.

The walled garden, part of Mrs. Shipman's 1936 design for the gardens of the original house, was planted with annuals. In the 1942 site plan, Mrs. Shipman showed the walled garden area as an herb-and-vegetable garden. Today it has been converted to a formal rose garden, featuring many varieties of floribunda roses. In New Orleans, roses bloom from April through November.

Edith and Edgar Stern delighted in bringing fresh flowers indoors, and there has always been a cutting garden at Longue Vue to provide flowers at every season of the year. Mrs. Stern considered indoor floral arrangements so important to a well-dressed room that the architects included a special room in the house for the purpose of arranging flowers.

The 1942 site plans called for a greenhouse, a lathhouse, cold frames, and a potting and storage shed. Additional greenhouses have been installed, and this nursery area is open to visitors. Permanent display gardens here include a bed of hybrid tea roses and an herb-and-vegetable garden.

Before she died in 1980, Edith Stern expressed the wish that "my house and garden will serve some public use, the garden as presently used for horticultural functions and exhibitions and the house as a museum of decorative arts." Mrs. Stern's wishes have been fulfilled beautifully. Longue Vue presents a spectacular and exciting horticultural display that is an inspiration to visitors. The Sterns learned well the lessons of philanthropy taught to them at an early age. It is our good fortune that they passed on this legacy to us in the form of Longue Vue House and Gardens.

CHEEKWOOD

In the 1870s Nashville, Tennessee, was a thriving little town. Because of its strategic location on the Cumberland River, the town soon developed into an important shipping center. Steamboats delivered tobacco and grain and then loaded their empty stores with ironware, household goods, and farm machinery from the small Broad Street wharf.

Among the most important arrivals to this little shipping town was a small group of settlers by the name of Cheek. Two branches of the family came to Nashville from Kentucky: The C. T. Cheeks from Glasgow, and the Joel O. Cheeks from Burksville. Both families went into the wholesale grocery business.

Joel Cheek's grocery business soon became highly successful, and before long this ambitious young man was exploring the coffee industry. In 1892, satisfied that he had developed a superior blend of coffee, Joel Cheek sold his grocery business and concentrated his efforts on coffee.

The other grocery, C. T. Cheek and Co., was owned by Leslie Cheek, his brother, and his father. All were financially successful, but Leslie was not satisfied; he began looking for more investments and finally decided to go into the coffee business with his cousin Joel. Their product was named for a hotel at the corner of Fourth and Church streets in Nashville—the Maxwell House. The Cheek cousins soon were very rich. In 1928 the company was pur-

Left. This early photograph of Cheekwood shows the mansion, the wisteria arbor, and a series of gardens. A stream leading from the reflection pool is easily viewed as it makes its way down the hill to the swimming pools below.

Below. Cheekwood boasts a fine iris collection. This is found in the Clarence P. Connell Garden, named for a brilliant iris breeder. The iris is the Tennessee state flower.

Far left. Siberian Iris (Iris sibirica)

South of the recreation room are the terrace and the arbor that is notable because of the huge wisteria vines covering it. The French statue and small grotto give this area a sophisticated elegance.

chased by General Foods (then known as Postum Co.) for $42 million.

Leslie Cheek had married Mabel Wood of Clarksville. The couple became extremely interested in Georgian architecture and frequently traveled to England to learn more. While on one of these trips, Mrs. Cheek purchased a tall Victorian mirror. When they brought it home, however, they found that it would not fit in the house and Leslie Cheek stored it at a warehouse. A few years later, he grew tired of keeping such an expensive antique at the warehouse. He came home and announced to his wife that either they would have to sell the mirror or build a house to fit it. Mabel Cheek called his bluff.

The couple began plans for a grand and glorious estate, to be built on a site eight miles southwest of Nashville bordering the Percy Warner Park. They bought a hundred acres and hired Bryant Fleming to design the house and grounds.

Fleming was on the faculty at Cornell University and was well schooled in both residential and landscape architecture. A written history of the estate says that "it is a question whether he designed the house to set off the gardens trailing down the hillside, or the gardens to ornament the house at the top of the hill."

They called the place Cheekwood (Mabel's maiden name was Wood). This collaborative name typified

the cooperation that Leslie and Mabel Cheek exhibited throughout the project. They began work in 1929; Cheekwood is one of the last great country homes built before the Depression.

Clearing the land for the house and grounds took approximately a year. During this time, the Cheeks took Fleming with them to study eighteenth-century homes and gardens throughout Europe.

When they returned home, they carefully considered every facet of the estate before beginning construction. The house is situated high on a hill and was placed to best take advantage of the cool evening breeze.

While Mabel Cheek divided her time and efforts between the house and gardens, her husband spent most of his time on the outdoors. He wanted a boxwood garden, and he spent a great deal of time finding the largest specimens in the Southeast. Cheekwood was built on a limestone hill, making it difficult to dig holes for the large transplanted boxwood. Leslie Cheek solved the problem with dynamite.

One of Cheek's large boxwoods came from rural eastern Tennessee. The owner agreed to sell it for $100—a tremendous amount of money in the Depression—but when the workmen came to dig it, the owner had changed his mind: his wife's great-grandmother was buried there, and he didn't want to disturb her. An extra $50 was parted with, for great-grandmother's sake, and the workmen dug up the boxwood, finding great-grandma's teeth in the process.

And what happened to the mirror that started it all? Mabel Cheek, claiming a lady's right to change her mind, had it cut down. It now hangs indoors, in a bathroom.

During the 1950s the Exchange Club of Nashville hoped to create a botanical garden for Nashville and the Southeast. The group approached the Cheeks' descendants, Mr. and Mrs. Walter Sharp, who still owned Cheekwood. In a marvelously generous act, the Sharps donated Cheekwood and fifty-five acres to be used as a botanical garden and fine-arts center.

Opposite. Cheekwood, home of Leslie and Mabel Cheek, is situated eight miles southwest of Nashville, bordering the Percy Warner Park. Today the grounds are made up of a series of different gardens including collections of herbs, wildflowers, daffodils, and scented plants.

There are several different gardens, covering a diverse range of horticultural interests—but a tour of the gardens really begins inside. Botanic Hall, built in 1970, serves as the staff office, houses an excellent botanical library, and contains many interesting horticultural displays. In the sun-filled atrium there is a fountain called *Summer Play*, created by Jesse Beesley, a Tennessee artist.

Directly across from Botanic Hall is the herb study garden, begun in 1983 by the Herb Society of Nashville. Groomed beds contain displays of various kinds of herbs: medicinal and culinary herbs at the center, with the occasional ornamental herb snuck in, surrounded by less formal areas where useful wildflowers and woody plants grow.

Just past the herb garden is the Hardison Daffodil Garden, which includes hundreds of different species and varieties of narcissus growing around a central sundial. The garden is an invaluable resource for local enthusiasts. The daffodil garden is naturally most spectacular in spring, but careful overplanting with marigolds makes this area attractive all year.

Designed to delight four of the five senses, the Burr Garden is particularly appealing to blind persons. Some of the planting beds are at waist level, offering easy access. The carefully chosen plants, such as mints and lamb's ears, provide pleasing aromas and textures. The sound of running water soothes, and brilliantly colored flowers climbing over an arbor and surrounding a sundial delight the eye. An old-fashioned knot garden weaves miniature hedges of barberry and dianthus.

During summer months a profusion of perennials creates a wonderful spectacle of color. Bright daylilies blend and contrast with purple balloon flower, daisies, and purple coneflowers.

The Howe Garden is a transplant from Nashville. It originally belonged to Cora Howe, an enthusiastic wildflower gardener who carefully planted native shrubs, flowers, and trees, creating an appealing habitat for birds and small mammals. Not content to keep this wonderful bit of wilderness to herself, Mrs. Howe first opened her garden to the public in 1929, and she continued to do so until her death in 1967. Through the generosity of her heirs, the entire garden—including a stone wall and a toolshed—was moved to Cheekwood in 1968.

In spring, Virginia bluebells and wild blue phlox bloom brightly beside white toothwort and bloodroot. Mayapple blossoms are hidden beneath large, umbrellalike leaves. Summer brings pale pink wild geraniums and the brighter pink-and-red fire pink. Jack-in-the-pulpit blooms in spring, but in summer puts forth startlingly bright spires of red berries.

One of the most exciting parts of the Howe Garden is the John C. Lambert Trillium Collection, which was donated to Cheekwood in 1985. It contains dozens of species of this beautiful native wildflower. In 1983 the Howe Garden received the prestigious Garden Club of America Founder's Fund Award for its work in propagating endangered native plants.

As you approach the house, which is now a fine-arts center, a series of streams, fountains, and pools becomes more and more apparent. The reflecting pond, close to the house, is home to an interesting display of water lilies in summer.

To one side of the mansion a lovely swan fountain overlooks Nashville's beautiful Percy Warner Park—a high panorama of Nashville and the distant hills. A grand wrought-iron arbor adjacent to the house supports an old wisteria vine, providing shade and color. Many of Leslie Cheek's boxwoods are in this part of the garden.

Close to the mansion is the Clarence P. Connell Garden, named for a brilliant iris breeder and collector. Connell won the prestigious Dykes Medal in 1929 for his hybrid 'Dauntless.' The iris is the state flower of Tennessee.

The koi ponds below the iris garden were part of Bryant Fleming's original landscaping. The ponds make a natural transition into the Japanese garden, designed by David Harris Engel, the best-known

American designer of Japanese gardens. The Japanese garden at Cheekwood is known as Shomu-en, or the pine-mist garden. Much of the garden is composed of a large raked-sand area, adorned with rocks and plants. A variety of evergreens, stoneware, and an elongated teahouse create peace and tranquility.

Returning up the hill from the Japanese garden, the visitor finds himself in back of Botanic Hall in the rose garden, which contains dozens of types particularly suited to the middle Tennessee area. Near the display greenhouses, a brightly colored fence and arbors provide support for many kinds of vines and trailing plants.

Cheekwood's blend of gardens is highly individual. From the stark simplicity of a Japanese garden to the opulent display of fragrant flowers and colorful perennials in the Burr Garden, each area has an aura of its own. Together they create a magnificent horticultural display.

DIXON GALLERY AND GARDENS

Amidst the bustle of Memphis, Tennessee, lies the peaceful quiet of the Dixon Gallery and Gardens, at the former home of Margaret and Hugo Dixon. A tall canopy of trees offers welcome shade, and a smattering of brightly colored flowers adds vibrancy to the

Above.
Margaret Dixon loved flowers of every hue but had a special fondness for white flowers. In deference to her wishes, the plants close to the house only have white flowers.

Left. A soft, open woodland is an essential part of Memphis's Dixon gardens. Home of Margaret and Hugo Dixon, this estate was developed into a public garden in 1974.

garden, like jewels on a dark green velvet dress. The house and grounds were developed into a public garden and museum after the death of the owners in 1974, operated under the auspices of a private non-profit organization. It was opened to the public in 1976 and a gallery was built the following year to house the permanent art collection.

The present site of the gardens was part of a land grant originally awarded to Geraldus Buntyn. At the time of his death in 1865, Buntyn's property included over forty thousand acres. The Dixons bought a small portion of this wild property in 1939 and began to work on their dream garden.

Margaret Oates Dixon was born in 1900 to a family of wealthy cotton merchants who moved to Memphis from Vicksburg, Mississippi. Hugo Dixon, whose father was a cotton broker on the Liverpool Exchange, was born in 1892 in England. Dixon began his career in cotton in Europe but after World War I joined his brother, Roger, in Dallas, Texas.

Margaret had met Roger Dixon and his wife aboard an ocean liner in the mid-1920s. So taken with the young woman, the Roger Dixons persuaded her to come to Dallas and meet Hugo. Hugo, even more enchanted, married Margaret at her Memphis home in 1926. The young couple moved first to Dallas and later to Houston. They returned to Memphis to live in 1939.

The Dixons had a great love of nature and had traveled throughout the United States and Europe, visiting gardens. They wanted to have a careful hand in planning the grounds of their new home. After careful consideration they asked Hugo Dixon's sister, Hope Crutchfield, to design the garden and grounds.

In 1940–41, real work on the garden began. The land was covered with open woodland and meadow, with several old trees and some new forest growth. The Dixons and Mrs. Crutchfield were careful to preserve as many of these old trees as possible. The resulting landscape gave the estate an air of great antiquity. Adding to this feeling is the quick growth of the plantings done in the early 1940s. Tiny box-

woods planted at the entrance of the gardens have grown swiftly in the rich environment of the mid-South and now tower over the visitor.

The design for the gardens, patterned after an English park with long vistas and a series of formal, intimate gardens, relied heavily on the arrangement and sequence of garden space. Hugo Dixon wanted to create a "cathedral" effect with a judicious use of tall-growing trees. His sister wrote to him: "I have circled in the trees, trying to get the cathedral effect that you have, on to paper, in order to determine if trees A and B would add to that effect.... Put in a tree around location F again *if* it *adds* to the cathedral."

Hugo Dixon became an avid gardener, and between 1955 and 1972 he kept a garden journal, noting the weather and the entrances and exits of his favorite plants. On March 15, 1962, he wrote: "In December temperatures on three nights were zero, +5, and +10 but plants were all dormant. Looks as if all ligustrums are dead and a lot of the English box completely frozen."

Because of the grand cathedral effect and the stunning vistas, as well as the smaller garden "rooms," it is impossible to see all of the gardens from any one spot. Instead, the visitor is lured from one small garden area to the next, each with its own character and personality.

According to Hope Crutchfield's plan, the gardens are on a cross-axis plan. The major axis runs from north to south and goes through the center of the south lawn, with the house at one end and a magnificent sculpture of Europa and the Bull at the other.

The center axis goes in front of statues of the four seasons, ending at the terrace on one side and the statue, *The Venus of Memphis,* on the other.

Grand old trees provide a framework for the rest of the garden. Oaks and hickories tower over an understory that includes dogwoods, azaleas, hemlocks, and boxwood. Ivy beds throughout the grounds weave a common thread throughout the different gardens.

One of the most exciting horticultural exhibits in the gardens is the camellia collection, which was

The slathouse at Dixon Gardens houses many tender plants. Here camellias and azaleas can be found in bloom in late winter and early spring.

donated by Mrs. Warda Stout in 1976. This exhibit of more than two hundred plants is housed in the camellia slathouse; they bloom from November to March, peaking in February.

Another colorful part of the grounds is the cutting garden, located behind the camellia house. Here are found dozens of different flowers that provide bright cheerful color indoors and out. In spring, narcissus, tulips, and other bulbs bloom spectacularly. But the true glory of this garden is seen in summer, when such old-fashioned favorites as nicotiana, phlox, hydrangeas, purple coneflower, daisies, and black-eyed Susans turn the garden into a paintbox of bright, bold colors.

From the cutting garden, neat paths wander down into the woodland garden. In spring this becomes a fairyland of delicate shades of pink and white from countless azaleas and dogwoods. Small wildflowers dot the forest floor, and ferns make a lacey green backdrop.

Returning to the house, the visitor now has a clear view of the south lawn, a rolling expanse of grass framed by forest. At the far end of the lawn stands an eighteenth-century statue of Europa and the Bull, which the Dixons purchased from the sculpture garden of an English castle. Before the Dixons bought the statue, they installed a cardboard replica in the garden to see it if was the right size and shape.

The east-west axis, called the "Venus allee," passes in front of Europa, and ends to the west at the old swimming pool. Perhaps the most changed part of the garden, the pool has been covered and is now used for small concerts or gatherings; it is also used as a reservoir. The allee, an avenue of deciduous and evergreen trees and shrubs that includes many different kinds of azaleas, leads to the Wheeler Williams statue *The Venus of Memphis*, which Hugo Dixon commissioned in 1963. In spring the area is especially beautiful, when the pink-pearl azaleas surrounding the statue are in bloom.

From the Venus allee brick paths lead the visitor through a series of three formal gardens. The upper

tier is planted with flowers of the season that provide brilliant spots of color in a forest of green.

Past the formal garden areas, close to the house, is the reflecting pool, which is best seen from the house. The reflecting pool now is home to a restored nineteenth-century cast-iron fountain acquired in 1990. Margaret Dixon, although fond of bright colors in the garden, preferred white next to the house. Thus all plantings in the area close to the residence include white flowers.

Throughout the garden, small benches of one sort or another are strategically placed. Alongside one azalea-studded path is a curved stone whispering bench. Because of the way the bench is curved, two lovers seated at either end could whisper back and forth, and their messages would carry perfectly—but the chaperone sitting between them would be unable to hear the conversation.

Seated quietly on one of the benches, surrounded by moss, ferns, and a multitude of wildflowers, the visitor might think that he has happened upon a wilderness. It is only the far-off sound of city traffic that brings him back to the present. The Dixons, with their love of nature and their desire for moments of calm and tranquility, would be happy that so many visitors have found a peaceful pleasure in their garden.

Left. The formal areas at Dixon Gardens have always been filled with colorful bedding plants. Today, as in the early days of the Gardens, old-fashioned favorites such as phlox, nicotiana, and daisies still bloom.

Opposite. The Dixons visited gardens throughout the United States and Europe, collecting ideas for their own garden. They were careful to preserve as many of the old trees as possible to give the gardens an air of antiquity.

{7}

Gardens for the People, 1925-1940

In the twentieth century, the United States experienced a renaissance of interest in plant exploration. Once the passionate pursuit of such learned men as Thomas Jefferson, plant exploration became again the province of scientific adventurers. This time, however, it was not our native plants that captured our enthusiasm, but the exotic plants of other lands. Callaway Gardens and Fairchild Tropical Garden were products of this burst of enthusiasm.

David Fairchild was the leading and most respected American plant explorer of the late nineteenth century. He traveled throughout the world searching for new plants, introducing thousands of new fruits and vegetables as agricultural crops in America. In 1930, a self-educated man called Robert Montgomery read Fairchild's book *Exploring for Plants*, and he became convinced that there was a need for a tropical botanical garden in the United States. After years of work and study, Montgomery created Fairchild Tropical Garden.

Cason Callaway's chief interest was the farming practices in his own area of western Georgia, bringing a businesslike, scientific approach to raising crops. On his own land Callaway experimented with farm mechanization, methods of erosion control, and fertilization. The results were highly successful, and his worn-out land, formerly a cotton field, was soon a demonstration farm, showing other farmers in the area what could be done with their own land.

Callaway desired to take a more active role in helping other farmers better their own land. To this end, he developed a program called "One Hundred Better Farms."

The basis of improving a farm financially, Cason felt, was in improving the soil. In 1944 he proposed that a group of businessmen in Atlanta, Georgia, form a hundred corporations. Each corporation would hire a farmer, buy a hundred acres of land, and spend about $40 per acre to improve the soil.

After three years the venture was considered a huge success. It was due, in part, to the charisma and energy of Cason Callaway. But it was also due to a willingness to accept more scientific methods of farming, to seek and listen to advice from government agencies designed to deliver such advice.

It was a time when Americans were proud of their accomplishments and ready and willing to share knowledge and experience with each other.

Opposite. The Callaways worked hard at rejuvenating land depleted by years of cotton farming. Their philosophy was if cotton robbed the land of its richness, money from cotton mills should help build it back up.

Page 158. Swirls of spring blossoms line the lawns at Callaway Gardens. Tulips and pansies provide a seemingly endless stream of color and fragrance.

Page 159. Cason Callaway loved to share his corner of heaven on earth. This photograph, taken in May 1957, shows the directors of the Chemical Bank fishing at Lake Florence south of Callaway Gardens.

This transfer of knowledge was not limited to the scientific community. Groups and clubs at all levels of society were formed. Troops of Boy Scouts and Girl Scouts, Future Farmers of America, and the 4-H clubs all catered to the needs of America's youth. And for the women? The Garden Club.

The idea of a garden club originated in Athens, Georgia, in 1891. It was an idea that spread like wildfire: soon there were garden clubs in communities throughout the country. The Founders' Memorial Garden in Athens pays tribute to those women who formed the first garden club in America.

Farther south, in Florida, the members of the Palm Beach Garden Club created their own demonstration gardens, proving that both traditional and tropical gardens could succeed there. The result is the beautiful Four Arts Garden, located behind the Society of the Four Arts Museum in downtown Palm Beach, Florida.

The natural union of art and gardening caught the imagination of other people around the country. In Murrell's Inlet, South Carolina, Archer and Anna Huntington dreamed of creating a sculpture garden that they could give to the public. Brookgreen Gardens, America's first sculpture garden, is the result. Here, among the camellias and azaleas, the boxwood and magnolias, are some of the finest examples of nineteenth– and twentieth–century American figurative sculpture.

Gardens are communal in spirit—a concept well understood by many men and women who planned gardens in the early twentieth century. We are indebted to these people for their foresight and their generosity. Through their efforts, we have been able to further our knowledge and understanding of plants and gardening. The beautiful gardens that they helped to create continue to be an inspiration.

CALLAWAY GARDENS

"Callaway Gardens, a man-made landscape in a unique natural setting, was conceived and created by Cason J. Callaway and his wife, Virginia Hand Callaway, for

The Callaway family so enjoyed their family retreat at Blue Springs they decided to share this woodland wonderland with others. Enthusiastic about the project, Cason Callaway created thirteen lakes and a nine-hole golf course.

L a u r a   C .   M a r t i n ' s
S o u t h e r n   G a r d e n s
162

the benefit of mankind. The purpose is to provide a wholesome family environment where all may find beauty, relaxation, inspiration and a better understanding of the living world." This stated mission directs and influences every decision made at Callaway Gardens. The founders' far-reaching vision has made Callaway Gardens a beautiful place in which to grow and to learn.

Cason Callaway was born in 1894 in La Grange, Georgia, a small town near the Alabama border. At the turn of the century, western Georgia—like much of the South—was still suffering from the consequences of the Civil War, which had ended only three decades earlier. The land was poor and the people even more so. Sharecroppers worked the tired land, eking out a living in this hot, dry climate.

The Callaways were wealthy, but they believed in the principles of generosity, philanthropy, and altruism—traits that Cason Callaway acquired at an early age and displayed throughout his life. First and foremost, however, Callaway was an astute and practical businessman.

Like his father before him, Callaway worked with the textile industry. After finishing school and serving in the navy during World War I, he returned to La Grange to help his father run the mills. At his death, Callaway took over the mills, increasing their size, number, and productivity.

When he turned forty-four, Callaway resigned from the mill, but his business career was far from over; he held directorships at many important corporations and financial institutions. But it was his relationship to his land that was to consume Callaway's greatest love and efforts.

While still intimately involved with his work at the mills, Callaway realized that he needed a retreat—a place where he "could just walk in the woods and look at the beauty that God had made, and think about things I hadn't had time to think about before."

Searching for such a place in 1930, Cason and his bride Virginia visited Blue Springs, thirty miles from their home in La Grange. At the foot of a flint cliff was a clear, blue pool, thirty-five feet across and nearly the same depth. Nearby Pine Mountain rises 1,300 feet above sea level and some geologists claim that it is the oldest land on the North American continent—the tailbone of the Appalachian Mountains, now weathered and worn to the size of a mere hill. The place spoke to the Callaways, who dreamed of owning this land and building a cabin for the family.

During the next few months, the Callaways came time and time again to Blue Springs. Cason hiked over a nearby ridge to the Barnes Creek watershed and found still more land much to his liking. He also found a beautifully colored azalea, blooming late in the summer—unlike other azaleas, which bloom in spring. He later found that this was the plum leaf azalea (*Rhododendron prunifolium*). This rare wild shrub only grows within a hundred-mile radius of Blue Springs.

The discovery of the plum leaf azalea was the turning point. Shortly thereafter, Cason and Virginia Callaway purchased the Blue Springs property and three thousand surrounding acres. A proud property owner, Cason immediately created a lake which he named for his mother, Ida Cason, and built a summer home beside it.

The family loved this summer retreat and spent a great deal of time here. The area was attractive to everyone, and sometimes strangers stumbled onto this haven.

The story is told that one day Callaway looked out the window of his house and saw a family setting out a picnic beside the lake. He strode out, determined to get the strangers off his land.

"What can I do for you, sir?" he asked the man sternly.

Unconcerned, the man turned to him and answered, "Well, we need some crackers for the baby."

An astonished Cason Callaway meekly went to the house and got some crackers. As he returned to the family he said, "This place is only open to the public today. Tomorrow it will be closed again."

In 1988 the Cecil B. Day Butterfly Center opened to the public. In addition to a 7000 square foot conservatory, there is a demonstration butterfly garden.

Pages 164–165. Spring at the Gardens is spectacularly beautiful. Callaway realized that people needed a place where they could just walk in the woods and look at nature's wondrous beauty.

It was, perhaps, the sight of this family happily picnicking beside the lake that gave the idea to Cason Callaway of creating a huge, beautiful picnic ground so that thousands of families could come and enjoy the serenity of the place.

By 1938 the Blue Springs property had grown to nine thousand acres, and eventually the Callaways purchased a total of forty thousand acres. In 1937 Cason dammed the Blue Springs lake, creating a swimming hole a quarter of a mile wide. During that time there were no swimming pools or safe swimming holes in Harris County. For two weeks during the summer, the Callaways opened the swimming hole to the children of the county; under the supervision of the Red Cross, hundreds of these children learned to swim in Blue Springs Pool.

The Callaways loved their spot in the woods and worked untiringly to rebuild the land. The land had suffered for many years from being planted exclusively in cotton. But Callaway said that it was only right that, if cotton robbed the land of its richness, then money from cotton textile mills should build it back up again. He would supervise: he once said that "the best fertilizer a land can have is the footprint of its owner."

Once started, Callaway was hard to stop. Using a team of earth-movers and bulldozers, Callaway filled in gullies, drained silt-laden bottomland, and gradually began to transform the landscape. When Virginia mentioned that she would like a magnolia tree, he planted five thousand of them. He also planted 700,000 pine seedlings. Seeds of the rare and lovely plum leaf azalea were planted; eventually twenty thousand plants filled the area with rich color in late summer. Along the creek, Callaway created a series of thirteen lakes, and around one lake he built a nine-hole golf course with broad fairways. And around the golf course he planted beautiful flowers and shrubs. Cason once said that if someone made the mistake of lifting his head on a shot, he wanted him to be looking at something beautiful.

Although his original idea was merely to create a beautiful retreat for family and friends, Callaway eventually decided to open the gardens—named for his mother, Ida Cason Callaway—to the public. This change, of course, called for a great expansion of his plans. He brought in thousands of tons of clean white sand to make the biggest inland white sand man-made beach in the world. He built bathhouses and an inn. Certain lakes were designated for fishing. Callaway once said, "It's all a matter of knowing how nature works. It takes fertilizer to make the algae grow. It takes five or six pounds of algae to make one pound of minnows, and it takes about six pounds of minnows to make one pound of bass. And it takes just one eight pound bass to make a two hundred pound fisherman the happiest man in the world."

The Callaways hoped the natural beauty of the place would bring people to visit and they developed many different kinds of gardens within the complex. Here could be found natural gardens full of the wildflowers of the Appalachians, and also formally planted exotic flowers from around the world. The woodland gardens soon became famous for their springtime glory when azaleas, rhododendrons, mountain laurel, magnolias, dogwoods, and thousands of wildflowers transformed the forest into a fairyland.

Cason Callaway did not forget his many lessons of farming in western Georgia. He was always experimenting with crops, and different ways to plant—anything and everything that would help teach Georgia farmers how to make their own lands more productive. He built "Mr. Cason's Vegetable Garden," which he was determined to make the most productive seven and a half acres in the Southeast. Designed as a demonstration garden, its produce provided fresh fruits and vegetables for the clubhouse and dining rooms.

Opening Blue Springs to the public greatly influenced the surrounding counties and towns. Through the employment opportunities created here for local residents, and through generous donations, the Callaways

Natural areas within the Gardens are filled with wildflowers and native trees and shrubs. Berries attract birds and other wildlife during fall and winter months.

transformed Harris County from one of the poorest and most backward of all Georgia counties to one of the most progressive.

Before he died in 1961, Cason Callaway explained why he spent a hard-earned fortune on creating this magnificent garden.

> I am a selfish man at heart. I want to use my money to do people good and make them happy while I am still alive to watch them enjoy it. When I stroll around the Gardens and see thousands of people on the beach and in the water, and on the golf course and fishing in the lakes, or just strolling in the woods listening to the birds sing, or looking at the flowers, it makes me feel a fine warm glow of selfish happiness.

Since Cason Callaway's death, Callaway Gardens has continued to grow in a way that would surely have pleased its founders addressing a critical need for conservation and horticultural education.

In 1984 the John A. Sibley Horticultural Center opened on the grounds. The Sibley Center is the most advanced greenhouse-garden complex in the world. This center, which encompasses five acres, includes a magnificent conservatory coupled with a horticultural display that integrates indoor and outdoor settings.

Within the conservatory itself are plants native to tropical regions of the world. A long, narrow walkway leads from the conservatory, and along it is a rock wall planted with azaleas, ferns, camellias, and citrus fruits. In this climate-controlled area, temperatures never dip below 40° Fahrenheit. Many of the plants in this area are native to China and Japan.

Behind a beautiful two-story waterfall is a fern grotto, whose warm, humid environment is suitable for plants such as wandering Jew, rainbow moss, and many different kinds of ferns.

The formal conservatory is a wonderful mass of color and excitement, where twenty-six major floral themes are featured annually. Outstanding plants in this area include lilies, fuchsias, geraniums, caladiums, impatiens, and coleus. During autumn, many different kinds of chrysanthemums create an astounding display.

Outside the conservatory areas, the visitor finds fanciful, exotic creatures such as dinosaurs or peacocks, created from carefully arranged groups of flowers. A wide, expansive lawn is bordered by shrubs and old-fashioned perennial and mixed borders. During spring, flowering bulbs create a breathtaking display of color. Later in the season the bulbs are replaced by various annuals and perennials. Toward the end of the year chrysanthemums take center stage.

In a superb educational and conservation effort, the Cecil B. Day Butterfly Center, in a 7,000-square-foot glass-enclosed octagonal conservatory, was opened to the public in September of 1988. The center is home to over fifty different species of tropical plants and tropical butterflies, which fly freely in the conservatory.

The center has between eight hundred and a thousand butterflies at any time of the year. The conditions are carefully controlled for its tropical inhabitants: The temperature remains a constant 78° Fahrenheit, and the humidity stays between 60 and 80 percent. Cascading flowering vines and shrubs provide nectar and moisture for the butterflies.

Outside the conservatory there are several small natural display gardens that teach visitors what plants to use to attract native butterflies to their own gardens.

Callaway Gardens is a marvelous example of how commercial ventures can support educational and conservation efforts. The after-tax proceeds from Callaway Gardens Resort, Inc., go to support the efforts of the Ida Cason Callaway Foundation. This foundation is dedicated to the concept of providing a beautiful and inspiring landscape for all visitors.

Cason Callaway once said, "I don't know what the soul is, but whatever it is, a sense of beauty and goodness must be at the heart of it." It is easy to walk around Callaway Gardens and see that Cason and Virginia Callaway put their heart and soul into this place of beauty and goodness.

Left. Early community support was important to the development of Fairchild Gardens. This photograph shows the Ladies of the Vine Committee standing in front of the Semple Vine Pergola.

Below. Hibiscus thrives in the heat of the south Florida sun. Brilliantly colored blossoms were used traditionally to make tea and dye cloth.

FAIRCHILD TROPICAL GARDEN

On a broad expanse of land just south of Miami, Florida, there is a living laboratory of exotic and spectacular tropical plants. Fairchild Tropical Garden is a botanist's dream, a place to learn and study, to admire, and to investigate some of the world's most exciting plants. It was the brainchild of Colonel Robert H. Montgomery, who, though not a botanist himself, had a passionate interest in plants. His dream was to create a botanical garden that would find a place among the great botanical gardens of the world.

The son of a Methodist minister, Montgomery moved so often during his childhood that a formal education was virtually impossible. Undeterred by a lack of schooling, Robert Montgomery educated himself. He did such a magnificent job of it that he excelled in accounting and the law.

In the mid-1930s, Montgomery decided to create a public garden to display his favorite plants. He approached his project with characteristic energy. Having read David Fairchild's *Exploring for Plants*, Montgomery realized that there was a great need for a tropical botanical garden in southern Florida. He contacted Fairchild to discuss this project, and the two soon developed a great friendship and enormous mutual respect. Fairchild worked as consultant for developing the garden that Montgomery named for him, and he served as director and president emeritus from 1945 until his death in 1954.

The garden was designed by William Lyman Phillips. At the time of his initial involvement, Phillips was superintendent of a Civilian Conservation Corps camp in Dade County. Phillips was a gifted designer, and his plans for the garden are still the bible for maintaining and developing the garden today.

Tropical plants are often protected by sharp leaves, spines, and thorns. Often hidden by this protective arbor are delicately beautiful flowers.

Montgomery gave Phillips free rein. According to Phillips, the only suggestions made by Montgomery were to have "palms on the one side and flowering trees on the other, that the place should be a garden rather than a park, and that palms looked best standing on a smooth lawn."

The basic design of the garden adhered to three main principles: variety, consistency, and contrast. To encourage visitors to explore all of the garden, Phillips designed it so that there is no central vantage point. Each oasis of plants, each circle of palms or cycads or native plants, must be discovered separately.

One of the first basic design decisions Phillips made was to group the collections according to botanical family. In this he said that both Montgomery and Fairchild "tolerated rather than supported" him. But Phillips insisted that in a garden whose collections were to expand gradually through the years, this design concept was the only practical one.

The next major design element was the inclusion of broad open spaces of lakes and lawns to offset groupings of plants. In Phillips's own words, "The entire plan is essentially an articulated complex of openings. The necessity of open spaces was obvious, for without well-defined openings no sense of organization, no scenic effects, would be possible." Fairchild Tropical Garden was developed as a symphony, with "chords" of palms and cycads, "melodies" of flowering plants, and "rests"—essential moments of complete silence—to show off these rich and varied tones.

Fairchild Tropical Garden is large—eighty-three acres, all of which are gracefully and generously planted. The visitor is therefore encouraged to take a tram ride to receive an introduction to the treasures that await. After the tram ride, the visitor can explore smaller areas at leisure.

Fairchild sometimes made suggestions and requests. In his memoirs, Phillips wrote: "Some time in 1941 Dr. Fairchild called me up and said, 'We've got to make a palm glade in the Garden.' I asked, 'What is to make a palm glade in the Garden.' I asked, 'What is a palm glade?' 'I don't know,' he said, 'but it's a good word. You go ahead.'"

With this suggestion, Phillips created the Bailey Palm Glade, named for Liberty Hyde Bailey, a professor emeritus at Cornell University and one of America's leading horticulturists of the time. This was probably the world's first palm glade.

Fairchild is a garden of shapes and textures. As the visitor wanders through the garden, or travels over the grounds in a tram, he is alternately beckoned and warned off. Sharp spines and swordlike leaves demand respect and suggest viewing from a distance. Arid rock-garden plants shout, "Look but don't touch!" And yet one is drawn closer by a fascination for these well-armored plants.

Closer inspection rewards the brave. Among the sharp, spiny dangers lie delicate flowers worth the journey. The flowers of the century plant, for example, are exquisite, intricate blossoms. Like a princess in a well-fortified tower, these blossoms are found only by those who pass through the fortifications.

In the rain forest section, bromeliads, orchids, and ferns grow high in the trees, just as they grow in the wild. Because southern Florida does not receive as much rainfall as does a true tropical rainforest, an outdoor sprinkler system sprays water both at ground level and high in the canopy. The rare plant house contains rare and difficult-to-grow tropical plants, such as the breadfruit tree, rare palms, bromeliads, and orchids.

The main attractions of the garden are the collections of palms and cycads. Almost three thousand species of palm grow worldwide; Fairchild Tropical Garden grows over seven hundred species, making it the largest collection of palms in the continental United States. Palms are of enormous economic value to many of the lesser developed countries, providing food, shelter, clothing, waxes, and oils. A history of palms and their uses can be found in the Palm Products Museum, located in the Montgomery Library and Museum near the bookstore.

Opposite. Before Hurricane Andrew in 1992, Fairchild boasted an unusual and beautiful rain forest area where bromeliads and orchids grew high in the tree canopy.

Above. Sun and shadows interplay on the lawn at Fairchild. There is no central vantage point in the Garden, and each section is designed to be explored on its own right.

Palms exhibit tremendous variety, growing tall and stately or short and squat. The bottle palm, shaped like a soda bottle, is big and round at the bottom and tapers at the top. The very names of some of these tropical palms are colorful—gingerbread, jelly, date, cherry, syrup, and sugar palms all sound like they came from a bakery; the lady, Cuban belly, and old man palms have a completely different connotation.

The next major collection at Fairchild is that of cycads. The cycads are an interesting group of plants. They have an ancient lineage, having flourished with the dinosaurs more than one hundred million years ago. Cycads resemble palms, but they produce seed-bearing cones, similar to the ones produced by conifers. At this time Fairchild grows 123 of the 150 species known worldwide. The collection is mostly in the upland sections of the garden and in the grassy area leading to the Bailey Palm Glade.

In spite of the importance of the palms and cycads, visitors who look for flowering plants are not disappointed. The flowering tropical plants here are startling in their beauty. Many—such as the red silk cotton tree, with its red, waxy flowers measuring four inches across—are uncommon.

The hibiscus collection is at its peak in late spring or fall but the flowers bloom throughout the year. The Semple Vine Pergola features a multitude of fragrant flowering vines, many of which were favorites of David Fairchild. One of the most beautiful is the blue clitoria, or butterfly pea.

Nearby, the yesterday-today-and-tomorrow shrub lives up to its name by showing off three distinctly different colors of blossoms. The first blossoms to come out are a deep lavender-purple color. As they begin to age they fade to a lighter lavender; just before they drop they turn pure white.

The arid rock garden is like a miniature sandy desert. Century plants show off their enormous spikes of delicate flowers. Closer inspection shows a tiny green frog peeking out from the folds of the leaves of this plant. Prickly-pear cactus is eerily beautiful with its sharp, needlelike spines. Several species of African aloe, with long, fleshy leaves in different shades of green, grow close to the ground.

Montgomery, Fairchild, and Phillips succeeded in their goals for the garden. Phillips's masterful design works beautifully, enticing the visitor from one group of plants to another. Rarely is a visitor disappointed, for the variety of plants and the beauty of these tropical treasures provide a lifetime of exploration.

FOUNDERS' MEMORIAL GARDEN

Gardeners love to talk. They enjoy sitting and swapping information, bragging about their own plants, and speaking wistfully of the gardens of other people. This love of garden chatter and a real desire to help beautify the community led to the founding of the first garden club in America—in Athens, Georgia, in 1891. Today there are an astounding number of garden clubs in this country. At last count, 9,286 were listed as members of the National Council of State Garden Clubs. The number of individual members is now well over 275,000.

These clubs range in size from less than a dozen members to over a hundred, and they can be found in remote little communities as well as every major city in the country. Each has its individual goals and challenges, varying from one part of the country to another. In Alaska, for example, the big problem under discussion is how to keep moose out of the garden—intruders that are hardly a major concern in the Bronx.

Garden clubs provide the perfect vehicle for gardeners to share their successes and failures with others. The clubs are of enormous value to individuals and communities; their civic and community projects have contributed a great deal to the beauty of America through the years.

The twelve women who formed the first garden club gathered in the drawing room of Mrs. E. K. Lumpkin to

The Founder's Memorial Garden in Athens, Georgia, was built in tribute to the women who began the first garden club in America. Today over 275,000 women in this country are members of local garden clubs.

Bamboo, decorative, useful, and fast-growing, is often used as a living screen or a green backdrop in this garden.

organize the "Ladies' Garden Club of Athens." Their purpose was to gather together periodically to discuss their own gardening ventures and to lend their expertise to the community. Education was a high priority for them—a tradition that continues even today.

During the next few decades many more clubs similar to this were formed, and in 1928 the Garden Club of Georgia was organized. Twenty-nine local Georgia clubs sent representatives to the Biltmore Hotel in Atlanta to establish goals and guidelines for the group. One year later, in 1929, the National Council of State Garden Clubs was formed. Throughout the state and country, garden club members felt that the founders of the first garden club should in some way be honored. What better way than with a living garden dedicated to them?

During the late 1930s, the Garden Club of Georgia began looking for a suitable location for the Founders' Garden. At the same time, the faculty of the School of Landscape Architecture of the University of Georgia, located in Athens, was trying to find a site for a collection of ornamental plants. The two groups combined their efforts.

In 1938 Professor Hubert Owens presented to the Garden Club of Georgia a faculty proposal suggesting that a two-and-a-half-acre memorial garden be developed on the north end of the University of Georgia campus. Staff and students of the School of Landscape Architecture would be responsible for the design of the gardens and would supervise the actual construction and installation of plant material. In addition the university would be responsible for perpetual care of the gardens. In return the Garden Club of Georgia would furnish the funds necessary for the project.

The Founders' Memorial Garden is not simply a living tribute to the women who first formed the Ladies' Garden Club of Athens; it also serves as a demonstration garden showing visitors and students ornamental plants that thrive in the Piedmont Region of Georgia. What is more, it provides an essential "laboratory" for students of landscape architecture at the University of Georgia.

In January 1940, the Board of the Garden Club of Georgia unanimously approved the project, and work began almost immediately. In addition to the garden area the site included a former faculty residence, a kitchen building, and a smokehouse. By 1964 these additional buildings were also used by the Garden Club of Georgia as their headquarters and museum.

The garden site contained many mature oak trees with a smattering of understory trees such as dogwoods and redbuds. These trees were incorporated into the design, aided by pruning. Smaller ornamental trees and shrubs were also planted. In addition, the design called for annuals, perennials, vines, and bulbs.

The year 1941 saw the completion of a white picket fence enclosing the boxwood garden, a gravel terrace area, and a serpentine brick wall surrounding the perennial garden. With the advent of World War II, all work on the garden ceased; when the project resumed in 1945, the plans included a small section dedicated to the sons and daughters of garden club members who had served in the war.

By 1951 the project was completed. The National Council of State Garden Clubs gave their Silver Medal Award to the Garden Club of Georgia in recognition of this outstanding garden. In 1954, to celebrate its twenty-fifth anniversary, the National Council of State Garden Clubs presented the Founder's Memorial Garden a sculpture by C. T. Posey. It was installed in the perennial garden.

At the center of the Founders' Garden is a graceful house dating from 1857. Originally a faculty residence, the restored house, along with its kitchen and smokehouse, serves as headquarters for the Garden Club of Georgia, Inc. Directly behind it is a small colonial boxwood garden. Dwarf evergreen hedges are cut and pruned to form clean, geometrical shapes intersected by brick walks. A central bed and garden borders are filled with various annuals appropriate to the season. The entire garden is enclosed by a white picket fence, softened by various climbing vines.

Opposite. Serpentine beds filled with colorful annuals and perennials line the lawn at Founder's Memorial Garden. This statue by C.T. Posey was presented to the Garden by the National Council of State Garden Clubs.

The Society of the Four Arts Garden was begun by the Garden Club of Palm Beach to demonstrate that gardening in south Florida was possible and pleasurable. Stoneware and statuary enhance the beauty of the plantings throughout the garden.

Just outside the gate is a small terrace overlooking a broad lawn surrounded by a serpentine brick wall. The borders of the lawn are planted with dozens of different kinds of perennials and annuals. At the end closest to the boxwood garden, the National Council statue stands against the rich backdrop of vine-encrusted steps and wall. A round pool with a few aquatic plants lies at the opposite end of the lawn. Behind this pool, a screen of living bamboo provides an evergreen backdrop.

On the other side of the boxwood garden is an informal area planted with trees and shrubs. An outstanding camellia collection here is dedicated to Hubert Owens, longtime dean of the School of Landscape Architecture and original landscape designer for Founders' Memorial Garden. The trees in this part of the garden have grown and matured, providing a great deal of shade.

There is plenty of sunlight, however, filtering through the branches, and pockets of sun-loving annuals create exclamation points of color throughout the area. Along the borders ferns, hostas, and impatiens form the backbone of this garden. Stone walks meander gracefully through the area, and steps lead to an upper level, a stone wall providing support for the necessary terracing. Rhododendrons and azaleas bring subtle color to this shaded garden during spring months.

Here, beside a small pool and fountain, is the inscription dedicated to those who served in World War II. A bronze plaque reads, TO THOSE WHO GAVE MUCH AND TO THOSE WHO GAVE ALL.

Garden Clubs are important organizations in almost every community in our country. Their members display a dedication to education, a love of gardening, and a determination to be good stewards of our natural world. Garden clubs enrich our lives in countless ways.

The Founders' Memorial Garden is a beautiful tribute to those women who created the first garden club. We are much indebted to their leadership, their inspiration, and their dedication.

FOUR ARTS GARDEN

The gardens at the Society of the Four Arts in Palm Beach, Florida, combine to weave a delightful tapestry—a landscape spanning the four corners of the earth and the moon itself.

In 1938, in an effort to show homeowners and gardeners what could be grown successfully in southern Florida, the Garden Club of Palm Beach planted seven small demonstration gardens. The result was stupendous. The seven distinct original areas within the Four Arts Garden complex included a moonlight garden, Chinese garden, jungle garden, Spanish façade garden, tropical fruit garden, rose garden, and British colonial garden. Today each of these gardens has a unique personality and aura, but each flows into the other to create a landscape of delight.

In spite of southern Florida's hot and humid climate, ravaging hurricanes and storms, and the challenge of having to use unfamiliar plant material, the transplanted ladies of the Palm Beach Garden Club were able to plant and maintain gardens that are still a beauty to behold, and still serve as model gardens for the community.

When the ladies of the Palm Beach Garden Club first began their gardening project, they were assured that it was impossible to grow roses in the southern Florida climate. They were determined to try, however, and the rose garden directly behind the Four Arts Library is testimony to their success. Two large beds are filled to bursting with roses of every hue. Thriving in spite of the heat, these roses add year-round color and beauty to the garden.

Across a patio from the roses are neat brick-lined squares filled to capacity with various herbs. The air is scented with the piny odor of rosemary and the sweet-spicy scent of basil. Other beds hold mint, thyme, parsley, and chives.

Large terra-cotta and stone pots, strategically placed around the perimeter of the patio, are filled with bright pink hibiscus and blue plumbago. Opposite the

A porphyry marble well head atop the mount was made into a fountain.

herb beds is a large bronze statue whose dark form shows beautifully against the white walls of the garden. The statue is of a young woman holding a child who is reaching for a frog. It adds a delightful sense of play to the garden.

At the end of the patio and rose garden area, the large, round moon-gate allows a tantalizing peek inside the Chinese garden. The elaborate ironwork in the gate is softened by Florida ferns, which grow and tumble over the base of the gate.

Over the entrance to the Chinese garden are the characters meaning "Happiness and Harmony." A plaque on the side wall of the garden describes the Chinese concept of a garden:

> To the Chinese the making of a garden is the effort of the individual to attain unity with the universe. In its inception the garden was a retreat. In China it was essentially an aid to contemplation.
>
> Exalted by beauty, lulled by its harmony the Chinese was able to comprehend truths beyond ordinary perception. A quiet space in which one found relief from tension.
>
> In the design for contentment which is the basis of Chinese philosophy, every individual possesses that which in his own mind is a garden.
>
> The Chinese feel that unless a man has a garden, he scarcely grasps the reason for existence.

The Chinese garden at the Society of the Four Arts is composed of a small pond surrounded by ferns, moss, and grasses. Impressive planning and attention to detail is evident in this garden. Great attempts have been made to make it appear as authentic as possible, not only adhering to Chinese design philosophies, but also incorporating the kinds of plants, stones, and statuary that would be found in the Orient. Water lilies add a touch of color to the black stillness of the pond. Many of the plants are Florida's answer to ori-

ental horticulture. For example, instead of locust, which is traditionally used in China, the Four Arts Garden has used red sandalwood. Podocarpus has replaced willow, and black olive is used instead of cedar.

Other plants are of Chinese origin but also grow in this climate. Many of these are rich in symbolism and meaning. Gardenias are symbolic of charm and grace, orchids of culture and nobility. The pomegranate means self-renewal.

The statuary, also, is symbolic. The four ancient Foo dogs are cast in the role of temple guard dogs. The male dog covers the world with his paw, and the female covers and protects her pups with her paw. Other statues of antique origin lend a feeling of authenticity to the garden.

Although the entire garden is enclosed by a high white wall, red-and-black-lacquered windows give the visitor the feeling of truly being in an outdoor room. Moss-covered stones are strategically placed throughout the garden, lending a sense of stability and permanence to this tranquil place.

Leaving the Chinese garden, the visitor comes into an open area, surrounded on three sides by a crescent-shaped bench of white stone that looks like a sliver of the moon. Surrounding the bench are lush tropical palms. Giant crinum lilies with stark white blossoms and fragrant ginger lilies are found behind the bench. A profusion of emerald ferns creates a delicate green background for the white blossoms. This is the moonlight garden.

The idea of a moonlight garden is not a new one. In 1639 the Mogul emperor Jahan built a moonlight garden in Delhi, India. He used fragrant white flowers such as jasmine, narcissus, tuberoses, and lilies.

The moonlight garden at the Society of the Four Arts is planted along the same ideas, and some of the same kinds of plants have been used. Traditionally the flowers within a moon garden are white, reflecting moonlight to perfection and seeming to emanate light themselves. Many of the lighter-colored flowering

Opposite. The ladies of the Palm Beach Garden Club succeeded not only in creating an opportunity for education but also a place of beauty.

plants have a sweet, heavy fragrance that attracts night-flying moths and insects. This fragrance adds greatly to the pleasure of visiting such gardens at night.

Daytime visitors to this moonlight garden are not forgotten, however, for two beautiful wooden bird-houses hang from elaborately carved hooks on each side of the center of the garden.

When the visitor enters the jungle garden, he is instantly surrounded by lush, tropical growth. The garden is crowded with blossoms usually seen only in the confines of a pot sitting in a sunny window. Different varieties of begonias and prayer plants look strangely out of place in this unaccustomed freedom. Ponytail palms, heliconia, and bromeliads complete a picture that, but for the lack of a boat, might resemble the setting for *The African Queen*.

A small dark pool is nearly hidden by palm and bamboo foliage. Bright pink caladiums, growing side by side with ferns of every shape and size, make spots of color. Maidenhair ferns grow in great profusion, adding delicate texture to this diverse and exciting garden.

The jungle garden is effective in showing the variety and number of tropical plants that can be used by the gardener. It opens the doors for new ideas in using familiar and unfamiliar plants in a natural setting.

The Spanish influence in Florida is evident in almost all parts of the state. At the Four Arts Garden, the Spanish influence is seen in the façade of a Spanish house, which includes the front door and a window complete with ornate ironwork. A beautifully elaborate blue-and-yellow tile bench and a small well nestled in the stone patio area complete the picture.

The plants used in this area are not necessarily of Spanish origin, but were selected to complement the color scheme. Behind the bench, the speckled leaves of yellow aucuba offer a glimpse of interesting foliage. Lady-of-the-Night (*Brunfelsia*) has bright yellow blossoms that gracefully complement the yellow tiles. Blue colors come from the blue birdvine on the wall, and allamanda, which droops gracefully from a blue tile planter.

The wishing well in the center is completely covered with creeping fig, and a pot of bright red impatiens hangs cheerfully from an ornate iron arch above the well.

Perhaps one of the most useful of all the demonstration gardens at the Four Arts is the tropical fruit garden. Many gardeners are interested in growing tropical fruits—but often find it a problem to include them within the home landscape. The tropical fruit garden provides answers.

At the center of the garden is a huge *Kigelia*, or sausage tree, with conspicuous, elongated sausage-shaped seedpods. These seedpods are inedible. In its native homes (Egypt and tropical Africa), this tree—whose flowers only open at night—is pollinated by bats. This specimen, apparently far from an obliging bat, is pollinated by hand by watchful and enthusiastic volunteer gardeners. This particular tree is now a Town of Palm Beach Historical Specimen Tree, and is legally protected.

The sausage tree is surrounded by lacy tree philodendron. Other trees in this garden include kumquat, zamia, macadamia nut, bottlebrush, and lime.

Another area of interest at the Four Arts Garden is the palm garden, where dozens of species of palms are displayed along with many different kinds of ferns.

The Madonna garden is a small enclosed area with a small round pool and a lovely Madonna fountain. The roof over the fountain is covered with stephanotis. Pink impatiens flank the pool and the moss-covered steps.

The former British colonial garden is now called the central, or fountain, garden. Laid out according to eighteenth-century English design principles, it is symmetrical with a large central square and a pool and fountain. This square is surrounded by walks bordered by neatly clipped hedges.

Beyond the fountain garden is the gate to the garden complex. Barely visible through the elaborate ironwork are whizzing cars, tall buildings, and the everyday world of Palm Beach.

Opposite.
The round moon gate allows the visitor a peek into the Chinese Garden. A plaque in this garden room suggests that "unless a man has a garden, he scarcely grasps the reason for existence."

L a u r a   C .   M a r t i n ' s
S o u t h e r n   G a r d e n s
180

The Spanish
Garden
includes the
facade of a
Spanish house
with its tile roof
and ornate
iron-work.

Opposite. *The
enclosed
Madonna
garden holds a
round pool
brimming with
water lilies. The
moss covered
steps are
flanked with
pink impatiens.
Skyscrapers in
the background
are reminders
that this oasis is
nestled in the
heart of town.*

Laura C. Martin's
Southern Gardens

It is a great tribute to the ladies of the Palm Beach Garden Club that their idea of creating gardens for the community has blossomed and grown from dream to reality. The gardens add not only to our education, but also to our pleasure.

BROOKGREEN

Archer Huntington, founder of Brookgreen Gardens, said that his gardens represented a "quiet joining of hands between science and art." Here in the lush South Carolina coastal area, horticulture and landscape design combine to provide a showcase for more than five hundred pieces of nineteenth– and twentieth–century American sculpture.

The sculptures found in this magnificent garden represent the talent and genius of American sculptors during the last century and up to the present time. The sculptures would create a sensation even if housed in a museum building. Here their appeal is augmented by the beauty and grace of a beautiful botanical garden.

Archer Huntington was married to Anna Hyatt Huntington in 1923. At the time of their marriage, Anna was at the height of her career as one of America's premier sculptors. It was her profession that brought the couple together: Huntington had commissioned Anna to design a medal for William Dean Howells.

Anna Huntington was remarkable in her ability to capture the essence of her subjects. She worked primarily with animals, diligently striving to recreate the shape and tone of the animals that she modeled. Stories of her childhood relate that she would sometimes sit for hours to see how a grazing horse's leg muscles changed when the animal shifted his weight.

The Huntingtons first heard of Brookgreen Plantation in 1929, when they read an advertisement for it. They fell in love with the place, and Archer Huntington bought not only Brookgreen but surrounding land as well. His holdings totaled a little over nine thousand acres.

Archer Huntington had inherited a vast fortune, and he handled it with uncommonly astute business sense. For this reason, he was able to purchase Brookgreen and many works of major American

sculptors. Soon the Huntingtons were on their way to creating a sculpture garden. It would be an excellent place to display Anna's work, as well as the work of other major American sculptors.

The first step in constructing the garden was to define the layout. A winding, openwork brick wall was built to establish boundaries; walks were laid in the shape of a huge butterfly with outspread wings, according to Anna Huntington's design. Many features of the old plantation were used, including some of the original plantings, natural forests, and swamp areas.

The Huntingtons began with great joy to purchase the art for their garden. The guiding principle of selection was one of creativity coupled with a high level of skill in execution. Archer Huntington said at one time, "Art is craftsmanship concealed by its own superiority."

The Huntingtons believed that stone and metal would be the sculpture materials best suited for the garden. The first of Anna's major works to be placed at Brookgreen was her magnificent *Youth Taming the Wild*. A large pool was built at the end of the walk leading from the entrance to the gardens. On each side, longleaf pines beckon one closer. In this pool stands Anna Huntington's rearing horse, with a young man trying to tame its great spirit.

This statue sets the mood for the remainder of the gardens, for just as the young man wants to tame the horse without breaking its spirit, so do the gardener and the artist desire to soften nature without trying to control it.

Today Brookgreen Gardens comprises a large formal garden (Anna Huntington's "butterfly design"), a dogwood garden, a palmetto garden, a memorial garden, and long expanses of lawns, interspersed with statue-bedecked fountains.

Incorporated into the butterfly design is a stunning live oak avenue. These oak trees lined the entrance to the original plantation and are thought to be about 225 years old. At the end of this impressive lane of grand old trees stands one of the most spectacular of all the statues, a gilded bronze of Dionysus by Edward McCartan. Glowing golden in the sunlight, this sculpture serves as a strong focal point for this section of the garden.

The plant material for Dionysus—and for all the sculptures—was chosen carefully with an eye for texture, color, and form. The large brick pedestal on which the statue rests is covered with creeping fig vine, creating a look of permanence and age. Small clipped hedges surround Dionysus, making a living frame for a magnificent picture.

West of this, facing the South Carolina Terrace, is a large pool and fountain built on the site of the original plantation house. This pool serves as a reservoir for water used to fill other pools in the garden. In this pool sits the *Alligator Bender* (1937), by Nathaniel Choate. Several different kinds of water plants grow close to the statue; these tend to soften the strong, muscular lines of the piece. Dark green evergreen foliage forms a permanent backdrop for the pale gray statue.

North of this area is the dogwood garden, which is a fairyland of soft white blossoms in early spring. At the eastern end of this garden is the gallery of small sculpture, in whose niches are miniature beasts, gods, and goddesses, and mortals of every description. A young boy with a kayak paddle stands here, ready for a morning workout. In a nearby pool, *Frog Baby* gurgles with delight as water splashes and sprays around him.

On the other side of the butterfly design is the old kitchen, dating from plantation days, and a series of pools, grassy lawns, and fountains. A large rectangular pool is home to the Fountain of the Muses, a series of five upright statues surrounded by three additional sculptures at the back of the pool. Variegated privet and tall, graceful plumes of pampas grass form the perfect backdrop for this series. Facing the Fountain of the Muses is a stark white Pegasus, the largest piece of sculpture in the garden. The work of Laura Gardin Fraser, it was carved on the site, requiring four years to complete.

Left. *The purpose of Brookgreen Gardens, as stated in its constitution, is to "exhibit the flora and fauna of South Carolina and objects of art." The gardens today are carefully maintained to meet this purpose.*

The palmetto garden is home to many different kinds of palmettoes, most of which are native to this part of South Carolina. Spiky palmetto leaves contrast sharply with the smooth, rounded curves in the figure of a young girl.

While the classics are well represented with many statues of mythical figures, native subjects are also represented. Native Americans and the West were tremendous influences on American sculptors, and much of this influence is well represented at Brookgreen. Frederic Remington's well-known *Bronco Buster* is here, as well as James Earle Fraser's *End of the Trail*, symbolizing the passage of the Indian way of life.

Everywhere the size, texture, and kind of vegetation chosen for the gardens beautifully match the sculptures. Like a finely tuned orchestra, these elements work together to create a visual harmony.

Sea Scape, a limestone statue by Herbert Adams, is framed by bright pink azaleas in early spring. Fig vine, symbol of immortal life, creates a rich backdrop for *Benediction*, a magnificent bronze statue of a blessed angel done by Daniel Chester French in 1919.

Although Brookgreen teems with visual pleasures, the sounds also delight. Visitors often find themselves speaking in hushed tones, as if in a church or a cathedral. The muted sounds of water splashing in the pools and fountains blend quietly with the gentle flow of water from the marsh. The call of the marsh hen adds a soprano voice, which is joined by the deep bass of the bullfrog.

It is easy at Brookgreen to allow the boundaries of magic and reality to blend a little. The statues are frozen moments of time—nature captured in bronze or stone. Our admiration extends not only to the sculptures, but also to the intricate perfection of nature.

It becomes difficult to determine what is real and what is created by the hand of some artistic genius. The sculptures are so magical that it's easy to imagine that they can move or create music. And soon there are more questions than answers. Is that egret in the marsh real, or a statue? Is that the sound of Pan's flute? Or merely a soft cry from a passing shorebird? There, in the distance, is that couple standing hand-in-hand a statue, or are they merely transfixed, momentarily turned to stone by the magic of Brookgreen Gardens?

{8}

Modern Gardens, 1940-Present

*A*merica has often been called the melting pot of the world. The same can be said of the development of garden design in this country—it reflects the varied tastes and skills of our diverse population.

From the very beginning the American South was influenced by people from every corner of the world. They came from France, Ireland, England, Spain, Italy, and Scotland. They came from Africa and Barbados, from China and Japan. And they learned from each other.

They planted camellias from Japan, ginger lilies from Africa, ginkgo trees from China, and boxwood from England. They built mounts and allees like the ones they had seen in France, and included grand vistas and small groves of trees like the ones that had inspired them in England. They put in Italian fountains and oriental bonsai. Each element added to our understanding of what a garden is.

The gardens we build today reflect what we love best. George Morikami built a Japanese garden in Florida in the hope that this would help Americans better understand his native land. Today thousands of schoolchildren and other visitors come to admire the garden's stark simplicity.

Ryan Gainey has taken the best from the past and mixed it masterfully with the best of the present to create an incomparable southern cottage garden. It is the garden of our grandparents and the garden of our children. It is the fairytale garden of our dreams, dripping with blossoms of every hue, heavily scented with the fragrance of a thousand flowers.

Dick Pope transformed a murky swamp into a botanical playground that he called Cypress Gardens. Today huge topiary creatures lend a sense of magic to this beautiful garden in spring while thousands of poinsettias change the winter landscape from green to red during the Christmas season.

It is the Gardens for Peace, however, that may represent the garden of the future. Gardens for Peace is a network of gardens whose purpose is to promote gardens as symbols of peace and understanding. It is hoped that these gardens will provide an environment where people can come and contemplate or meditate and enjoy the quiet solitude of nature.

Page 192.
Unexpected but beautiful, a waterfall tumbles into a dark pool in southern Florida's Morikami Garden. This Japanese garden skillfully uses tropical plants to illustrate an Oriental style. Water and rocks are both important elements in the garden.

Page 193.
Called the Water-ski capital of the world, Cypress Gardens has presented water skiing shows since the summer of 1942. Dick Pope holds the honor of being the world's first barefoot water skier.

Left. *A glossy black arched bridge gracefully spans dark, still waters at Morikami Gardens. The museum building, garden architecture, and plant material blend to create an oriental aura.*

Below. *George Morikami (at right), founder of the Gardens, came to the United States in 1906 as part of the Yamoto community. The members were to establish a farming community to grow silk, tea, tobacco, pineapple, and rice.*

It has been said that we will only understand what we see, and only care for what we understand. In the garden we might finally find our salvation, not only individually, but as a global community; for it is in a garden that we begin to see the astounding beauty and diversity of nature, and in seeing to understand.

MORIKAMI GARDENS

The hot, flat landscape of southern Florida is filled with scrub pine and sand. Mosquitoes hum and swarm, waiting for prey. Birds cry and call, seemingly unimpressed by the heat of the sun. Little seems to break the monotony of this scene. When a gracefully arched black bridge suddenly interrupts the barren landscape, one has to stop, shake one's head, and wonder if it is mirage or reality that greets the eyes.

Closer inspection assures the visitor that this is not the result of sunstroke, not a figment of the imagination, but the entrance to an unusual and lovely place, Morikami Gardens in Delray Beach, Florida. Located nearly an hour north of Miami, Morikami Gardens was made possible by the generosity of a Japanese gentleman who made his home in southern Florida at the turn of the century.

George Sukeji Morikami came to the United States in 1906 with other Japanese farmers as part of the Yamato community, a Japanese colony established through the dreams and visions of an American-educated expatriate, Jo Sakai. It was the intention of Sakai and the purpose of the colony to develop a Japanese farming community, and to grow silk, tea, tobacco, pineapples, and rice.

The original visions of the community never came to fruition. One after another, these enterprising Japanese met with disappointment and disaster. A few colonists were killed by a typhoid epidemic. Others lost money in a pineapple blight in 1908. Still others, trying to make a living by growing tea, silk, and tobacco, found theirs an impossible task in the southern Florida climate. Most of the Japanese settlers became disillusioned and returned home. George Morikami

Above.
A tsukubai is found just outside a structure holding the bonsai collection. Japanese custom dictates that visitors wash their hands before entering a building.

Right. *Basic to the design of a Japanese garden is a quiet stillness and a reverence for nature. A single tree can be the focal point for an entire area.*

probably would have been among these, but he lacked the funds for a return voyage. He stayed, and the Yamato colony, through his generosity, has had a beneficial and lasting effect on southern Florida.

Morikami stayed with the colony until it finally disbanded in 1942. At the age of nineteen, he found himself virtually alone in a strange country. He had no money and could not even speak the local language. Determined to get a formal education, Morikami enrolled in the local elementary school to learn to read and speak English. While he attended school with the local children, Morikami rented a small piece of land and began to grow vegetables to sell at the market.

Perseverance, frugal living, and shrewd real-estate purchases finally paid off. When Morikami reached the age of eighty-nine, he was a wealthy man desirous of doing something to pay back his adopted country for the opportunities it had given him. He decided to give land, designated for a park and garden. This area is now called Morikami Park. Before his death in 1976, Morikami donated a generous two hundred acres to Palm Beach County.

Today Morikami Gardens presents an unexpected but authentic reproduction of a Japanese garden in the southern Florida landscape. The climate of Delray Beach and Tokyo are literally worlds apart, so the planners and planters of Morikami adapted Florida plants to a Japanese design. The result is pleasing to the eye and a balm for the soul.

At the center of the garden is the Morikami Museum, whose exhibits show aspects of everyday Japanese life, pictures and stories of the first Yamato colony, and examples of various Japanese-style fine arts.

The museum building is surrounded on all sides by a veranda. In the center of the building is a court-yard garden, with a wide expanse of raked sand and a few plants and rocks. The very scarcity of plants causes one to stop to examine the ones that are there. The sun creates sharp shadows against the clean white sand, and every detail of the plants can be enjoyed in shadow as well as in shade.

In keeping with the Japanese idea that a building and the land around it should present an uninterrupted unity, the gardens were developed at the same time that the museum was built.

Basic to the concept of Japanese garden design is a feeling of peace and stillness, and a reverence for nature. Although color from blooming plants often adds interesting emphasis, the basis of the garden is form and pattern created by evergreens, water, and rocks.

Like many Japanese gardens, Morikami is a garden of green and black with exclamation points of color. Dark, still pools reflect strong lines and myriad forms of trees and shrubs. Water is everywhere, tumbling over rocks in a rare Florida waterfall, in lakes and ponds, and in a canal surrounding the museum, which serves as a boundary between the Florida brush and the intricate and delicate designs of the garden.

Morikami is not a garden that will overwhelm with grandeur and color. It is a garden, instead, that invites the visitor to sit and study, to take time and discover the beauty of the understated and the joy of the tranquil.

A tour of the gardens begins on the cleanly raked paths. The first of these paths leads to the Bonsai Memorial Garden, at whose entrance is a *tsukubai* where clear, cold water slowly flows out of a bamboo pipe. A *tsukubai* is a common sight in Japan, where custom dictates that a visitor wash his hands before entering a home.

Within the ordinary bamboo walls of this open-air structure are some very extraordinary plants. Bonsai is the art of growing dwarf potted plants by using specialized pruning and wiring methods. These twisted miniature trees and shrubs seem like wizened old men bent with age; their cultivation embodies the ancient Japanese spirit of patience and perseverance. An entire grove of maple trees is grown in a pot measuring only three feet long, the slender trunks and tiny leaves as perfect as those of their ordinary-size cousins.

The path winds out of the bonsai garden and continues around the museum, skipping in and out of plants native to countries all over the world. Indigenous Florida cattails stand beside exotic Egyptian papyrus. A zigzag bridge spans the distance over the water; one Japanese tradition says that demons can only run in a straight line. A bridge with turns and curves will stop a demon's progress.

Underneath the bridge, fat koi fish swim lazily. Fed by a multitude of children who visit the garden, the fish seem almost too fat to swim. Across the water is a hillside studded with palms and ferns of all shapes and kinds. Water tumbles over the rocks onto a miniature black beach below, spilling into a pool filled with still, black water.

Leaves from the seagrape tree fall into the water, going nowhere. On the banks of the pond, old and new bamboo spring forth from the same clump. Brown, brittle leaves from last year give way to the supple young green shoots of the new growing season.

Outside the garden proper, paths lead to the nature trail, a less formal but equally beautiful part of the garden compound. At the head of the trail, a Japanese haiku sets the mood for a quiet visit.

How cool the breeze
the sky is filled with voices
pine and cedar trees.

Just past the memorials for George Morikami and the Oki family, who were also a part of the original colony, other memorials can be found. One recent addition was a large stone lantern donated in memory of the crew of the space shuttle *Challenger*.

A small enclosed garden along the nature trail adds a bit of formal beauty to the unstructured garden beyond. Pink azaleas grow beside large hollow stones filled with water. Raked paths give a feeling of order and neatness. Strangely shaped rocks convey a feeling of the unknown and the unknowable.

This garden spot is filled with a union of opposites. Hard rocks create a backdrop for soft, delicate

Opposite.
Bonsai is the art of growing dwarf potted trees and shrubs using special wiring and pruning techniques. The bonsai collection here holds intricate forms of tiny trees.

The bungalow where Ryan Gainey has created his own version of the Garden of Eden had a stark landscape devoid of flowers in 1915.

blossoms. Sharply angled branches throw shadows on the gentle curves on the path. Sunshine plays hide-and-seek in the shadows, a black-and-white portrait in the garden.

Here Japan seems much closer than a half a world away. The garden has a miraculous way of reminding us that we are a global community, that the peace and tranquility found in this bit of Japan can also be found in that island nation so far away.

LE JARDIN DES FLEURS

Anyone who is going to be a gardener does so for self-expression. We were expelled from the Garden of Eden and we spend our entire lives trying to recreate it.

—Ryan Gainey

Looking around Ryan Gainey's garden it is easy to understand why he gets philosophical about his plants. Visiting this garden is almost a religious experience. For flower lovers, the vibrant hues of the multitude of blossoms make it sheer heaven. For the more sophisticated landscape design student, Gainey's use of color and incorporation of garden ornaments makes it an exciting, unusual, yet surprisingly familiar landscape.

Le Jardin des Fleurs began in 1981, when Gainey bought a small bungalow and three lots in Decatur,

Georgia. The land was the former location of an early twentieth-century nursery. Using some of what was already there, adding much skill and knowledge of plants and garden design, and polishing it all off with legendary imagination and flair, Gainey has created one of the South's most beautiful private gardens.

It is, in his words, a southern cottage garden and, more importantly, an American garden. Here are influences from all over the world, and from many stages of garden history. Flowers from his native South are planted in ways that remind him of his travels throughout the world.

Ryan Gainey now owns several successful gardening shops in the Atlanta area. He is not native to the city, however, but to the small town of Hartsville, South Carolina. His childhood garden consisted of a dirt yard swept with dogwood switches, three chinaberry trees, cannas outside the back door, and a flat trellis covered with kudzu vine. Because both his parents were from rural farming families, more emphasis was placed on the family's large vegetable garden than on the smattering of ornamental plants around the house.

Gainey gives credit to three ladies in his cotton-farming community for his love of flowers. It was largely due to their influence that he turned down an art scholarship to go to Clemson University and study horticulture.

Though Gainey gained formal training at Clemson, this was only one of many influences contributing to his ideas of gardening and design. Perhaps one of the greatest influences was a visit to Giverny, the famous retreat and garden refuge of Claude Monet. Many horticulturists feel that Monet's gardens were as magnificent as his paintings. While Gainey was at Giverny, he absorbed many ideas of the great Impressionist artist.

Gainey visited Giverny in the fall when there was a great exuberance of color. He made careful notes and added to a list of plants and flowers that had a special meaning for him. When he returned home, he began incorporating many of these ideas into his own garden.

Opposite. Creatures of the garden are not neglected at Le Jardin des Fleurs. A bright pink azalea standard stands at the entranceway to a collection of elaborately painted birdhouses.

Other influences also came from Europe. Peter Coat's book *Gardens for Connoisseurs* was important to him, as was Rosemary Verey's work.

Although Europe may have influenced Gainey's ideas of design, it was the flowers of his homeland that tugged at his heart. In his own words, he began "to *see*" the flowers along the roadsides and in abandoned homes and gardens.

With this new insight, Ryan Gainey began to collect southern plants. Some of these were old-fashioned varieties, long gone from the current catalogs. Others were native plants, blooming in quiet beauty along the roadsides. Everywhere he went, he dug plants from ditches and fields, or begged or traded for seeds, cuttings, or plants of hundreds of different varieties.

Much of what he brought home he included in his own garden. Much more of it went to friends and fellow flower enthusiasts. Due to his efforts, many old-fashioned varieties that would have been lost are now thriving.

"It is an experience of learning," Gainey says. "You see something in bloom and fall in love with it and that's what you end up with."

Ryan Gainey's southern cottage garden is a cornucopia of colors and textures, ideas, humor, and philosophy. Traditionally a cottage garden is found in the front of a house—and usually the house is rather modest and informal, the yard fenced to keep out livestock.

A cottage garden is generally made up of many different kinds of plants—perennials, annuals, bulbs, shrubs, roses, herbs, and vines, and even an occasional vegetable patch.

Ryan Gainey has all these elements in his cottage garden. The house can best be described as a bungalow—small but full of personality. Along the sidewalk in front of the house stretches a length of fence, covered with vines, and an arbor covered with the climbing form of 'The Fairy' rose.

The three original lots are now combined to present a series of gardens, each of which presents a different vignette and creates a slightly different aura.

Just to the right of the house is a small, elegant garden room. The gate and fence surrounding this first little garden are made from twigs and branches and the garden itself is a simple circle bordered by white impatiens, begonias, and purple phlox. Upon entering the garden, the visitor at once feels at home. A small sign to the right, saying "Please Come In," makes this hospitality perfectly clear.

Leave this garden, pass under an eleagnus arbor, and you are on your way to the greenhouses. Three are left over from the turn-of-the-century nursery originally found on the property. Along this stone path, a wrought-iron Victorian birdhouse stands fifteen feet above the garden, and wind chimes catch the breeze.

In one direction, the plants are huge and exuberant; in another direction they are diminutive and fragile.

"The garden should be simple, natural and beautiful," Gainey says. "It is our opportunity to manipulate and embrace nature simultaneously."

His manipulation of his garden is masterly.

There is beauty everywhere. Much of it is traditional beauty. A picket fence is bordered by old-fashioned phlox, cleome, and other annuals. Rosebushes trained into standards, surrounded by dwarf clipped hedges, create a pattern in the vegetable garden. Beautiful old coping stones surround a quiet circle of grass.

But much of the beauty found in this garden is spontaneous, innovative, and exciting. Birdhouses are

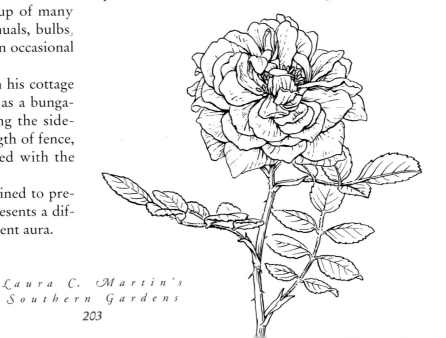

Old-fashioned Rose (Rosa rugosa)

found everywhere and come in every shape, size, and form imaginable. A miniature white church stands close to a small green cottage complete with chimney—all ready for feathered friends. Close to the birdhouses stands a poet's cupboard painted in purples and blues that states:

I gaze upon the garden
My heart grows peaceful still
From its color comes my being
From its spirit comes my will.

Everywhere in this garden is personality—the soul or spirit of the garden which, according to Gainey, is so critical to the creation of any garden. His advice to other gardeners? "Don't change anything too much, for the garden itself has a soul. Move plants around but don't throw them out, for everything has a spirit."

Toward the entrance to the garden is a large blue gazing ball that reflects the entire garden on its shiny surface. Gaze into this crystal ball of the garden and you will see the past in every color of the rainbow. Antique roses, grandma's hollyhocks, and old-fashioned phlox all combine to give you a sense of the beauty of the garden in days gone by.

Look again and you will see the future, for in the garden the future builds on the past. The gardens of tomorrow will be planted with the flowers of yesterday and today. It is easy to see the spirit of the garden

in this crystal ball and to know that this is the tie that binds gardeners from past and future from all parts of the world.

CYPRESS GARDENS

If it ain't fun, then the heck with it!
—Dick Pope

Dick Pope, Sr., was a flamboyant publicity man who moved to Florida from Iowa. Originally a real estate salesman, Pope was hit hard by economic disaster in the mid-1920s. In looking around for another means of supporting himself, Pope heard that Johnson Motors was interested in launching a big publicity campaign from the company headquarters in Waukegan, Illinois. Pope immediately left for Waukegan, stopping at every major city along the way to wire the company president to "hold all publicity plans until I get there." Not surprisingly, this gregarious and assertive man got the job.

Dick Pope put to use an equal amount of enthusiasm and aggressive spirit to form Cypress Gardens. In 1931 he joined the Lake Region Canal Commission near Winter Haven, Florida. Using his persuasive skills, he convinced the group to put up $2,800 to drain a large swamp on the shores of Lake Eloise.

The locals and the Canal Commission soon became disenchanted with the project and called Pope such names as the "Swami of the Swamp" and the "Maestro of the Muck." Because they wanted to abandon the project, Pope was faced with a tough decision. He could either invest his own funds and continue with his dreams of creating a garden out of the swamp, or he could give it all up and turn to something else to earn a living.

Family legend says that Dick and his wife, Julie, flipped a coin to decide their future. Fortunately for all of us, the coin landed "heads," and Dick Pope continued work on the project as a private investment. To start, he payed back the Canal Commission and hired forty day laborers at one dollar per day each. Always

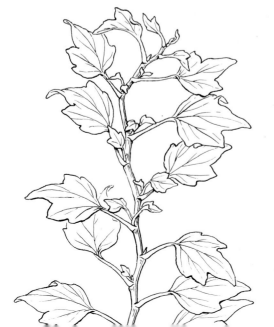

*English Ivy
(Hedera helix)*

Ninety percent of all plants grown at Cypress Gardens are native to tropical or subtropical areas. This tumbling waterfall gives the visitor the feeling of being in the tropics.

with an eye on publicity, Pope designed the gardens using a camera viewfinder to establish one of the most beautiful and photographic spots in the world.

Cypress Gardens opened on January 2, 1936. To publicize the gardens, which were located miles from a major city, Dick employed some fairly innovative marketing techniques. He had seven full-time photographers take hundreds of pictures which he sent out all over the country. He established Florida's first flower queen contest and offered to let corporate and advertising agencies shoot publicity photographs at the gardens free of charge. The result was favorable; Cypress Gardens was soon attracting visitors by the thousands from all over the world.

Dick Pope came to gardening and horticulture through a circuitous route. When he first began the garden project, he knew virtually nothing about flowers. One story about Pope tells that when he discovered he did not know how to spell "azalea," he suggested to his secretary that they just call it "flame vine."

While he lacked a background in gardening terms, he certainly had a flair for the advertising business and an ability to attract visitors. Even as a young man he managed to attract attention. He and his

brother Malcolm were the first water stunt men in Florida. Malcolm was the first to jump over obstacles in a motor boat, Dick the first to jump on water skis. In the *Guinness Book of World Records* Dick is featured as the first barefoot water skier.

During the summer of 1942 six soldiers arrived at Cypress Gardens, observed the boats on the lake, and asked when the show was going to begin. Although at this point there had never been a water ski show at Cypress Gardens, Julie Pope, like her husband, disliked missing an opportunity. She quickly answered, "around 3:00 P.M.," picked up her daughters and a few friends from school in Winter Haven, and told them to get ready to put on a water ski show.

The performance was such a success that the soldiers returned the next weekend bringing eight hundred of their friends with them. Ever since, the water ski show has been an exciting attraction of Cypress Gardens. In fact, the gardens are often called the "Water-ski capital of the world."

Although many visitors enjoy the water ski shows, the water skiing competitions, the model railroad exhibit, the performing bird show, and the Kodak tower that stands 153 feet above the gardens, it is the beautiful displays of flowers that attract gardeners by the thousands. The gardens offer a striking blend of color, texture, balance, and composition—all factors that make it a unique and rewarding experience to photograph the floral displays.

As visitors enter the gardens, they are immediately struck with the immaculate cleanliness of this large public park. The walkways are wide and spacious, the grounds manicured to perfection.

The Florida climate is perfect for growing a multitude of tropical plants—many of which other gardeners can only grow during the short summer months. Bougainvillea, bromeliads, orchids, and roses offer spectacular color all year long.

Ninety percent of the plants grown at Cypress Gardens are native to tropical or sub-tropical habitats. The gardens boast over eight thousand varieties of plants originating in seventy-five countries. Although Florida's weather is almost always warm enough to support these plants, there are occasional cold spells that endanger the health of these tropical plants.

Because Cypress Gardens is dependent on its spectacular floral displays, the horticultural staff has made elaborate preparations to ensure the continued health and survival of these plants if inclement weather should occur. The sixteen acres of original gardens, where the most important and beautiful botanical displays are found, are irrigated by an extensive watering system. If frost is predicted, this watering system is used to spray warm water throughout the area, effectively raising the ambient temperature several degrees.

For even colder temperatures, natural gas heaters are used to increase the temperature even more. Some of these heaters are even placed on poles to warm the tops of the tropical trees.

There are many ways to enjoy the botanical displays at Cypress Gardens. A series of walks connects the various types of gardens, or a slow electric boat ride allows a visitor to view the plants from a different perspective.

Within the botanical gardens area are included an Oriental Garden, a French Garden, and an All-American Rose Garden showing more than five hundred of the most popular rose varieties grown in America.

A man-made Mediterranean waterfall creates an unusual but dramatic addition to the flat Florida landscape. An Italian fountain, made with over ten thousand handmade tiles, creates another cool oasis. But the prevalence of gray-green Spanish moss gently swaying in the breeze from a multitude of cypress trees is a constant reminder that this is a garden of the American South.

Sweeping lawns intersect the various floral displays. Here southern belles dressed in long hoop skirts welcome you to the shade of a white gazebo or will oblige the enthusiastic photographer with a smiling pose.

Although the flower display at Cypress Gardens is impressive every day of the year, the gardens now sponsor three annual floral festivals.

The Spring Flower Festival lasts from mid-

Pages 208–209. Glorious beasts such as this finely petaled peacock grace the grounds at Cypress Gardens during the Spring Flower Festival.

Cypress Gardens grows over eight thousand varieties of plants. The warm Florida climate makes it possible to have outstanding horticultural displays throughout the year.

Ducks and rabbits stuffed with plants such as begonias form creatures beloved by children and adults. In addition to floral displays, Cypress also offers a model railroad, a bird show, and the 153-foot Kodak tower.

March to mid-May. During this time, huge topiary figures are featured. Dominating the festival, these oversize blooming creatures are shaped like swans, ducks, peacocks, rabbits, and other animals. During this time over one hundred fifty thousand spring annuals, such as pansies, impatiens, and begonias are on display.

Beginning in November the gardens are dressed up with over two million chrysanthemum blooms for the Chrysanthemum Festival. These beautiful plants are found in topiaries, hanging baskets, and cascading over rocks, waterfalls, and walls. One of the most exciting of all displays is the chrysanthemum archway that visitors walk through at the entrance to the gardens.

The Poinsettia Festival celebrates the holiday season by transforming Cypress Gardens into a wonderland of color. Over thirty thousand poinsettia blooms cascade down waterfalls or are carefully placed to create huge living trees. Blossoms are found in pink, red, and creamy white. The Poinsettia Festival lasts from mid-December until mid-January.

Strolling through Cypress Gardens, the visitor is often reminded of Dick Pope's basic philosophy—"If it ain't fun, then the heck with it." His sense of fun, his genius for publicity, and his flair for the beautiful have provided us with a garden that delights and amazes the young and old alike.

GARDENS FOR PEACE

Gardens are a union of plants and people. The selection of plants used and how people have arranged these plants varies from location to location and even from one time period to another. But the basic concept of a garden never varies. It is a place of beauty, a spot where people can enjoy the wonders of the natural world in peace and solitude.

Gardens for Peace is an international organization founded in 1984 by Atlanta native Laura Dorsey Rains. Its primary purpose is to promote worldwide peace by recognizing and promoting gardens around the world as symbols of peace. The organization's stated mission is "to identify and link established gardens throughout the world where contemplation and meditation by individuals and communities will foster respect for the environment and a climate for peace among all peoples."

Ms. Rains grew up in Atlanta, and it was here that she first began to love plants and gardens. But it was far from her home in Atlanta that she first envisioned creating a network of gardens. During the Vietnam War her husband, who had been wounded in combat, was taken to a hospital in Japan, and Ms. Rains traveled there to care for him. During her three-month stay in Japan, she often went to Japanese gardens to enjoy a few moments of peace and solitude. These visits to the gardens became an important part of her stay in Japan. After she returned home, the memories of the peaceful feelings she experienced in these gardens caused her to realize how important a garden was for personal meditation and reflection.

Later, as she walked through gardens in England, she also came to the conclusion that although gardens in different parts of the world may not look the same, they all offer the same oasis of quiet stillness. She realized that the feelings of peace we get from gardens transcend world conflict.

Ms. Rains began dreaming of a network of gardens whose primary purpose would be to promote world peace. Transforming her ideas from dreams to reality took much work and effort, but with the help of her mother, Laura Whitner Dorsey, and her friends and business acquaintances, the concept of Gardens for Peace became an actuality.

The Swan Woods Trail at the Atlanta History Center was chosen as the first garden in the network. In the fall of 1987, the site was shown to a group of visitors from Atlanta's sister city Tbilisi, in Georgia (of the former U.S.S.R.). The visitors were so impressed with the concept of Gardens for Peace that they offered their help. It was suggested that Tbilisi be the site for the second garden in the network.

One of the visitors, a well-known artist, offered to design and donate a sculpture interpreting the Gardens for Peace logo. The logo, which was recognized for excellence in the 1987 Print's Regional Design Annual, shows a tree whose leaves become a bird in flight.

On April 22, 1988, the Swan Woods Trail was dedicated as the first garden in the international network. The lifesize bronze sculpture from the Soviet Union, *The Peace Tree*, was installed on September 24, 1989. Laura Rains said of this statue, "*The Peace Tree* represents a symbol for the future and challenges us as a global community to discover and claim peace as we unite gardens around the world."

The sculpture is a combination of the Gardens for Peace logo and a logo used at a Friendship Force meeting in 1987. It is composed of five lifesize figures holding hands around a fourteen-foot tree. Nearby is a bronze plaque commemorating the dedication.

The Swan Woods Trail is located just minutes from downtown Atlanta. At the entrance to the gardens the visitor can look through the trees and see nearby skyscrapers and hear the dull roar of never-ending traffic.

But once the visitor begins to walk on the trail, city sounds and city tensions and pressures slip away as if by magic. The Swan Woods Trail is located behind the historic Swan House on the grounds of the Atlanta History Center. The trail winds through ten acres of woodlands and has been developed as an outdoor laboratory.

Within this garden, many different stages of forest growth are represented. The area has been greatly altered through the years, as is evidenced by many invasive cultivated plants such as English ivy. The upper part of the area is an oak-hickory-pine forest, the lower part, formerly a cotton field, is in a stage of advanced secondary growth with many pines and shrubs.

Native Georgia wildflowers are planted along the trail, including many plants that appear on Georgia's Protective Plant list. Pink lady's slipper, fothergilla, Oconee-Bells, and false hellebore are examples of endangered plants found within the woodland area.

It is by the stream at the bottom of the woodland area where the Gardens for Peace statue is found. It is the most beautiful part of the woodland. Ferns grow along the stream, a rich green canopy intertwines overhead, and a sprinkling of wildflowers add a touch of gay color to this peaceful, almost churchlike spot.

On May 24, 1989, dedication ceremonies were held in Tbilisi, making a garden site in the heart of this city the second in the network. At this time a sculpture designed by Atlanta artist Sergio Dolfi, entitled *Birds*, was unveiled and installed in the garden.

The third garden was dedicated on the grounds of the Royal Botanical Garden in Madrid, Spain, on November 7, 1991. A Spanish sculptor, Julio L. Hernandez, was commissioned to create a sculpture to place in the garden.

The criteria for selecting gardens to be included within the network are clearly spelled out. The Neel Reid Scholarship Fund of the Peachtree Garden Club in Atlanta, Georgia, awarded a research fellowship at the University of Georgia to a British student, Simon Downs. The purpose of the fellowship was to allow Mr. Downs to develop the guidelines for choosing specific areas as Gardens for Peace.

At the end of his studies Simon Downs wrote, "Throughout the history of civilization, man's view of his position in the universe has been expressed through the garden. During much of this history he has been at peace neither with himself, nor with the rest of nature, but has still created gardens as sanctuaries from the rest of the world. The garden has thus become one of the most universal symbols of peace."

Each of the gardens considered for inclusion in the network must be open to the public, although it is understood that some gardens must charge admission to ensure proper maintenance.

Left. The Swan Woods is filled with plants and wildflowers native to the southeast. Bright orange blossoms from the turk's cap lily shine like brilliant jewels against dark green native ferns.

Opposite. The "Peace Tree" installed at the Swan Woods Trail in 1989 is said to be a "symbol for the future and challenges us as a global community to discover and claim peace as we unite gardens throughout the world."

The garden must include familiar patterns of design but also variety or diversity of plant material that ensures the interest of the visitor. Other considerations of design include enclosure—the sense of being protected by a canopy, the use of mystery to draw people into the garden, water, visual stimuli in the form of texture and color, and other stimuli such as sweet or unusual fragrances, bird song, or the sound of running water. The gardens must be a part of, not separate from nature.

Most importantly, the garden must have a feeling of peace and tranquility and it must present an atmosphere of safety and refuge.

The Gardens for Peace organization also sponsors educational programs, through which it hopes to make people of all cultures and nations more aware of the historical and symbolic significance of the garden.

According to Laura Rains, "the founders of Gardens for Peace believe that by promoting the concept of the garden as a place of peace and meditation, the organization will make a contribution to the general social welfare of all and to the elimination of tensions, discrimination and prejudice that are inconsistent with the harmony and peace symbolized by the garden."

Appendices

T he gardens featured in this book present a marvelous opportunity for some interesting trips. Although the gardens described in each chapter are grouped by historical period, they are not necessarily located in the same area. To help plan tours of these gardens, seven trips are suggested. Each tour covers as many gardens as possible in the same general locale. The most outstanding gardens are marked with an asterisk (*). Following these lists, specific travel information about each garden is given alphabetically by state.

1. Georgia and North Carolina

ATLANTA

Ryan Gainey's "Jardin des Fleurs" (only open to public second weekend in May)

Gardens for Peace

PINE MOUNTAIN, GEORGIA *(90 miles south of Atlanta)*

*Callaway Gardens

ATHENS, GEORGIA *(75 miles northeast of Atlanta)*

Founders' Memorial Garden

ASHEVILLE, NORTH CAROLINA *(156 miles north of Athens)*

*Biltmore

2. North Carolina

WINSTON-SALEM

Old Salem

MANTEO *(317 miles east of Winston-Salem)*

*Elizabethan Gardens

NEW BERN *(122 miles south of Manteo)*

Tryon Palace

WILMINGTON *(80 miles south of New Bern)*

Orton Plantation Gardens

3. South Carolina

CHARLESTON

Heyward-Washington House

Magnolia Gardens *(14 miles west of Charleston)*

*Middleton Place

MURRELLS INLET

*Brookgreen *(88 miles north of Charleston)*

4. Tennessee

NASHVILLE

Cheekwood

The Hermitage

MEMPHIS *(219 miles west of Nashville)*

Dixon Gallery and Gardens

5. Florida

MIAMI

*Vizcaya

Fairchild Tropical Garden

DELRAY BEACH *(72 miles north of Miami)*

Morikami Gardens

PALM BEACH *(18 miles north of Delray Beach)*

*Four Arts Garden

TAMPA

Cypress Gardens *(60 miles east of Tampa.)*

6. Mississippi, Louisiana, and Alabama

NATCHEZ, MISSISSIPPI

Elms Court (open only during spring and fall pilgrimages)

Monmouth (open only during spring and fall pilgrimages)

ST. FRANCISVILLE, LOUISIANA *(60 miles south of Natchez)*

Rosedown

*Afton Villa

NEW ORLEANS, LOUISIANA *(160 miles south of St. Francisville)*

*Longue Vue

MOBILE, ALABAMA *(153 miles east of New Orleans)*

Bellingrath Gardens

7. Virginia

WASHINGTON, D.C., AREA

*Dumbarton Oaks

*Mount Vernon

WILLIAMSBURG, VIRGINIA *(164 miles southeast of Washington, D.C.)*

Williamsburg

*Governor's Palace

George Wythe House

Benjamin Waller House

CHARLOTTESVILLE, VIRGINIA *(117 miles west of Williamsburg)*

*Monticello

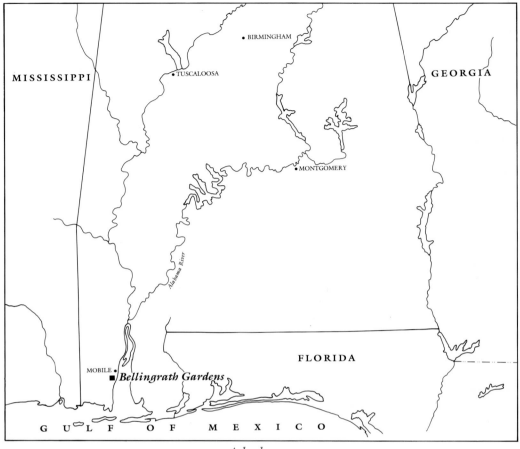

Alabama

Cypress Gardens is a one-hour drive from Tampa or Orlando. For information write Cypress Gardens, P.O. Box 1, Cypress Gardens, FL 33884, or call (800) 237–4826.

Hours
Open daily, 9:00 A.M.–6:00 P.M.

Admission
A fee is charged for adults and children (3–9). Children under 3 admitted free.

Seasonal Displays
Spring: amaryllis, anthuriums, azaleas, Easter lilies, gardenias, golden shower tree, pansies, shrimp plant, spathiphyllum, thunbergia.

Summer: bird-of-paradise, caladiums, bedding plants (marigolds, dusty miller, begonias, impatiens), Canna lily, Crinum lily, hibiscus, mimosa, oleander, water lilies.

Fall: floss silk tree, chrysanthemum, coleus, ginger.

Winter: flame vine, fuchsias, poinsettias, bedding plants (petunias, phlox, salvia, snapdragons, verbena), kapok tree.

Alabama
BELLINGRATH GARDENS
Travel Information
Bellingrath Gardens is located just south of Theodore, Alabama, close to Mobile. For information write Bellingrath Gardens and Home, Theodore, AL 36582, or call (205) 973-2217.

Hours
Gardens open from 7:00 A.M. to one hour before dusk; house open in winter 8:00 A.M.–4:30 P.M.; in summer, 8:00 A.M.–5:30 P.M.

Admission
A fee is charged for admission to the garden for adults, students, and children over 6. Children under 6 admitted free. A fee is charged to all for admission to the house.

Seasonal Displays
Late winter/early spring: camellias, azaleas, daffodils, hyacinths, tulips.

Summer: roses, bedding plants, hydrangea, alamanda, salvia, chenille, copper plants.

Fall: chrysanthemums.

Christmas season: red, pink, and white poinsettias.

Florida
CYPRESS GARDENS
Travel Information
Cypress Gardens is located forty minutes southwest of Walt Disney World off U.S. Route 27 near Winter Haven in central Florida.

FAIRCHILD TROPICAL GARDEN
Travel Information
Fairchild Tropical Garden is located just minutes from downtown Miami, Coral Gables, and South Miami on scenic Old Cutler Road.

L a u r a   C.   M a r t i n' s
S o u t h e r n   G a r d e n s
216

For information write Fairchild Tropical Garden, 10901 Old Cutler Road, Miami, FL 33156, or call (305) 667-1651.

Hours
Open daily, 9:30 A.M.–4:30 P.M. Tram tours leave hourly. Closed Christmas Day.

Admission
A fee is charged for adults. Children 12 and under admitted free when accompanied by an adult.

Seasonal Displays
Fairchild Tropical Garden offers outstanding horticultural displays all year. Among the most exciting plant collections found in the garden are palms, cycads, flowering trees, shrubs, and tropical vines; ficus trees, ground covers, bromeliads, aroids (philodendrons), and Bahamian plants. In addition, the rare plant house is home to many rare and difficult-to-grow tropical plants including rare palms and giant tree ferns, orchids, and bromeliads.

FOUR ARTS GARDEN
Travel Information
The Society of the Four Arts is located in Palm Beach, Florida. For information write the Society of the Four Arts, Four Arts Plaza, Palm Beach, FL 33480, or call (407) 655-7226.

Florida

Hours
Call for current hours.

Admission
No fee.

Seasonal Displays
Year-round: herbs, ferns, orchids, begonias, palms, bromeliads, tropical fruits.

Spring: crinum lily, ginger lilies.

Winter: roses, hibiscus, gardenia, caladiums.

MORIKAMI GARDENS
Travel Information
Morikami Museum and Gardens is located at 4000 Morikami Park Rd., Delray Beach. For information call (407) 495-0233.

Hours
Open Tuesday–Sunday, 10:00 A.M.–5:00 P.M. Closed Mondays, Easter, Thanksgiving, Christmas, and New Year's Day.

Admission
Donation requested.

Seasonal Displays
Florida's tropical climate makes for year-round horticultural displays of bonsai, water lilies, Japanese maples, nandina, carissa, pride-of-Bermuda, clipped junipers, bamboo, podocarpus, and bald cypress.

Spring: trumpet trees, crape myrtle, iris.

Summer: daylilies.

Fall: white ginger, bird-of-paradise.

Winter: camellias.

VIZCAYA
Travel Information
Vizcaya is located just south of the Rickenbacker Causeway in Miami. For information write Vizcaya, 3251 South Miami Avenue, Miami, FL 33129, or call (305) 579-2813.

Hours
Open daily, 9:30 A.M.–4:30 P.M. Closed Christmas.

Admission
A fee is charged for adults, students, children 6 and over, and senior citizens. Children under 6 admitted free.

Seasonal Displays
Throughout the year: bedding plants, evergreen shrubs, ferns, palms.

Georgia
CALLAWAY GARDENS
Travel Information
Callaway Gardens is located on U.S. Route 27 in Pine Mountain, Georgia, 70 miles south of Atlanta. For information, write Callaway Gardens, Pine Mountain, GA 31822, or call (404) 663-5187.

Hours
Open during daylight hours.

Admission
A fee is charged for adults and children (6–11). Children under 6 and members admitted free. An annual membership may be purchased for adults and children.

Seasonal Displays
Spring: wildflowers, azaleas, camellias, magnolias, narcissus, flowering crabapples, oakleaf hydrangeas, annuals, perennials.

Summer: rhododendrons, wildflowers (daisy, black-eyed Susan, coreopsis, butterfly weed), annuals, perennials, crape myrtle, daylilies, plum leaf azalea.

Fall and winter: Chrysanthemums, goldenrod, fall foliage, pansies, holly, nandina, pyracantha.

FOUNDERS' MEMORIAL GARDEN
Travel Information
Founders' Memorial Garden is located at South Lumpkin Street and Bocock Drive, University of Georgia, Athens. For information, write Headquarters Secretary, The Garden Club of Georgia, Inc., The University of Georgia Campus, Athens, GA 30602, or call (404) 542-3631.

Hours
Garden open daily, sunrise to sunset; house open Monday–Friday, 9:00 A.M.– noon and 1:00 P.M.–4:00 P.M. Also by appointment. Closed on holidays.

Admission
No fee.

Seasonal Displays
Spring: tulips and other bulbs, redbud, azaleas, camellias.

Summer: boxwood garden, summer annuals, perennials, magnolia.

Fall: fall foliage, bamboo screen.

GARDENS FOR PEACE
Travel Information
Gardens for Peace—The Swan Woods Trail is located at the Atlanta History Center, 3101 Andrews Drive, NW, Atlanta, GA 30305. Call the center at (404) 261-1837 for holiday hours, ticket prices, tours, lectures, and other educational offerings.

Hours
Open Monday–Saturday, 9:00 A.M.–5:30 P.M.; Sunday, noon–5:00 P.M.

Admission
A fee is charged for adults; children under 6 are admitted free. An annual membership may be purchased for adults and children.

Seasonal Displays
Spring: woodland wildflowers and shrubs (fothergilla, bloodroot, foamflower, green and gold, mayapple, trillium, dwarf crested iris, lady's slipper).

Summer: ferns and meadow flowers (black-eyed Susan, coreopsis, purple coneflower).

Fall: fall foliage, aster, goldenrod, sweet shrub.

Le Jardin des Fleurs
Travel Information
Le Jardin des Fleurs is privately owned but is always included in the "Gardens for Connoisseurs" tour, sponsored each Mother's Day weekend by the Atlanta Botanical Garden. For information call the Atlanta Botanical Garden, (404) 876-5859.

Seasonal Displays
Spring: spring bulbs, sweet blue phlox, roses, flowering shrubs, peonies.

Summer: annuals and perennials, crape myrtles, daylilies, cleome, herbs, hydrangeas, hollyhocks.

Fall: goldenrod, asters, moonvine, fall-flowering shrubs, stone mountain daisy, white and blue ageratum.

Louisiana
Afton Villa
Travel Information
Afton Villa is located on U.S. Route 61, 3 1/2 miles north of St. Francisville, Louisiana. For information write Afton Villa Gardens, 7020 Green Street, New Orleans, LA 70118, or call (504) 861-7365 or (504) 635-6773.

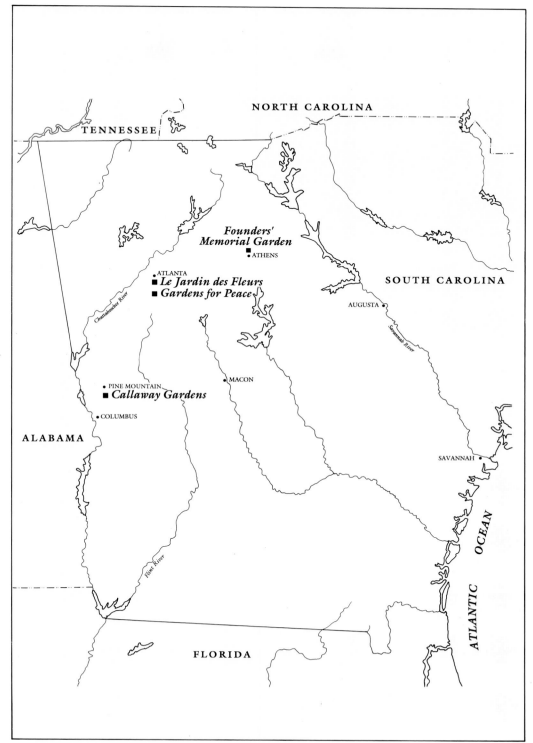

Georgia

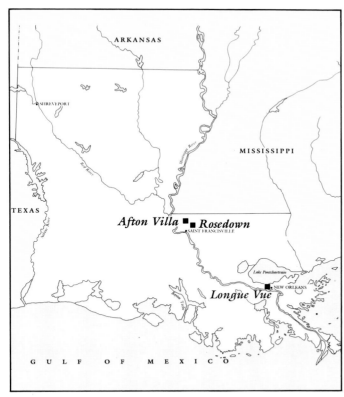

Louisiana

Hours
Open daily, March through June, 9:00 A.M.–4:30 P.M. Closed July through February.

Admission
A fee is charged for adults; children under 12 admitted free.

Seasonal Displays
Spring: bulbs (narcissus, tulips), azaleas, iris, dogwood, hydrangeas, mock orange, wisteria, pansy, blue phlox, gardenia, spring-flowering annuals.

Summer: hosta, caladium, summer bedding plants (begonia, impatiens, mari-gold, penta, loosestrife, salvia, dianthus, vinca).

LONGUE VUE
Travel Information
Longue Vue is located at 7 Bamboo Road, New Orleans, LA 70124; write to this address for information, or call (504) 488-5488.

Hours
Open all year, Monday–Saturday, 10:00 A.M.–4:30 P.M.; Sunday, 1:00 P.M.–5:00 P.M. Closed on major holidays.

Admission
A fee is charged for adults and children.

Seasonal Displays
Spring: azaleas, wildflow-ers, dogwood, Lady Banksia rose, mountain laurel, pansies, red bud, violets.

Summer: bedding plants, lantana, butterfly vine, magnolia, oleander, plumbago, roses.

Fall: begonias, chrysanthe-mums, roses, sansanqua, cassia, hollies.

Winter: camellias, jonquils, ornamental cabbage, poinsettias, sweet olive.

ROSEDOWN
Travel Information
Rosedown Plantation is located in St. Francisville, Louisiana, at the juncture of the Great River Road (U.S. Route 61) and Route 10. For information write Rosedown Plantation and Gardens, P.O. Box 1816, St. Francisville, LA 70775, or call (504) 635-3332.

Hours
Open daily, March through October, 9:00 A.M.–5:00 P.M.; November through February, 10:00 A.M.–4:00 P.M. Closed Christmas Eve and Christmas Day.

Admission
A small fee is charged to help with the upkeep of the plantation.

Seasonal Displays
Spring: azaleas, gardenias, spring bulbs, wildflowers, roses.

Summer: hydrangeas, summer annuals, roses, caladium.

Fall: bright orange seed-pods of hip gardenia, fall foliage, chrysanthemums, rose hips, live oaks, Spanish moss.

Winter: camellias, pansies.

Mississippi
ELMS COURT
Travel Information
Privately owned, Elms Court is included as part of the biannual Natchez pilgrimage tours, held dur-ing the spring and fall. For information and dates write Natchez Pilgrimage Tours, Canal at State Street, P.O. Box 347, Natchez, MS 39121, or call (800) 647-6742.

Seasonal Displays
Spring: hostas, violets, spring bulbs, pansies, azaleas, banana shrub, wisteria, old-fashioned roses (Lady Banksia, Cherokee, Eglantine), irises (Louisiana, Siberian, European).

Summer: annual and perennial bedding plants, camphor tree, calycanthus, sweet olive, and ginger.

Fall: lycoris in five colors—red, white, pink, yellow, orange; also fall foliage, ginger, Louisiana iris.

Winter: camellias (*japonica* and *sasanqua*), pansies.

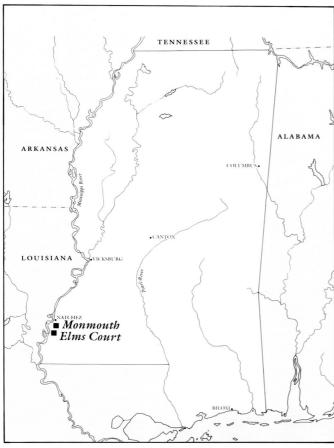

Mississippi

MONMOUTH

Travel Information
Monmouth is a privately owned bed-and-breakfast inn. For information write Monmouth, 36 Melrose Avenue, Natchez, MS 39120, or call (601) 442-5852. Monmouth is on the biannual Natchez pilgrimage tours held during the spring and fall. For dates or information write Natchez Pilgrimage Tours, Canal at State Street, P.O. Box 347, Natchez, MS 39121, or call (800) 647-6742.

Seasonal Displays
Spring: narcissus, iris, crocus, azaleas, banana shrub, violets.

Summer: water plants, summer bedding plants, herbs, boxwood, cut flowers.

Fall: fall foliage, lycoris.

Winter: camellias, pansies.

North Carolina

BILTMORE
Travel Information
The Biltmore Estate is located in Asheville, North Carolina, 35 miles east of the Great Smoky Mountains National Park on Interstate 40. For information write the Biltmore Estate, One North Pack Square, Asheville, NC 28801, or call (704) 255-1130.

Hours
Open daily, 9:00 A.M.–5:00 P.M. Closed Thanksgiving, Christmas, and New Year's Day.

Admission
A fee is charged for adults and children (6–17); children 11 and under admitted free with a paying parent.

Seasonal Displays
Spring: flowering shrubs and trees (forsythia, magnolia, spirea, flowering cherries, dogwood, azalea); 50,000 tulips and other spring bulbs.

Summer: roses, perennials, marigolds, salvia, geraniums, rhododendron, mountain laurel.

Fall: chrysanthemums, fall foliage.

ELIZABETHAN GARDENS
Travel Information
The Elizabethan Gardens are located on U.S. Route 64 in Manteo, North Carolina. For information write the Elizabethan Gardens, P.O. Box 1150, Manteo, NC 27964, or call (919) 473-3234.

Hours
Open daily, 9:00 A.M.–5:00 P.M.; closed Saturdays and Sundays in December and January. During the summer months the gardens stay open later.

Admission
A small fee charged for adults; children 12 and under admitted free when accompanied by an adult.

Seasonal Displays
Spring: azaleas, dogwoods, pansies, jasmine, bulbs, spring annuals.

Summer: roses, magnolias, crape myrtle, lilies, hydrangeas, summer annuals, hibiscus.

Fall: potted geraniums, chrysanthemums, sasanqua camellias, impatiens.

Winter: live oaks with underplantings of *Camellia japonica*s and giant daphne.

OLD SALEM
Travel Information
The town of Old Salem is located at Old Salem Road and Academy Street in Winston-Salem, North Carolina. The majority of the gardens are found behind Salt Street. There are nine exhibition buildings open to the public and eleven recreated gardens. For information call (919) 721-7300. To arrange a garden tour write the Visitors' Center, Old Salem Inc., Box F, Winston-Salem, NC

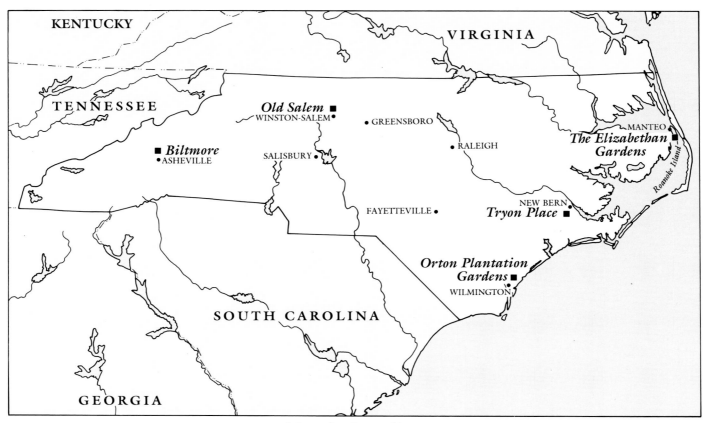

KENTUCKY

VIRGINIA

TENNESSEE

Old Salem ■
WINSTON-SALEM ●

● GREENSBORO

MANTEO

Biltmore ■
● ASHEVILLE

SALISBURY ●

● RALEIGH

**The Elizabethan
Gardens** ■

NEW BERN

FAYETTEVILLE ●

Tryon Place ■

**Orton Plantation
Gardens** ■

WILMINGTON

SOUTH CAROLINA

GEORGIA

North Carolina

27108, or call (919) 721-7345 or (800) 441-5305.

Hours
Visitors' Center and buildings open Monday–Saturday, 9:30 A.M.–4:30 P.M.; Sunday, 1:30 P.M.– 4:30 P.M. Closed Thanksgiving and Christmas.

Admission
Gardens are free to the public. A fee is charged for a tour of all buildings.

Seasonal Displays
Spring: spring vegetable gardens, flowering shrubs and trees (quince, snow-ball, roses, lilacs, kerria rose, dogwood, blackhaw, fringe tree, redbud), fruit trees (peach, cherry, apple), narcissus, Roman hyacinth, satin hyacinth, Star-of-Bethlehem, Johnny-jump-up, blue phlox, candytuft, stock, iris, peonies, Carolina yellow jessamine.

Summer: vegetables and field plants (corn, pump-kins, cotton, tobacco), perennials, fruit (gooseberries, currants), grapes, gourds, hop vines, native clematis, herbs, crape myrtle.

Fall: color from tulip-poplars, maples, cool-season vegetable gardens, red peppers, late annuals such as cockscomb and globe amaranth.

ORTON PLANTATION GARDENS

Travel Information
Orton Plantation Gardens is located close to Wilmington, North Carolina, on Route 133, 15 miles from U.S. Route 17. For information call Orton Plantation Gardens (919) 371-6851.

Hours
Open March through August, 8:00 A.M.–6:00 P.M.; September through November, 8:00 A.M.–5:00 P.M.

Admission
A slight fee is charged to offset cost and maintenance of garden.

Seasonal Displays
The height of the blooming season is spring. There are periods during the year with little or no floral display.

Spring: azaleas, flowering fruit trees, camellias, banana shrub, rhododendron, dogwood, pansies, Lady Banksia rose.

Summer: annual bedding plants, palms, wisteria, Cherokee rose, magnolia, crape myrtle, iris.

TRYON PALACE

Travel Information
Tryon Palace is located in New Bern, North Carolina, at the intersection of U.S. Route 17 and Interstate 70. The Palace is at the intersection of George and Pollock streets, one block off U.S. 17 (Broad Street). For information write Tryon Palace, Box 1007, New Bern, NC 28560, or call (919) 638-5109.

Hours
Open Monday–Saturday, 9:30 A.M.–4:00 P.M.; Sunday, 1:30 P.M.–4:00 P.M. Closed Thanksgiving, December 24–26, and New Year's Day.

Admission
A fee is charged for adults and students (grades 1–12).

Seasonal Displays
Spring: Thousands of tulips and other spring bulbs fill the formal beds in the scroll garden. One Sunday in April is designated as Gardener's Sunday, with free admission to the palace gardens from 9:00 A.M. to 5:00 P.M.

Summer: espaliered fruit (including flowering

crabapple, cherry, peach, and apple trees), vegetables, herbs, summer annuals.

Fall: chrysanthemums, including a Chrysanthemum Festival in October.

South Carolina
BROOKGREEN

Travel Information
Brookgreen Gardens is located on the west side of U.S. Route 17, 18 miles north of Georgetown, directly across from Huntington Beach State Park, between the communities of Murrells Inlet and Pawley's Island. For information write Brookgreen Gardens, U.S. Route 17 South, Murrells Inlet, SC 29576, or call (803) 237-4218.

Hours
Open daily, 9:30 A.M.–4:45 P.M. Closed Christmas.

Admission
A fee is charged for adults and children (6–12).

Seasonal Displays
Spring: dogwood, azaleas, wildflowers.

Summer: bedding plants, water plants.

Fall and winter: live oaks, palms, American holly.

HEYWARD-WASHINGTON HOUSE

Travel Information
Heyward-Washington

House is found at 87 Church Street, Charleston, SC 29401. For information call (803) 722-2996.

Hours
Open daily, 9:00 A.M.–5:00 P.M.

Admission
A small fee is charged for the house and garden tour.

Seasonal Displays
Spring: pink tulips and other spring-blooming bulbs, Atamasco lily, blue scilla, daffodils, white stock, violas, mock orange.

Summer: snapdragons, phlox, obedient plant, purple coneflower, pomegranates, pink crape myrtles.

Fall: *Camellia japonicas*, tea olives.

MAGNOLIA GARDENS

Travel Information
Magnolia Plantation and Gardens is 10 miles northwest of Charleston, South Carolina, on Route 61. For information write Magnolia Plantation and Gardens, Route 4, Charleston, SC 29414, or call (803) 571-1266.

Hours
Grounds open daily, 8:00 A.M.–5:00 P.M.; house open daily, 9:30 A.M.–5:00 P.M. Tours every half hour.

Admission
Write or call for current fee schedule.

Seasonal Displays
Spring: spring bulbs (anemones, daffodils, tulips), forsythia, gardenia, iris, flowering fruit trees, rhododendron.

Summer: bedding plants, bougainvillea, caladium, daylily, hibiscus, impatiens, lantana, lilies, roses.

Fall: beauty-berry, cassia, ginger lily, herbs, pampas grass, nandina, holly, pyracantha, aucuba.

MIDDLETON PLACE

Travel Information
Middleton Place is located on Route 61, fourteen miles northwest of Charleston. For information write the Middleton Place Foundation, Ashley River Road, Charleston, SC 29414, or call (803) 556-6020.

Hours
Garden open daily, 9:00 A.M.–5:00 P.M. House open Tuesday–Sunday, 10:00 A.M.–4:30 P.M.; Monday, 1:30 P.M.–4:30 P.M.

Admission
A small fee is charged to support the nonprofit Middleton Place Foundation.

Seasonal Displays
Spring: azaleas, flowering bulbs, wildflowers.

Summer: annuals, bedding plants, crape myrtles.

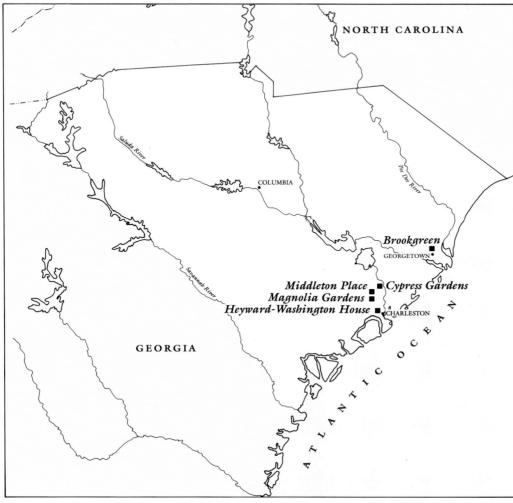

NORTH CAROLINA

COLUMBIA

Brookgreen
GEORGETOWN

Middleton Place *Cypress Gardens*
Magnolia Gardens
Heyward-Washington House CHARLESTON

GEORGIA

ATLANTIC OCEAN

South Carolina

annuals, roses, wisteria (swan garden), container plants (Japanese garden).

Fall and winter: camellias, orchids, evergreens (Japanese garden), cloud-forest greenhouse, tropical plants (Botanic Hall).

DIXON GALLERY AND GARDENS

Travel Information
Dixon Gardens is located on Park Avenue between Getwell and Perkins roads, across from Audubon Park, in eastern Memphis. For information, write Dixon Gardens, 4339 Park Avenue, Memphis, TN 38117, or call (901) 761-2409.

Hours
Open Tuesday–Saturday, 10:00 A.M.–5:00 P.M.; Sunday, 1:00 P.M.–5:00 P.M. Closed Mondays, Thanksgiving, Christmas, New Year's Day, and Independence Day.

Admission
A small fee is charged for adults, students, children, and senior citizens.

Seasonal Displays
Spring: dogwood, azalea, viburnums, woodland wildflowers.

Summer: hardy ferns, perennials, annuals.

Fall: colorful foliage and fruit (poplars, viburnums, dogwoods, hydrangeas).

Winter: camellias.

Fall: cool-weather vegetables, fall foliage, live oaks, hydrangeas.

Winter: camellias, evergreens, ornamental grasses.

Tennessee
CHEEKWOOD
Travel Information
Cheekwood is found at

1200 Forrest Park Drive, Nashville, TN 37205-4242. For information or to schedule a guided tour, write, or call (615) 356-8000.

Hours
Open Monday–Saturday, 9:00 A.M.–5:00 P.M.; Sunday, noon–5:00 P.M.

Admission
A fee is charged for adults,

senior citizens, and school-age children.

Seasonal Displays
Spring: woodland wildflowers (Howe Garden), narcissus (Hardison Daffodil Garden), iris (Connell Garden and Wills Garden), dogwood, redbud, various spring bulbs.

Summer: herbs (herb study garden), perennials and

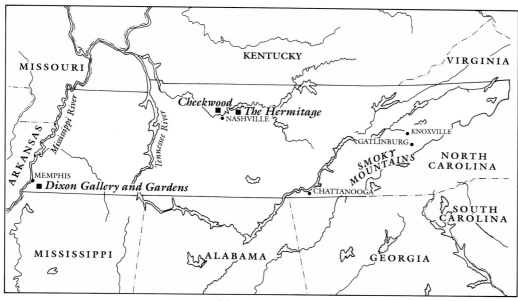

Tennessee

THE HERMITAGE

Travel Information

The Hermitage is located just off Old Hickory Boulevard in Hermitage, Tennessee, four miles north of Interstate 40 (Exit 221) and nine miles south of Interstate 65 (Exit 92). For information write the Hermitage, 4580 Rachel's Lane, Hermitage, TN 37076, or call (615) 889-2941.

Hours

Open daily, 9:00 A.M.–5:00 P.M., except Thanksgiving, Christmas, and the third week in January.

Admission

A fee is charged for adults, senior citizens, and children (6–18). Children under 6 admitted free.

Seasonal Displays

Spring: dogwoods, azaleas, peonies, iris, spirea, daylily, sunflower, hollyhock, herbs, crape myrtle.

Virginia

MONTICELLO

Travel Information

Monticello is located near Charlottesville, Virginia, on Route 53. For information write Monticello, P.O. Box 316, Charlottesville, VA 22902, or call (804) 295-8181.

Hours

Open November through February, 9:00 A.M.–4:30 P.M.; March through October, 8:00 A.M.–5:00 P.M.

Admission

A fee is charged for adults, children, and senior citizens.

Seasonal Displays

Spring: flowering fruit trees in the orchards, early vegetables in the vegetable garden, spring-blooming bulbs (narcissus, tulips, crocus), wildflowers, dogwoods, redbud, hardy annuals, biennials, perennials.

Summer: vegetables in the vegetable garden, perennials and summer annuals in the roundabout, fruit trees.

Fall: tree foliage in the grove, chrysanthemums.

MOUNT VERNON

Travel Information

Mount Vernon is located in Mount Vernon, Virginia, on the Mount Vernon Memorial Parkway. For information write Mount Vernon, Mount Vernon, VA 22121, or call (703) 780-2000.

Hours

Open every day; March through October, 9:00 A.M.–5:00 P.M.; November through February, 9:00 A.M.–4:00 P.M.

Admission

A fee is charged for adults, senior citizens (62 and older), and children (6–11).

Seasonal Displays

Spring: crabapple, dogwood, redbud, oak-leaf hydrangea, carnations, English daisy, lily-of-the-valley, pansy, scilla, iris, crocus, peony, tulip, blue phlox.

Summer: vegetables (beans, cabbage, carrots, lettuce, kale, peppers, peas), herbs (lavender, marjoram, mint, parsley, rue, sage, thyme), fruit (grapes, peaches, apples, cherries), cardinal flower, bachelor's button, cockscomb, frittilaria, hollyhock, larkspur, roses, phlox.

Fall: euonymous, buckeye, maples, Franklinia, aster, calendula.

[map labels] MISSOURI · KENTUCKY · VIRGINIA · Mississippi River · Tennessee River · Cheekwood · The Hermitage · NASHVILLE · KNOXVILLE · GATLINBURG · ARKANSAS · MEMPHIS · Dixon Gallery and Gardens · SMOKY MOUNTAINS · NORTH CAROLINA · CHATTANOOGA · SOUTH CAROLINA · MISSISSIPPI · ALABAMA · GEORGIA

WILLIAMSBURG
GOVERNOR'S PALACE
GEORGE WYTHE HOUSE
BENJAMIN WALLER
HOUSE

Travel Information
Colonial Williamsburg is located midway between Norfolk and Richmond on Interstate 64. It is 50 miles east of Richmond, Virginia, and 150 miles from Washington, D.C. For information write the Visitors' Center, Colonial Williamsburg Foundation, P.O. Box 1776, Williamsburg, VA 23187-1776, or call (804) 229-1000.

Hours
The Visitors' Center is open daily from 9:00 A.M.–5:00 P.M., 8:30 A.M.–8:00 P.M. during summer.

Admission
A fee is charged for adults and children (6–12).

Seasonal Displays
Spring: spring bulbs, flowering ornamental and fruit trees.

Summer: annuals and perennials (hollyhocks, daylilies, globe amaranth, ageratum).

Fall: annuals and perennials, fall foliage (usually peaking in early November).

Washington, D.C.
DUMBARTON OAKS

Travel Information
Dumbarton Oaks is located at R and Thirty-first streets in Georgetown, Washington, D.C., 1½ blocks from Wisconsin Avenue. For information write Dumbarton Oaks, Washington, DC 20007, or call (202) 342-3200.

Hours
Open daily, April through October, 2:00 P.M.–6:00 P.M.; November through March, 2:00 P.M.–5:00 P.M. Closed on national holidays and during inclement weather.

Admission
A small fee is charged for adults, children under 12, and senior citizens. Senior citizens admitted free on Wednesdays. Free admission for all from November through March.

Seasonal Displays
Spring: spring bulbs, cherry trees, forsythia, wisteria, azaleas, dogwood, lilacs, akebia, star magnolia, perennial borders, clematis, roses, peonies, fringe tree.

Summer: perennial borders, clematis, roses, grandiflora magnolia, canna, daylilies, fuchsia, gardenias, agapanthus, oleanders.

Fall: chrysanthemums.

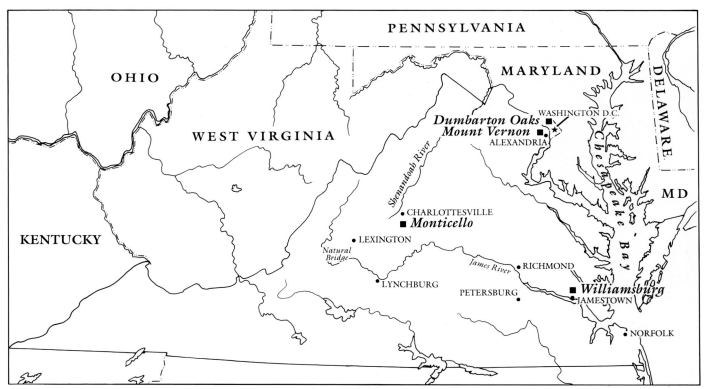

Virginia

*P*art of the magic of visiting gardens is in trying to duplicate a bit of it in your own gardens at home. The following notes have been written to help you do just that. Each garden is represented by an outstanding plant, group of plants, or design concept. Horticultural information is given to help you incorporate these into your own gardens. Happy Gardening!

Alabama

Bellingrath Gardens

The chrysanthemum show at Bellingrath Gardens is one of the most exciting in the world. Chrysanthemums have been cultivated since ancient times; Confucius wrote about them as early as 500 B.C., and they were well-known flowers in ancient China.

Like Walter and Bessie Bellingrath, the ancient Chinese botanist T'ao Ming-yang grew such beautiful displays of this plant that people traveled from far away to see them. Soon his village became known as Chuh-sien, or the City of Chrysanthemums.

CHRYSANTHEMUM
Chrysanthemum spp.
Chrysanthemums are generally divided into several different classes, based on the physical characteristics of the flowering head. These classes include pompom,
quill, spider, brush, thistle, single, incurve, and spoon.

How to Grow

Chrysanthemums adapt to many different types of growing areas. Generally, they like rich, well-drained soil in full sun. It is important that these perennials receive regular moisture throughout the year. Although most chrysanthemums bloom during autumn, they are often planted in the garden in early summer. Persistent pinching back of the flowering buds during early summer will result in a fall display of numerous, lovely blossoms. These plants should be divided every two years. The center woody sections should be discarded, and only the outer sections replanted.

Florida

Cypress Gardens

Topiary is the art of creating whimsical live sculptures. The plants are sculpted by clipping, pruning, and training or growing small flowers in wire frames that are formed to various shapes. The art of topiary was first discovered by the Romans over two thousand years ago.

Cypress Gardens has taken the art of topiary and expanded it to create fantastic creatures of enormous size. The home gardener,
too, can enjoy the art and craft of topiary, perhaps on a slightly smaller scale.

One of the easiest and most versatile kinds of topiary for the home gardener is to create small shapes from wire frames. Plants are then trained to cover the outside of the frame, which gives it a basic shape.

The frame can be used in two different ways. The first method is to stuff the frame with a mixture of sphagnum moss and potting soil, effectively creating a shaped potting container. In the second method, the plants (usually vines) are planted in the container and trained to cover the frame.

Placing plants in moss-stuffed frames is easy and gives instant results. Plants used for this kind of topiary should show a variety of colors and textures. Ideally the plant should root easily, have a shallow root system, and a close, even growth habit.

Some of the best plants to use include:

BABY'S TEARS
Soleirolia soleirolii
Tiny leaves give this plant a mosslike appearance. The thin stems root easily wherever they touch.

CREEPING FIG
Ficus pumila
This common vine has small, shiny leaves and is adaptable

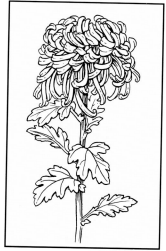

chrysanthemum

to a wide range of temperatures and light levels. It roots easily and is rarely bothered with pests or disease.

ENGLISH IVY
Hedera helix
This is a popular choice because there are so many different varieties to choose from ranging in color and leaf size.

Caring for the Topiary

Topiary creations need to be kept in a sunny place where there is good air circulation and a moderate temperature. It will be necessary to rotate the topiary every few days to ensure equal light for the entire creation.

The topiary should stay evenly moist. The amount of water needed will depend on the kind of plant material, the exposure to the sun, and the absorption properties of the potting mixture.

Topiaries should be fed with a liquid fertilizer at least once a month.

Fairchild Tropical Garden

Fairchild Tropical Garden has an outstanding collection of palms—over 700 different kinds. Palms are a lovely and fascinating group of trees, showing enormous diversity and economic importance. Palms also constitute important landscape plants as well. Many kinds of palms can be grown in warm regions of the United States.

COCONUT PALM
Cocos nucifera
This palm has a straight trunk that grows to be 100–130 feet tall at maturity. A large tuft of graceful, nodding leaf branches originates from the crown; each branch is 12–18 feet long. The evergreen leaves are shiny green and leathery. This tree is often used to line streets in tropical areas. It is tolerant of salt spray and pollution.

DATE PALM
Phoenix canariensis
This palm grows to a height of 50–60 feet at maturity. The gracefully arching evergreen leaves are 15–20 feet long and grow from the center of the top of a large, stout trunk.

MEXICAN FAN PALM
Washingtonia robusta

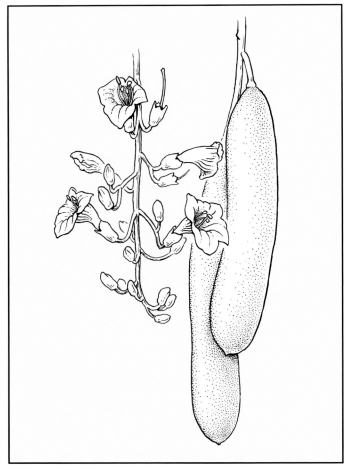

sausage tree

This palm grows about 90 feet tall and has large, segmented leaf blades that create a fan effect. This species is commonly grown in California, along the Gulf Coast, and in Florida.

How to Grow

Coconut palm grows in zones 8–10 and thrives in full sun and sandy soils. Both Mexican fan palm and date palm grow in zones 9 and 10. Both do best in rich, well-drained soils and full sun. Mexican fan palm does well in dry conditions.

Four Arts Garden

The Four Arts Garden has a diverse collection of tropical trees, including such culinary favorites as key limes, sweet orange, coffee tree, kumquat, date palm, guava, and pomegranate. The most unusual tropical tree here has no culinary value. It is the sausage tree. So unusual is this tree that the town of Palm Beach has declared it a Historic Specimen Tree.

The flowers of the sausage tree begin to open at dusk, at which time they begin to emit a mousy odor that attracts its primary pollinator, the bat. Bats receive both pollen and nectar from the flowers, which last only a single night. To induce the tree to produce its sausage-like fruit, the staff at the Four Arts Garden fertilizes the tree by hand at about the time of the full moon in September.

SAUSAGE TREE
Kigelia pinnata
This tree grows 20–40 feet tall and bears sausagelike fruits 1–2 feet long. The brown, oblong fruits hang from cordlike stalks. Dark purplish green, cup-shaped flowers are about 4 inches long; they are found on drooping spikes and develop on old wood. Because they hang downward, they are easily accessible to pollinators.

This tree is native to Egypt and grows well in tropical areas.

Morikami Gardens

The popularity of Japanese gardens in the United States is increasing rapidly. The combination of simplicity and serenity is becoming more and more appealing to harried and hurried American families.

Morikami Gardens provides a good source of inspiration to those interested in creating a Japanese garden.

The Japanese garden emphasizes respect and reverence for nature. Water is generally an important part of the design, because it is thought to bring peace and stillness to the soul. Interesting texture as well as unusual leaf or tree forms are also part of the design principles of Japanese gardens. Colorful blossoms are usually used only as adornment, not as the backbone of the garden. Plans generally show different shades of green.

Historically Japanese gardens are grouped into four different styles. The first of these, the *funa asobi*, or pleasure-boat style, was centered on an oval pond where courtiers went boating. The *shuyu*, or stroll garden, had a path that led from one point to another in the garden, allowing the visitor different vantage points of the same scene. The *zaken*, or contemplation garden, is viewed from within a central structure. The garden is composed of elements that suggest a picture or a scene that is suitable for long viewing. The *kaiyu*, or "many-pleasure" style, comprises many different kinds of gardens, such as tea gardens, all centered around a pond.

No matter what type of Japanese garden is created, the perimeter is almost always enclosed, often with a stone or bamboo fence.

Symbolism is important in the Japanese garden. Waterfalls or groupings of rocks provide a decorative focal point. According to myth and legend, the four corners of a garden are ruled by four deities. The east was considered the source of purity, the west the outlet for impurities. Thus streams running through the garden always run from east to west.

Vizcaya

The fern grotto at Vizcaya is an intriguing part of this exciting garden. Arching rocks provide the shade that, coupled with an abundance of water, creates ideal conditions for growing many kinds of ferns. Although most homeowners are not lucky enough to have a stone grotto, many kinds of native ferns thrive in normal garden conditions. One of the most satisfactory of these is the small maidenhair fern.

Maidenhair fern is attractive in numerous landscape settings. Planted singly, the plant shows its form and texture to advantage. Planted in a mass, it creates a wonderfully graceful, exciting display. This fern can even be

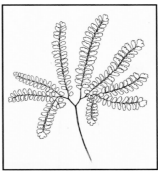

maidenhair fern

grown in a pot if given sufficient moisture.

MAIDENHAIR FERN
Adiantum pedatum
The lacy, delicate fronds of maidenhair fern make it a favorite plant to include in any shady garden. Many gardeners consider it the most beautiful of all our native ferns. The fronds are so thin and silky that they flutter with the slightest breeze. Generally these plants will attain a height of 18–24 inches. The stems are shiny dark reddish brown; the leaflets are found on radiating ribs that create a fan shape.

How to Grow

Maidenhair fern prefers to be placed in deep, rich, well-drained soil in filtered sun to deep shade. Even moisture through the year provides a good growing environment for this plant. If possible, place this delicate fern where it will be protected from high winds. Maidenhair fern can be

propagated in fall. The rhizomes should be dug and divided. Each segment should contain at least one frond or bud and be at least 2 inches long. These divisions are best planted 12 inches apart and should be frequently treated to a fine, even mist.

Georgia

Callaway Gardens
The Cecil B. Day Butterfly Center at Callaway Gardens is a treat for all the senses. Although the butterflies here are tropical, native species can also be delightful in a garden. It is easy to make your own "butterfly garden," with flowers and shrubs that will attract native butterflies. First, find out which butterflies are commonly found in your area; then learn which plants best serve their needs.

Plants suitable for attracting butterflies will fall into two main groups: those that supply nectar for the adult butterflies, and host plants, which supply food for the caterpillars and a place for females to lay eggs.

A successful butterfly garden should be planted in a sunny location and offer a wide variety of plant material. Nectar can be obtained from annuals and perennials such as verbena, phlox, tithonia, cosmos, butterfly weed, pentas, candytuft, and asters. Many wildflowers and even weeds have much to offer butterflies.

Flowering shrubs such as butterfly bush and lantana are also good nectar sources and provide shelter at the same time.

Caterpillars feed on many different plants, but the larva of each species is selective. Vegetables, herbs, garden flowers, weeds, and wildflowers are good food sources for caterpillars. Some of the best wildflower host plants include rabbit tobacco, everlasting, cassia, plantain, asters, violets, thistle, milkweed, and clover. Vegetables and herbs such as carrots, parsley, and dill are good host plants as well.

To attract the greatest number of butterflies, plan your plantings carefully. Have food sources available from early spring through late fall.

Never use chemical pesticides if you hope to attract butterflies. These delicate insects are highly susceptible to poisoning.

For more information on how to create your own butterfly garden, contact the Callaway Gardens Education Department, Callaway Gardens, Pine Mountain, GA 31822, or call (404) 663-5153.

Founders' Memorial Garden

The bamboo screen at the Founders' Memorial Garden provides a wonderful backdrop for the flower border and fountain, screening the garden from nearby university buildings and providing a hint of the exotic Far East.

BAMBOO
Several different genera of Bamboo are suitable for cultivation in this country. Among the best are:

Arundinaria variegata: Has white striping on green leaves. The slender stems die back in winter and should be cut back to the ground to stimulate new growth.

Bambusa multiples: Its reddish green leaves have silvery undersides. This relatively slow-growing species is the best bamboo for hedges, and forms nice clumps.

Phyllostachys aurea: Has rigid yellow stems with narrow leaves about 5 inches long. The stems turn black as they mature, showing white bands beneath each joint. This species will become invasive and should be kept in close check.

How to Grow

With bamboo, the difficulty lies not in getting it to grow, but in keeping it

from becoming invasive. Bamboo grows at an alarming rate. Most species prefer full sun and moist conditions. Top growth should be cut back severely every 2 years to stimulate fresh, young growth.

Gardens for Peace

The key to creating a successful natural garden is to match the plants to the environmental conditions that exist in your area. "Right plant in the right place" is a maxim as true in a wildflower garden as it is anywhere else.

There are several investigative steps that need to be performed before you begin digging or buying plants for your woodland garden. First determine the ratio of sun to shade. There are many different kinds of shade. Deep shade occurs when the area receives no direct sunlight. Few plants will flower under these conditions, though there are many kinds of foliage plants that survive admirably well. High, open shade allows early morning and late afternoon sunlight to filter through but offers protection from the hot noonday sun. Filtered or dappled sunlight means that the area receives some spots of sun throughout the day.

Next, determine the type of soil you have. Woodland soils vary in richness and in

Virginia bluebells

acidity. For the greatest success with the wildflowers you grow, choose those that suit your type of soil.

Finally, determine the amount of moisture your area receives, and if you are willing and able to supplement this moisture during the growing season. Many of the woodland plants prefer a rather damp environment, others like a dry, shady area.

The glory of the woodland garden comes in spring when a multitude of small, ephemeral wildflowers bloom profusely. It is possible, however, to extend the growing season by including both summer- and fall-blooming plants.

The following list includes many shade-loving, easy-to-grow wildflowers. For the best results, check the specific environmental needs of each of these plants.

Spring: bloodroot, green and gold, Virginia bluebells, columbine, foamflower, dwarf crested iris.

Summer: cinnamon fern, Christmas fern, Turk's cap lily, Indian pink.

Fall: joe-pye weed, cardinal flower, aster.

Le Jardin des Fleurs

Many of the flowers in Ryan Gainey's garden—like many of our own—were not purchased at a garden center. They came wrapped in damp paper towels, or plopped down in a tin bucket. Many of these plants are hand-me-downs from the gardens of friends and relatives.

Some of these hand-me-downs can be found everywhere, while others are now gone from the general trade and are only found growing in the gardens of friends who have passed them along. Generally these slips of plants or bits of seeds come with ample advice—where to put them, how to treat them, what they like to eat, how much water to give them—almost as if they were favorite children rather than plants out of the garden.

It is a new and exciting horticultural experience to branch out and grow plants that your grandmother

grew. And it is a hobby that can easily become a passion. Soon everywhere you look you will find a new kind of plant that it would be fun to try to grow. And everywhere you will find friends who want to help you grow it.

One of the best places to find heirloom plants is at state fairs. Here country gardeners will bring their best and most unusual plants, ones with such promise that they have been reintroduced into the horticultural trade. Others are simply pretty and sweet and will continue to

be passed around only through the generosity of gardening friends.

Interest in heirloom plants is increasing at a rapid pace. Throughout the country gardeners are beginning to realize not only the fun but also the importance of saving and growing these plants.

For more information about heirloom plants write the Thomas Jefferson Center for Historic Plants, Monticello, P.O. Box 316, Charlottesville, VA 22902; or the Southern Garden History Society, Old

Salem, Inc., Drawer F, Salem Station, Winston-Salem, NC 27108.

Louisiana

Afton Villa

The valley at Afton Villa is transformed in spring into a wonderland of color as thousands of narcissus blossoms turn the landscape yellow and white. People have loved narcissus for many centuries. British settlers to this country brought with them the bulbs of some of their favorite kinds. The poet's narcissus is a species that has been cultivated a very long time, having grown in England since 320 B.C. One of the favorite old-fashioned cultivars developed from this is 'Old Pheasant's Eye.' Another species that was often included in plantation gardens is *Narcissus magalis*.

POET'S NARCISSUS

Narcissus poeticus

Poet's narcissus grows about 18 inches tall and has fragrant, pure white flowers and a small, shallow, yellow cup tinged with red. The flowers measure 2–3 inches across and come in mid-to-late April.

How to Grow

Narcissus is among the easiest of all plants to grow. The large bulbs

Old-fashioned rose

poet's narcissus

should be planted in fall in an area that receives sun half the day. These plants like rich, well-drained soil. In fall, after the weather has turned cool but before the soil has frozen, plant the bulbs at a depth of 1½ times their height. The bulbs need time to develop roots before winter. After the plants bloom, remove the faded flower heads and allow the foliage to die back naturally but do not cut off the leaves. They provide food essential for the following year.

Longue Vue

Mrs. Stern considered fresh flowers an essential part of interior decor. Arranging her own flowers was a favorite pastime; like many gardeners, she set aside

an area in which to grow the flowers she would eventually bring indoors.

A cutting garden, large or small, is an advantage for almost any garden. Many of the flowers that look best in an arrangement do not always work well in the landscape. Zinnia blossoms, for example, are exquisite, but the stems and lower leaves are often subject to mildew and can be scraggly and unattractive.

The kinds of flowers in a cutting garden depend on location and the preferences of the gardener.

When planning a cutting garden, start indoors. Look around to determine which rooms you will be using flowers in most often. Note the colors in these rooms and imagine what floral arrangements would look best here.

Then begin to fill your cutting garden with the flowers that will be most useful. Most cutting gardens are made up of a combination of bulbs, annuals, and perennials. Try to include plants that will give you cut flowers throughout much of the year—foliage plants for winter color are a wonderful addition to any cutting garden.

The following plants will grow well in most southern gardens with little care or trouble.

Bulbs: narcissus, iris, tulips, crocus, lilies, anemone, dahlia, gladiolus.

Shrubs: azalea, spirea, forsythia, pussy willows, hydrangea, mahonia, pyracantha.

Perennials: chrysanthemum, black-eyed Susan, coreopsis, daisy, helleborus, daylilies, hosta, peony, phlox, primrose, sedum, rose, aster, goldenrod.

Annuals: snapdragons, nicotiana, zinnia, salvia, poppy, marigold, geranium, coleus.

Rosedown

When Catherine Fondren Underwood first saw Rosedown in the spring of 1956, it was the huge old shrubs and trees that caught her eye and convinced her of the possible beauty of these gardens. The long avenue of live oaks, dripping with Spanish moss, formed the perfect setting for the graceful old house at the end of the lane. A professor of forestry from Louisiana State University, Thomas Hansbrough, was hired to identify and determine the age of the old trees. Using an increment borer, he found that the trees had been planted in the early 1800s.

In colonial times, live oaks were cut extensively for use in making ships. The wood is hard, dense, and

strong, and heavier than any other North American tree. Until live oak was used in the shipbuilding industry, boats and seagoing vessels were not expected to last longer than about ten years. With the introduction of live oak wood, however, the normal life expectancy of a ship increased dramatically.

Live oak trees are attractive even when young, but attain their full beauty as they age and take on the characteristic gnarled look. Before the Civil War this tree was called *Quercus virens*, or living oak. The name was given to this tree because, unlike other oaks, it is an evergreen. Live oak is a wonderful specimen to use in a coastal area because it is tolerant of salt spray and sand.

LIVE OAK
Quercus virginiana

Live oak usually grows to a mature height of 60–80 feet and spreads an equal distance. The branches appear gnarled and twisted, and the bark is grayish. The leaves are 1–3 inches long and are dark green and leathery.

How to Grow

Live oaks prefer full sun and very rich, acid, well-drained soils. If temperatures dip below 0° Fahrenheit, the leaves will be killed.

wisteria

A hardy perennial vine, wisteria is covered with graceful cascades of flowers during early summer months. Although purplish blue is the most common flower color, cultivars bearing white flowers have also been developed. The vines can be grown on a wall, trellis, or fence, or can be trained into a standard—a form resembling a tree. The flowers put forth a luscious honey scent.

How to Grow

Wisteria needs a spot in full sun. The soil should be well drained and rich in organic matter. Soils high in nitrogen might produce more foliage than blossoms. If flowering is poor, try a bit of selective pruning on the roots. Once established, wisteria is drought tolerant. Under ideal growing conditions, the vine grows astoundingly fast—up to 30 feet in a single year.

Monmouth

According to excerpts from journals and diaries and the reports of many visitors to Monmouth, it is clear that small woods violets grew in great profusion at Monmouth. Although they probably started out in a neat, orderly formal bed, the exuberance of these small flowers soon overflowed the confines of a planting bed.

White violets have been grown for more than 2,000 years for their sweet scent. Only recently has this scent been replaced by a synthetic one in the perfume industry. Violets also

Mississippi

Elms Court

Nothing can bring back a memory as quickly or acutely as a fragrance. The sweet scent of wisteria in bloom works powerfully on the imaginations of those lucky enough to remember it. Chinese wisteria (*Wisteria sinensis*) was brought to England from China in 1816 and quickly made its way into American gardens. *Wisteria floribunda*, now more commonly grown, was brought from Japan in 1830. Wisteria soon became a favorite porch plant in the United States. It is a long-lived vine, easy to grow and beautiful when in bloom. When not held in check, wisteria can become so aggressive it is considered a nuisance.

WISTERIA
Wisteria floribunda

violet

have medicinal and culinary uses. Violet leaves are very high in vitamins A and C and can be eaten raw (in salads) or cooked like other spring greens. Violet flowers are sometimes used as garnishes, particularly when the petals are candied and used on cakes and pastries. Fresh violet leaves can also be placed in cold fruit soups or punches. Violets are close relatives of little Johnny-jump-up and the larger pansies.

WHITE VIOLET
Viola odorata
The little white violet grows only 3–4 inches tall. The leaves and flowers occur on separate stalks. The flowers are white, the lower petals often found with a single purple vein. This flower blooms during April and May.

How to Grow

White violets need rich woodland soil and partial shade. Small plants can be set out in fall or early spring and should be provided with ample moisture.

North Carolina

Biltmore
Much of the past and present beauty of the Biltmore Estate is found in its magnificent collection of native azaleas. Most of the azaleas native to the southeastern United States are deciduous, and have delicate, sweet-smelling blossoms.

Several native azaleas are good for including in a natural woodland garden. Among the best are coastal, Cumberland, and Florida azalea.

COASTAL AZALEA
Rhododendron atlanticum
Native to North and South Carolina and coastal regions as far north as Maryland. The fragrant bloom is white or red and white and appears in May and June.

CUMBERLAND AZALEA
Rhododendron bakeri
Found most often in open woodland areas at higher elevations north to Kentucky and south to Georgia. This June-blooming shrub has bright orange-red blossoms.

FLORIDA AZALEA
Rhododendron austrinum
Has fragrant yellowish orange blossoms with a distinctive, citruslike scent.

coastal azalea

The blossoms appear in March or April. This azalea is generally found in the southern part of the region in Florida, southwestern Georgia, and southern Alabama.

How to Grow

Native azaleas prefer soils that are slightly acid, well drained, and rich in organic matter. Because the roots are shallow, the plants should be mulched with leaf mold or bark chips. Cultivating around the base of the shrubs is discouraged because the roots can be easily damaged. Generally these azaleas prefer dappled sun or shady conditions and regular moisture.

Elizabethan Gardens
Sometimes called the "lilac of the South," crape myrtle trees provide spectacular color at the Elizabethan Gardens during summer. The most common bloom color for this slender tree is bright pink, but the blossoms also come in white, light pink, and lilac purple.

CRAPE MYRTLE
Lagerstroemia indica
Crape myrtles generally reach a height of about 30 feet and spread to a similar width. The outstanding summer blossoms are the most conspicuous and attractive feature of this tree, but the bark is also beautiful and adds interest and texture to the garden

crape myrtle

throughout the year. The outer gray bark often peels away in sheets, exposing a paler, almost mottled inner bark.

How to Grow

Crape myrtles will grow in shady areas, but for the best blooms they need full sun. They grow well in horticultural zones 7–9, need well-drained, slightly acid soils and plenty of moisture while becoming established. Once the root system has developed, the tree is considered drought tolerant. Crape myrtles are surprisingly adaptable to a wide range of conditions. They perform well when planted close together to form a hedge or screen, but also thrive singly. Given sufficient moisture, they will even grow well in a tub or container.

Old Salem

Herbs were essential to the health and well-being of the Salem community. Not only did these plants provide a bit of beauty to the garden, they were also absolutely necessary as medicines and flavoring in the cooking.

Many different types of herbs were grown in early Salem. These were found mixed in with other flowers and vegetables. One of the most important, and also one of the most attractive of the herbs grown here, was feverfew. This medicinal herb has been in use for centuries. The ancient Greeks used it as an aid during childbirth, and a seventeenth-century herbalist suggested that it was useful for many ailments such as arthritis, kidney stones, infant colic, constipation, and insect bites.

Today scientists have rediscovered the usefulness of this lovely herb. A 1985 British medical journal reported that feverfew was useful in alleviating the pain of migraine headaches.

FEVERFEW
Chrysanthemum parthenium

Feverfew looks like a miniature daisy. The blooms appear in great profusion at the ends of plant stems and have white ray flowers and yellow centers. The plants only reach a height of 2–3 feet. Feverfew generally blooms in midsummer through fall. Because of its neat, compact growing habit, feverfew is useful in rock walls, or in window boxes or porch boxes.

How to Grow

This little herb is tolerant of rather poor, infertile soils. It will grow best in well-drained soils and full sun. It can be easily propagated by dividing the plants in spring.

Another herb important to the early Moravian settlers was tansy. Like feverfew, tansy is also in the daisy family. Tansy was at one time used extensively as a folk medicine. Today its use is restricted because the plants contain a mildly toxic substance that can be harmful. In the seventeenth century, it was also commonly used as a strewing herb—it was tossed on the floor to release a pleasing, though pungent, aroma when crushed.

TANSY
Tanacetum vulgare
Tansy has dark green, fern-like leaves and clusters of yellow flowers. This perennial will spread with alarming speed if not kept in check. Tansy grows to a height of 3–4 feet.

How to Grow

Tansy tolerates a wide variety of environmental conditions, from rich soil full of organic matter to dry, infertile soils. Full sun will cause the plant to bloom more profusely and will intensify the scent and flavor of the leaves.

Orton Plantation Gardens
A woodland walk through Orton Plantation Gardens is a delight to the senses. One can hear the call of birds flying over the old rice fields, or can smell the incomparable fragrance of the forest. Perhaps the sweetest of all the woodland scents is that of winter daphne.

WINTER DAPHNE
Daphne odora
This is a dense, low-growing shrub with rosy-purple flowers appearing in late winter or early spring. The narrow leaves are 2–3 inches long. The leaves and berries are **poisonous**.

How to Grow

Daphne is not considered an easy plant to grow. It is short-lived at best, and does not like to be transplanted. The wonderful scent of the blossoms,

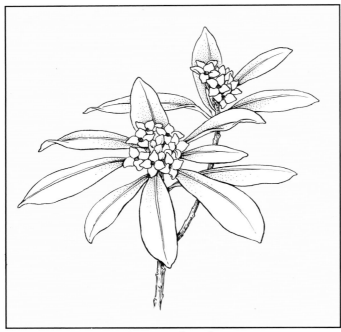

winter daphne

however, makes it well worth trying. Daphne likes filtered sun or partial shade. Protection from the summer midday sun is particularly important. Good drainage is also important; the roots have a tendency to rot easily. For best results the soil should be loose, sandy, and slightly acid. Where temperatures drop below freezing, mulch the small shrubs heavily with a combination of limestone grit and leaf mold. To help prolong the beauty of this plant, prune after it flowers.

Tryon Palace
Espalier gardening is the art of training trees and shrubs against a wall or fence—a challenging style of gardening, well represented by the fruit trees at Tryon Palace. Grapevines are trained against the extensive brick walls, and crabapple, pear, and apple trees against a network of fences.

To create a horizontal espalier, you must gradually train the branches to the desired position. It is easiest to start the process with young, unformed plants, but gardeners can also use older, more established trees and shrubs. The first step, no matter what the age of the specimen, is judicious and vigorous pruning to remove side shoots and unwanted buds.

Plant the tree or shrub in front of a wall or fence. In general, the trees should be spaced about 10–15 feet apart. A young, one-year-old specimen should be cut back to a bud or shoot about 14 inches above the ground.

Place a support wire (or use a fence pole) about a foot above the ground. Choose two buds on opposite sides of the stem located close to the training pole or wire. Leave these two buds and the top bud and remove all other buds along the length of the stem. Carefully make a small notch above the lower bud to stimulate growth.

The following summer, growth should have advanced so that real training can begin. The first year, tie both side branches to bamboo stakes at a 45-degree angle. Also offer support to the top branch with a taller bamboo stake so that the center branch will remain straight. If you like, choose two more opposite buds to obtain another pair of horizontal branches. Remove all other buds.

Not until the third summer can the lowest two branches be tied to stakes horizontal to the ground. At this time, follow the same procedure with two more branches farther up the

trunk. The first year train at 45-degree angles; the following summer, lower them to a full horizontal position.

The number of horizontal branches you train will depend on personal preference and the location of the espaliered trees. If a low fence is used, generally only two pairs of branches will work.

Using espaliered trees is a neat and orderly way of growing fruit. Very often, fruit develops faster on espaliered vines and trees than it does on a free-form plant.

South Carolina

Brookgreen
In spring the delicate white blossoms of dogwood turn the dogwood garden at Brookgreen into a wonderland of white blossoms. The number and variety of dogwoods here make this part of the gardens a favorite of visitors from all parts of the country.

FLOWERING DOGWOOD
Cornus florida
This is not a particularly large tree, only growing to a mature height of 15–40 feet. The true flowers are small and inconspicuous, but the more showy part of the blossom is composed of four large white or pink bracts. In fall, bright red

berries form in clusters, and the attractive foliage turns scarlet as the weather cools in autumn. The bark of the tree is gray and is divided into small, squarish plates.

Several cultivars of *C. florida* are available commercially. 'Rubra' has red or pink bracts. 'Pluribracteata' is a double-flowering form. 'Apple Blossom' shows a blush of pink in the bracts. 'Barton' has large white bracts and blooms early in the season.

How to Grow

Dogwood trees should be transplanted when young and should be planted in an area where the soil is acid and well drained. Although they can grow in full sun, partial shade is also acceptable. Mulch should be placed around the tree to keep roots cool in summer.

Heyward-Washington House

Mock orange trees provide a delightful part of the garden display at the Heyward-Washington House. Both deliciously fragrant and beautiful to look at, the mock orange was an important ornamental plant in the American colonies.

Spectacular in bloom, it unfortunately has little to offer at other seasons.

MOCK ORANGE
Philadelphus falconeri
This shrub grows to be about 8 feet tall and has narrow leaves, about 2½ inches long. The single white flowers are found in clusters of three to seven. *P. inodorus* has dull green foliage and a compact growing habit. It attains a height of about 10 feet. The flowers are rather large (2–2½ inches wide) and occur in clusters of two or three. *P. coronarius* has very fragrant flowers. The cultivar 'Avalanche' grows to be 4–5 feet tall and has single, fragrant blossoms, 1 inch wide.

How to Grow

In general mock orange is an easy plant to grow. It should be planted in full sun in relatively rich, well-drained soil. It will do best if mulched heavily to retain moisture and protect the roots from great fluctuations in temperature.

Prune the shrubs after they bloom. Pruning should effectively remove old, crowded branches, or branches where flowering has occurred. Mock orange tolerates imperfect conditions and is rarely troubled by pests or disease.

mock orange

Magnolia Gardens

The profusion of color during fall and winter months at Magnolia Gardens is proof that a garden can be beautiful throughout the year. Brightly colored berries and winter fruit not only make the garden lovely to look at, but also useful in attracting birds and wildlife to the area. Among the more outstanding "off-season" shrubs are nandina, pyracantha, holly, and aucuba.

NANDINA
Nandina domestica
This small evergreen shrub grows 6–8 feet tall and 2 feet wide. White flowers appear in late spring, but it is fall's bright red berries that are the real showpieces of this plant. Dwarf cultivars, which grow only 2 feet tall, are also available.

flowering dogwood

holly

How to Grow

Nandina needs to grow in well-drained soil in either full sun or partial shade. This shrub likes the acid soils found in many parts of the South. To increase the berry yield, plant these shrubs in large groups to encourage heavy cross-pollination.

PYRACANTHA

Pyracantha angustifolia
This shrub has brilliant red pulpy berries. Freestanding, it may grow to be about 3 feet tall, but it can grow as high as 12 feet against a wall. Clusters of tiny white flowers appear in spring.

How to Grow

Pyracantha grows in zones 7–10. It needs rich, fertile, well-drained soil and full sun. Protection from drying winter winds will result in healthier, more robust plants. Once established, pyracantha will tolerate both drought and pollution.

HOLLY

Ilex spp.
There are many different species of holly that grow beautifully in the South. English holly (*Ilex aquifolium*) has dark green shiny leaves and bright red round berries that last all winter. Chinese holly, *Ilex cornuta*, has thick, spiny, triangular leaves, bright yellow showy flowers, and red berries. Chinese holly is particularly useful in the landscape because it will grow berries without the presence of a male shrub. One of the favorite cultivars of this species is 'Burfordii.'

How to Grow

Hollies perform best if grown in full sun in rich, moist, acid soil. Chinese holly is tolerant of a wide variety of cultural conditions and is particularly good for use in southern landscapes. All hollies should be pruned and sheared in early spring before growth starts.

AUCUBA

Aucuba japonica
This shrub, which grows to a height of 6–8 feet, has thick green leaves that are often splotched or edged with gold. Purple flowers appear in spring; berries follow in fall and persist all winter.

How to Grow

Aucuba prefers moderate-to-deep shade and rich, moist, acid soils. Once established, these shrubs are tolerant of drought and air pollution. To produce berries, both male and female shrubs are needed.

Middleton Place
Camellias bring unexpected and welcome color to the winter landscape of the South, and also thrive in areas of California. Ranging in color from white to red and pink, camellia are among the most beautiful of all flowering shrubs.

CAMELLIA

Camellia spp.
The most common camellia is *Camellia japonica*. This is a rounded evergreen shrub with outstandingly beautiful blossoms, single or double. The dark green leaves are thick, glossy, and leathery. The shrub generally reaches a height of 5–12 feet.

How to Grow

Soil preparation is important in growing camellias. They like a light, rich, slightly acid soil (pH 5.5–6.0). When planting, dig the hole approximately 1½ times the size of the root ball. Remove the dirt

camellia

from the hole and mix with generous amounts of compost, leaf mold, or peat moss. Before planting, add 1/2 cup azalea-camellia fertilizer in the back fill of each hole. Camellias like partial shade and well-drained soil. After the shrub has bloomed, prune to maintain an attractive shape.

Camellias can be used for a variety of purposes in the landscape. They are lovely enough to be used alone as specimen plants or in small groupings as accents. Also useful in foundation plantings, or as hedges, these look wonderful in large groups.

There are thousands of named cultivars that have blossoms of different colors and sizes and that bloom at different times.

Tennessee

Cheekwood

Many outstanding irises grow at Cheekwood. Worldwide, there are over 200 known species of iris, and many more named cultivars. Cultivated varieties fall into two large categories: bearded and beardless.

Bearded iris have a "standard"—petals that stand upright—and a "fall"—petals that hang downward. The "beard" is at the center of the fall. Bearded

Siberian iris

iris, which bloom in May and June, are found in almost every color except a true red or true black.

Beardless iris have petals that are all more or less horizontal rather than divided into standards and falls. The blossoms are generally smaller, and the leaves narrower.

How to Grow

Relatively adaptable to a wide range of soil conditions, beardless iris are easier to grow than the bearded varieties. They need full sun.

Bearded iris need abundant moisture while in

bloom but will withstand relatively long dry spells at other times. The roots need very well drained sandy or gritty soils. Before planting the iris bulbs, dig the soil to a depth of about 6 inches, adding generous amounts of organic matter.

In fall, place the bulbs so that the rhizomes are just about at soil level. After they bloom, allow the leaves to yellow and dry on the plants; do not mow or cut them back.

Dixon Gallery and Gardens

As Margaret Dixon worked with Hope Crutchfield, she made it very clear to her sister-in-law that she wanted white flowers close to the house and the more colorful blossoms farther away. Her preference in this regard is one shared by many sophisticated gardeners throughout the world. The white garden at Sissinghurst, England, is a famous example.

White flowers bring a clean simplicity to any garden. With a backdrop of dark green ivy, or evergreen shrubs, these flowers seem to be almost illuminated. Although white flowers can be enjoyed at any time of day, they take on a magical charm as shadows deepen and the garden slips into night. Sometimes

called a moon garden, a landscape planted all in white will catch the light of the moon and create a place of peace and serenity.

Many different kinds of flowers bear white blossoms. You can start your season early with white spring bulbs, include white azaleas during mid-to-late spring, move into a series of white annuals and perennials for summer, and end the season with a glorious display of white chrysanthemums.

The following plants are suggested for a stunning white southern garden:

Spring:

Glory-of-the-snow (*Chionodoxa luciliae* 'Alba'). This bulb is good for a woodland area. Plant it in fall for bloom in early April.

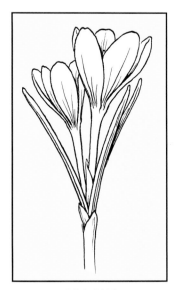

crocus

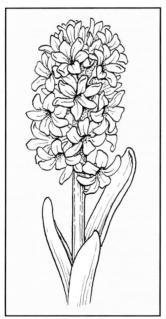

hyacinth

Crocus (*Crocus chrysanthus*). 'Snow Bunting' is a white crocus with a bit of lavender color on the outside. Plant bulbs in fall for bloom in February or March.

Hyacinths (*Hyacinthus* 'Carnegie'). These plants bear creamy white flowers on 12- to 15-inch stems in May. Plant bulbs in fall.

Narcissus (*Narcissus*). 'Stainless' is a pure white narcissus that blooms in midseason and grows to 18 inches tall. 'Ice Wings' is a small white narcissus, only 12 inches tall. Plant bulbs of both varieties in fall.

Summer:

Lily (*Lilum*). 'Casa Blanca' is a pure white oriental lily

that grows 4 feet tall and blooms in early August. Plant bulbs early in summer.

White Yarrow (*Achillea ptarmica*). 'The Pearl' blooms from June through September. This perennial can be planted in fall or early spring.

Astilbe (*Astilbe* x *arendsii*). The variety 'Avalanche' has pure white flowers on 30- to 36-inch stems. A perennial, it can be planted in fall or early spring.

Shasta daisy (*Chrysanthemum superbum*). 'Polaris' is the classic white Shasta daisy. A perennial, it can be planted in fall or early spring.

Phlox (*Phlox carolina*). The variety 'Miss Lingard' has tall spikes of pure white flowers and grows to 36

phlox

inches tall. This perennial can be planted in fall or early spring.

Impatiens (*Impatiens*). White varieties of this annual should be planted in spring after all danger of frost has passed.

Fall:

Chrysanthemum (*Chrysanthemum*). The variety 'Spotless' is a perennial with white blossoms and creamy centers on 16-inch stems. Plant early in summer.

The Hermitage

There is, perhaps, nothing as graceful and downright southern as a magnolia tree. Tall and stately, this broadcast evergreen puts forth huge, creamy blossoms with an unforgettable fragrance. These are long-lived trees, and one of the most beautiful and significant of these can be found close to Rachel Jackson's tomb at the Hermitage.

SOUTHERN MAGNOLIA

Magnolia grandiflora

A large, gracefully spreading tree, southern magnolia grows to heights of 50–80 feet and sometimes reaches as much as 40 feet across. Young branches are rusty brown. The leaves are large, about 6 inches long, shiny green on top, rusty brown and rough underneath. The large blossoms appear in early summer,

have 6 petals (sometimes 9 or 12), and are strongly scented. The fruit is a long, heavy seedpod with bright red berries that ripen in fall.

How to Grow

Magnolias should be planted from small, nursery-grown plants in spring or fall. Soil that is rich in organic matter and well drained will provide the best growing conditions for this tree. In spite of their size, magnolias are susceptible to damage during periods of drought. Mulching and watering during dry periods will ensure the continued health of the tree. Once the trees have been planted, do not disturb the root system, even by planting bulbs nearby. This tree is native from North Carolina south to Florida and west to Texas.

Virginia

Monticello

Thomas Jefferson's eight-acre vegetable garden and orchard were an important and beautiful part of his estate. The development of this part of the grounds took many years. The vegetable garden was first planted in 1770 but did not reach its peak until 1812.

Although Jefferson at one time grew as many as 450 varieties of fruits, vegetables, nuts, and herbs, many of these were merely experimental. He said "I am curious to select only one or two of the best species or variety of every vegetable and to reject all others."

The English pea was Jefferson's favorite vegetable and he grew as many as fifteen different varieties, searching for the sweetest, fastest growing, healthiest cultivar possible. For many years Jefferson participated in a local "pea contest" with his neighbors, the winner being the one who brought the first spring pea to the dinner table.

The planting of peas was so important to Jefferson that during his presidential term in Washington, he wrote to Monticello reminding them to plant "Ravenscroft peas, which you will find in a canister in my closet."

Peas are still a staple in early spring gardens throughout the country. Through the years many different varieties have been cultivated offering the gardener peas that vary in size, height, and resistance to heat and diseases.

Mount Vernon
George Washington seemed to love trees all of his life. When he was sixteen he wrote in his jour-

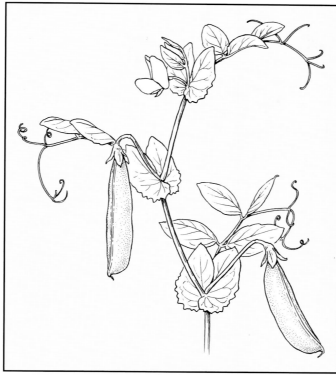

English pea

nal, "Spent the best part of the Day admiring the Trees & the richness of the Land." In 1914 the Mount Vernon Ladies' Association requested the services of Professor Charles Sprague Sargent, director of the Arnold Arboretum at Harvard University. Professor Sargent surveyed the trees on the Mount Vernon estate and offered advice as to their care: "No trees planted by man have the human interest of the Mount Vernon trees. They belong to the nation and are one of its precious possessions. No care should be spared to preserve them and as they pass away they should be replaced with trees of the same kind." Few of the trees that Washington actually planted himself still survive at Mount Vernon today. Among those that do survive, perhaps none are as exciting or beautiful as a pair of towering tulip-poplars.

TULIP-POPLAR
Liriodendron tulipfera
Tulip-poplars are native to eastern North America from Ontario south to Florida and west to Wisconsin. These magnifi-

cent trees grow to a height of 100 feet or more. When they grow in a forest habitat, branching occurs only high up in the tree. When they grow singly, branching generally occurs throughout the tree. The leaves, which turn bright yellow in autumn, are deeply lobed and blunt across the top. Once the tree has reached the age of about ten years, it will begin to produce large, showy, green-and-orange flowers. These are usually borne high in the tree and often go unnoticed until they fall to the ground.

How to Grow

Because Tulip-poplars put forth a huge root system, they need plenty of room and deep, rich, well-drained soil. Optimum growing conditions include full sun and slightly acid soils. They are long-lived but are susceptible to damage from drought and aphids, and are particularly sensitive to chemical herbicides.

Williamsburg Governor's Palace
At the heyday of the popularity of formal gardens, boxwood—more than any other single plant—conveyed the feeling of an English manor garden. The first boxwood was brought to America by Nathaniel Sylvester in 1652 and soon after this, all the southern

colonists were clamoring for "slips" of box to plant in their own gardens. Boxwood was used extensively in the colonies in formal gardens, among the most beautiful of which were found in Williamsburg. In England the plant's favor declined markedly under Queen Anne, who directed that it be removed from her own palace gardens.

ENGLISH BOXWOOD
Buxus sempervirens
Boxwood is a small evergreen tree or large shrub. The leaves are shiny dark green, measuring about 1 1/4 inches across. The flowers are numerous but inconspicuous. Legend tells us that this is because Apollo cursed the boxwood, declaring that its

flowers would never appeal to man. *B. sempervirens* can grow to about 20 feet tall. A shorter species, *B. microphylla*, called littleleaf box, only grows to about 3 feet tall. Japanese boxwood, *B. japonica*, has paler green leaves, grows about 6 feet tall, and is grown extensively throughout the United States.

How to Grow

Boxwood needs full sun or partial shade and very rich, well-drained soil. The roots are shallow and benefit from heavy mulching. Boxwood will withstand frequent clipping and pruning, making it a good specimen to use in a hedge or border. Unfortunately, once a boxwood develops bare

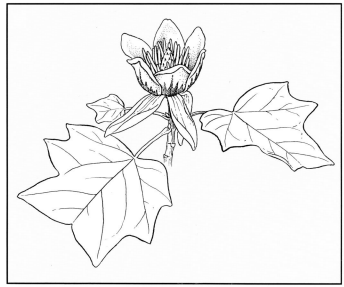

tulip-poplar

areas, it is difficult to get it to fill out again; few growth buds are found on old stems.

Benjamin Waller House
The privet grown by Benjamin Waller and his family is a plant native to Great Britain that rural British gardeners used extensively. Imagine the surprise of the early English settlers when they discovered that privet, so widely grown at home, grew nowhere in their new land!

The colonists soon brought a remedy—slips of privet to be planted in their new gardens. Up until the early nineteenth century, only European privet (*Ligustrum vulgare*) was grown in the United States. At that time a new species, *Ligustrum japonicum*, was introduced from Japan to gardeners in California. This species gained instant popularity because it was so easy to grow and adaptable to a wide range of environmental conditions. Today it is the most widely grown shrub in the United States.

PRIVET
Ligustrum japonicum
This evergreen shrub grows 6–10 feet tall and has glossy, dark green leaves. The blossoms are small spikes of scented white flowers.

How to Grow

Privet is extremely adaptable to many different environments and will thrive in any soils except for those that stay constantly wet. It will perform well in either full sun or partial shade.

Privet's tolerance of air pollution has made it quite valuable as an urban plant. It is useful as a hedge because it will take heavy pruning or shearing. Privet is also frequently made into topiary.

George Wythe House
In the early eighteenth century, many Virginia planters and homeowners found figs an important fruit. Both Thomas Jefferson and George Washington, among others, were known to have grown tasty figs. Although figs are generally considered a subtropical fruit better suited to California and the southwestern desert areas, many varieties also do well in colder regions. Figs were commonly found in many of the Virginia garden estates, indicating that even eighteenth-century varieties were tolerant of cold weather.

(Thomas Jefferson wrote of the Marseilles fig that it was "incomparably superior to any fig I had ever seen.")

English boxwood

FIG

Ficus carica

In warm regions, fig trees can grow as tall as 15–30 feet. In colder areas, they rarely grow taller than 10 feet. A fig is not technically a fruit at all, but a collection of closed flowers. Most fig trees bear fruit twice a season. The first, heavier, crop is borne on old wood from the previous season. A second crop is borne on new wood of the current season. Pruning the tree or cutting it back will generally eliminate the first crop.

How to Grow

Figs do best if planted in full sun but will grow well enough in any garden area with well-drained soil. The roots sometimes become vigorous and invasive. It is important to keep the numerous suckers at the base of the tree pruned out and to maintain a single, strong trunk. The trees benefit from regular watering during dry periods.

Washington, D.C.

Dumbarton Oaks

The herbaceous border at Dumbarton Oaks is rich in color and fragrance. In midsummer when the flowers are at their peak it is the epitome of the perfect flower garden, with blossoms spilling over one another in unabashed and resplendent glory.

Creating an English-style perennial or mixed border is perhaps one of the most challenging of all gardening projects. It takes time, effort, money, and persistence. It is worth the effort, however; there is little that can compare with a thriving flower border.

The first step in creating a border is to improve the soil. This task must be done before the first plant is placed in the ground. Because perennials return year after year, it will be difficult to work with the soil after the plants have become established. A soil test (which you can perform yourself, or ask a local gardening service to perform) will provide you with invaluable information about your soil's particular needs. The test will tell the pH of the soil and also which elements are weak or missing. Till the soil deeply and treat it to copious amounts of organic material. Well-rotted leaf mold, cured compost, and manure are good soil amendments.

Choosing the best and most appropriate plants is not only necessary, it is also pure fun. It is in this "dreaming stage" that your flower border might look its best. Be careful to choose plants that will perform well in your area. No matter how much you might love a particular flower, if it is not suitable to grow in your area, heartache is just about a sure bet. Select plants that are pleasing to you, but also choose flower colors that will work well together. As Beatrix Farrand pointed out, putting together a flower border is a good deal like painting a picture. Pay close attention to when the different plants bloom. By making careful choices, you can extend the season and enjoy your garden for many months of the year.

Generally, plants should be grouped by height and color. Taller flowers, of course, should be planted toward the back of the border, smaller flowers toward the front.

The location of a flower border is critical to its success. Most brightly colored perennials and annuals need full sun—at least six or seven hours a day. Without this amount of sunlight, flowering will be disappointing at best. Also consider a source of water when planting your border. While establishing the plants and during dry spells, water the border frequently.

After planting, mulch the area heavily. A good mulch offers many benefits, discouraging weeds and helping soil to retain moisture. Both factors are important attributes in a garden.

Once the border is planted, mulched, watered, and prayed over, sit back and be patient. There is a saying about perennials: "The first year they sleep, the second year they creep, and the third year they leap." The results are certainly worth waiting for.

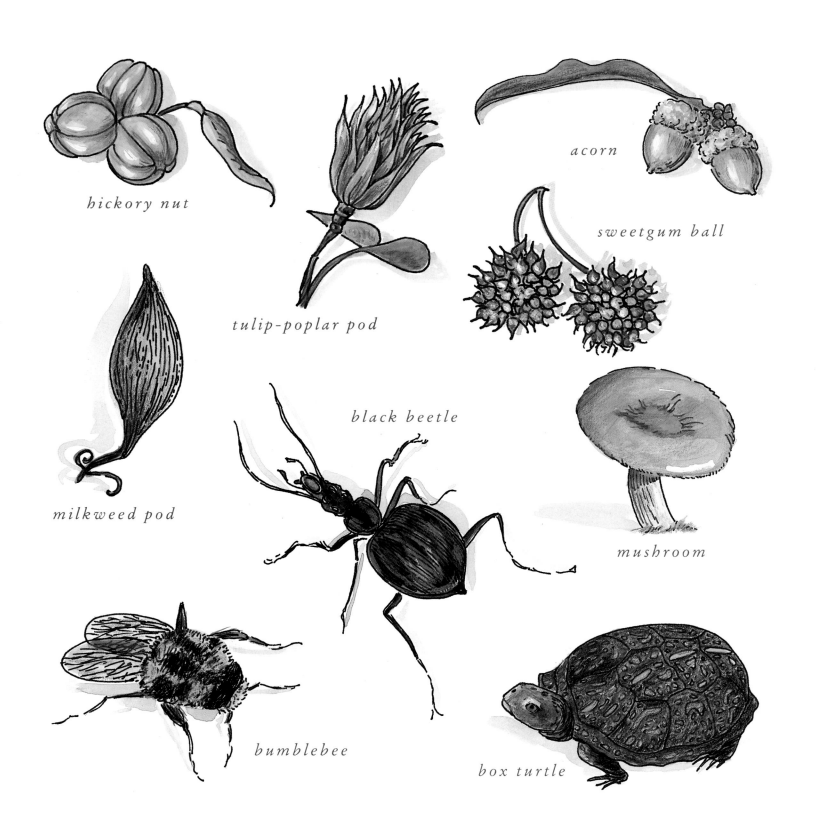

hickory nut

acorn

sweetgum ball

tulip-poplar pod

milkweed pod

black beetle

mushroom

bumblebee

box turtle

Gardens almost always attract some uninvited guests. Acorns and hickory nuts may litter the garden in fall, bumblebees and garden spiders may take up temporary residence in spring. The following is a list of plants and creatures that may make their way into the garden. None are harmful, and each can add its own bit of magic.

ACORNS—Jewels from a hickory tree, acorns come in a variety of shapes and sizes. Most show the characteristic round little head and "top hat."

HICKORY NUTS—Bitternut, pignut, or mockernut hickory nuts can all be found in southern gardens. Thick, hard outer shells quickly turn from green to brown and split, exposing the inner nut.

MILKWEED PODS—Seed pods from milkweed plants open with an explosion that sends the light, airy seeds drifting through the air. The pods themselves, rough and warty, have a charm all to themselves.

MUSHROOM—Wild mushrooms in the garden can be delicious or poisonous and only the experts can tell them apart. They are perhaps best enjoyed for their bright colors and unusual shapes.

SWEETGUM BALLS—Round little balls covered with star-shaped points, the fruit of the sweetgum tree matures in autumn but persists throughout the winter months.

TULIP POPLAR PODS—We sometimes forget that towering trees may also have beautiful flowers. The unusual orange and green flowers from the tulip poplar tree are wonderful reminders of this.

Animals

BLACK BEETLE—With his shiny black armor, the little black beetle is often found under logs or stones in the garden. Adult beetles emerge in late summer.

BLUE-TAILED SKINK—As these long, lazy lizard-looking creatures bask in the sun, their bright blue tails glimmer in the light. The young hatch in late summer and hibernate in the soil during winter.

BOX TURTLE—These creatures are found most often during the day. They prefer to eat earthworms and wild strawberries and may spend their lives in an area no larger than a football field.

BUMBLEBEE—The hairy black and yellow bumblebee drones endlessly in the warm summer sun. These creatures have smoky black wings and baskets on their hind legs used for collecting pollen.

CHIPMUNK—This striped little animal scurries in and out of gardens as far south as Alabama and Georgia. Its underground burrows can hold as much as a half bushel of nuts and other food.

CRICKET—Long considered a harbinger of good luck, the cricket makes a continuous trilling noise. Male crickets make noise by rubbing a scraper of one forewing against a series of 50–250 teeth on the opposite forewing.

GARDEN SPIDER—Oh what a tangled web they weave! Black and yellow garden spiders spin a web vertically in trees and bushes and then hang head downward at the center, waiting for the unsuspecting insect.

GARTER SNAKE—More friend than foe, garter snakes are often found in the garden. They have live young and shed their skins in one long piece rather than in small pieces.

GRASSHOPPER—A footstep in the garden is likely to create a circus of leaping grasshoppers. These long legged green creatures sometimes hold their broad wings over their bodies like a tent when at rest.

LADYBUG—The ladybug is not only the subject of favorite nursery rhymes but also is beloved by gardeners and farmers for eating such pests as aphids, scales, and mites.

PRAYING MANTIS—This insect is useful, for it is a voracious eater and will eat many garden pests. The name "diviner" was given to this creature by the ancient Greeks, for they believed it held supernatural powers.

SPRING AZURE BUTTERFLY—In April clouds of blue settle on puddles in the garden as this small butterfly emerges. The underside of the wings has rows of dark spots.

SPRING PEEPER—A chorus of these small tan-gray creatures sounds like a high-pitched chorus. These are commonly found in the garden at night during the warm months. They hibernate under logs and loose bark.

TIGER MOTH CATERPILLAR—The black and orange "woolly bear," or caterpillar, is a familiar sight in the garden. Superstition holds that the woollier the "bear," the colder the coming winter.

TIGER SWALLOWTAIL—The tiger swallowtail is one of our most beautiful common butterflies. The females, which look like the poisonous pipe swallowtail, are rarely eaten because of this.

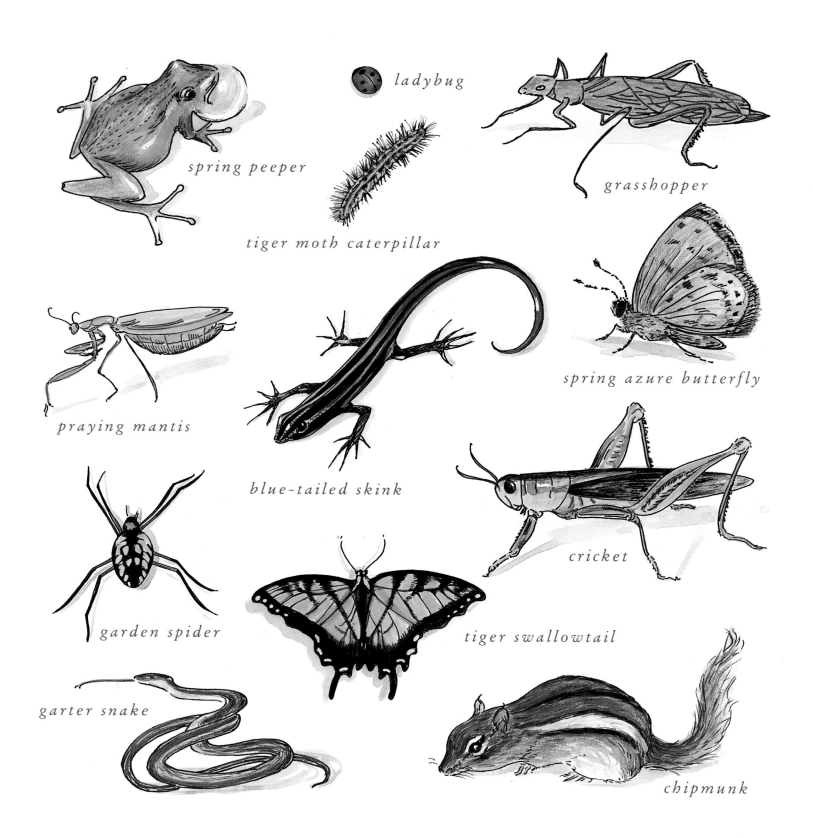

spring peeper

ladybug

grasshopper

tiger moth caterpillar

praying mantis

blue-tailed skink

spring azure butterfly

garden spider

tiger swallowtail

cricket

garter snake

chipmunk

Index

Picture Credits

All photography by David Schilling except the following:

2–3 Monticello; Thomas Jefferson Memorial Foundation
9 far left, 94, 95 Turnbull-Bowman Family Papers, Louisiana and Lower Mississippi Valley Collections, LSU Libraries, Louisiana State University
29, 35 top, 40 Courtesy of Colonial Williamsburg Foundation
39 top right Modern drawing by Richard Stinely, after sketch by Luty Blow, ca. 1807. Photograph courtesy of Colonial Williamsburg Foundation
42 Division of Archives and History, N.C. Dept. of Cultural Resources
46 bottom left Courtesy of The Charleston Museum, Charleston, South Carolina
58 bottom left and right Courtesy of Magnolia Plantation
60 top, Cape Fear Museum, Wilmington, North Carolina
65, 66 right, Courtesy of The Mount Vernon Ladies' Association
66 left, 67, 71 © "Wildlife Matters"
72 top left, The Historical Society of Pennsylvania, Philadelphia
72 top right, Charles Shoffner/Photographer
83 bottom left and right Courtesy Old Salem Restoration, Winston-Salem, N.C.
88, 91 bottom The Hermitage: Home of Andrew Jackson, Nashville, TN

103 bottom left and right Courtesy The Historic New Orleans Collection, Acc. No. 86-941-RL
104 Laura Martin
109 left Courtesy of Dr. and Mrs. Tom Gandy
109 right Courtesy of Monmouth Plantation
112 center and right Courtesy of William Garbo, Landscape Architect
115, 118 top, center, bottom center and right © The Biltmore Company, 1991
126 top left and right Vizcaya Museum and Gardens, Miami
133 bottom left Courtesy of Bellingrath Gardens/Photograph by The Overbey Studio
133 bottom right, 134 top Courtesy of Bellingrath Archives
141 bottom right By permission of the Harvard University Archives
144 Courtesy of Longue Vue House and Gardens
156 Courtesy of Dixon Gardens
159 Troup County Archives, Callaway Gardens Collection
169 left Photo by William M. Houghton/Courtesy of Fairchild Tropical Gardens
179 Society of the Four Arts, Palm Beach, FL
184 Brookgreen Gardens Photo, Murrells Inlet, SC
193 Courtesy of Cypress Gardens
195 bottom Courtesy of the Morikami Museum and Japanese Gardens
200 Courtesy of Ryan Gainey